To dear ~~[redacted]~~

Wishing you only
the best

Love

Christine

TOMORROW! ■ VÁCLAV HAVEL

This semi-documentary about the founding of the Czechoslovak Republic was written anonymously in 1988 for the revue *Rozrazil* - the 'living newspaper'. Scarcely more than a year later, the about-to-be President Havel and his colleagues found themselves acting out aspects of the play in real life . . . First ever publication in English.

GAMES ■ IVAN KLÍMA

In this semi-absurdist play written while Klima was still a banned writer, an initially genial house-party begins to turn deadly serious. 'In games we fake seriousness,' wrote Klima. 'But finally our true nature glimmers through, and for a moment, we see our real selves . . .' First staged in Britain in 1990.

CAT ON THE RAILS ■ JOSEF TOPOL

Mirroring the situation in Czechoslovakia before 1989, *Cat on the Rails* depicts two lovers waiting at a station for a train that never comes. Topol is possibly the most highly regarded practising playwright in his own country, though hardly known in the world at large. First publication in English.

BETWEEN DOG AND WOLF ■ DANIELA FISCHEROVÁ

In *Dog and Wolf* Fischerová, the leading Czech woman playwright, takes the trial of the French poet, François Villon, as an exemplar of the clash between the artist and society. First staged in Britian in 1993.

CZECH PLAYS

MODERN CZECH DRAMA

TOMORROW! ■ VÁCLAV HAVEL

Translated by BARBARA DAY

GAMES ■ IVAN KLÍMA

Translated by BARBARA DAY

CAT ON THE RAILS ■ JOSEF TOPOL

Translated by GEORGE & CHRISTINE VOSKOVEC

DOG AND WOLF ■ DANIELA FISCHEROVÁ

Translated by A. G. BRAIN

SELECTED AND INTRODUCED BY BARBARA DAY

Nick Hern Books
London

A Nick Hern Book

Czech Plays first published in Great Britain in 1994 as an original paperback by Nick Hern Books, 14 Larden Road, London W3 7ST

Typeset, printed and bound by Seagull Books, Calcutta, India

A CIP catalogue record for this book is available from the British Library

ISBN 1 - 85459 074 X

Acknowledgements

I would like to thank for their advice and guidance at various times: Karel Brušák, Jitka Martinová, Petr Oslzlý and David Short.

Introduction

In the centre of Prague on the evening of 17 November 1989, a student procession was attacked by police. The procession was to commemorate the date in 1939 when the Nazis closed the Czech universities; the attack was part of a power struggle between two factions in the ruling Communist party. The aim of both was to ensure the continuation of the Communist regime in Czechoslovakia; that night saw the beginning of the end.

One student who escaped the attack, which took place on a main boulevard a few yards from the National Theatre, made his way to a suburban fringe theatre. The 'Junior Klub na Chmelnici' is scarcely a theatre; it's a bare hall used as an occasional venue by rock groups, amateur shows, provincial tours and avant-garde performers who were not welcomed by the authorities in central Prague. On the night of 17 November, the student, whose home town was Brno, knew he would find performers from Brno's avant-garde companies Divadlo Na provázku (Theatre on a String) and HaDivadlo (HaTheatre).

The two companies were staging a joint production which they described as a 'living newspaper', *Rozrazil* (*Break through*); this 'issue' – so far the first and only – was 'On Democracy'. The show consisted of sketches, poetry, dance, and a short play, a semi-documentary – author uncredited – called *Tomorrow!* about the beginnings of the Czechoslovak state. I had seen a performance the previous October (in the meantime the production had been banned) and been struck by the straightforward, factual treatment of themes which under the Communists had been ideologised, and by the emotion of the audience's response. On 17 November 1989 the response must have been still stronger, for the student came onstage in the course of the performance to describe the drama he had just witnessed in central Prague – quite a scoop for a 'living newspaper'. Other students telephoned their friends in the theatres, and by the next afternoon a meeting had been convened in the Realistické divadlo (Realist Theatre) at which actors from the Prague theatres decided to cancel further performances and read to the audiences a manifesto issued by the students and theatre people.

It was not by chance that the first people to support the students were the actors and their colleagues from the theatres. A network of theatre people who opposed the Communist régime had come together over the previous two years – a network which ranged from such 'official' people as the head of the theatre department in the state literary agency, through the 'semi-dissident' playwrights Daniela Fischerová and Karel Steigerwald, to the notorious jailbird Václav Havel. Stealthy gatherings took place in the smoke-filled offices of the Realist Theatre. At meetings of the Union of Theatre Artists, dramaturges risked their careers by demanding the inclusion in the repertoire of plays by forbidden playwrights. (Goaded to a defensive reply at one of these meetings, one bureaucrat found his unguarded words recorded and published in a samizdat newspaper; cf *Plays International,* April 1989.) From the beginning of 1988 the atmosphere was confused and sometimes threatening. In January 1989, when most people still thought it was impossible to stage the work of a Charter 77 signatory, Josef Topol's *End of the Carnival* was revived in the provincial town of Cheb; in June, Topol was led onto the stage of Prague's Vinohrady Theatre to acknowledge the applause at the première of his new play, *The Voices of Birds.* And Václav Havel – although under threat of another prison sentence – was everywhere that summer; attending a student revival of Daniela Fischerová's *Dog and Wolf* (banned for the previous ten years) at a cellar theatre in Řeznická Street; taking the lead in a public seminar held on the highly 'official' premises of the Writers' Union (a sleight-of-hand by the playwrights which did not go unchallenged by the authorities). These were the open manifestations of a new ordering of forces which was barely in place when the secret police precipitated the events of 17 November.

The people from whom the first government of the new era was largely formed – and who held their first meetings on the stages of the Činoherní klub (Drama Club) and the Laterna magika (Magic Lantern) – included a high proportion of theatre workers. Amongst their tasks they had to ensure not only the smooth stage-management of the massive crowds, but also that the content of the meetings engaged the public's interest and understanding. The handling of these spontaneous demonstrations was the culmination of decades of theatre as a subversive force against a totalitarian régime. Afterwards, Petr Oslzlý – *de facto* director of the Theatre on the String and one of the organisers of the spectacles – described how the outdoor demonstrations gave him the impression he was witness to one of the great theatrical performances of ancient Greece.

This unity of actor and action was found not only in Prague but across the country; the 'striking' theatre workers organised themselves into troupes with a mission to spread the news of the extraordinary events in Prague – not only from their own stages, but from improvised platforms in village halls and factory canteens. These stages were almost the only source from which ordinary people could find out what was going on, since the old régime still struggled to keep control over radio, TV and the press.

In the Czech lands, the use of theatre as a didactic tool dates back to the late eighteenth century. There had been a lively theatre tradition in the Middle Ages, when a considerable standard was reached in liturgical plays and sacred farces, but its development was interrupted by the Hussite wars. It was not until the end of the eighteenth century that Czech plays – usually adapted from German originals – began to be performed by amateur groups of Czech patriots. Performances took place at first in inns and halls, and later at matinées and on holidays in the established theatres. The first permanent public theatre had been built in Prague in 1737, for the performance of Italian opera and German plays; in 1781 Count Nostitz built an opera house known today by its nineteenth-century title, the Stavovské divadlo (Theatre of the Estates). Drama, for the Czech patriots of the early nineteenth-century 'National Revival', was central to their aspirations. Translations into Czech, especially of Shakespeare's plays (already known in Bohemia through performances by travelling English players, but in the eighteenth century translated from German) helped to prove it a language capable of elevated expression. But the first attempts at original Czech plays were for the most part didactic and nationalist.

The situation did not change until the opening of the Prozatimní divadlo (Provisional Theatre) in 1862. Its building was a preparation for the Národní divadlo (National Theatre), a project which had been adopted after the political disappointments of 1848. Now, at last, a permanent repertoire in theatre and opera could be established; the Czechs had no golden age to be nostalgic about, and the actors, musicians and theatre workers knew that it was up to them to create a Czech theatre comparable with the theatres of other European nations. Bedřich Smetana led the opera company, and *The Bartered Bride* was premièred in the Provisional Theatre in 1863; it was Smetana's opera *Libuše*, glorifying the history of the Czech nation, which opened the National Theatre in 1881. (The Czech National Theatre is unique in having been paid for, not by the state or a patron, but by the people themselves.)

The establishment of a permanent professional Czech theatre, opened the way for a new generation of dramatists. In a late emergence of the realist movement, many of them wrote plays in a genre known as the village drama, in which the writers used their knowledge of the traditions and way of life of the Bohemian and Moravian countryside. Plays such as *Maryša* by the Brothers Mrštík and *The Farmer's Woman* by Gabriela Preissová are not only powerful dramas, but vivid evocations of the society of the time, and of the struggle of the non-conformist – especially a woman – against convention. The plays are still unknown to the English-speaking public, except for Preissová's *Her Foster-Daughter* – the source for Janáček's opera *Jenůfa* (premièred in his native Brno in 1904). Czech opera also prospered, and by the turn of the century opera and drama performances at the Czech National Theatre were second to none in Europe.

By this time, there were many other professional Czech-language theatres in Prague and the provinces, as well as popular outdoor summer arenas frequented by the working class and country visitors. These were non-didactic theatres, showing spectacle, farce, operetta, and the popular genre of fairy-tale drama. There were also the *šantány* (a Czech version of the *café chantant*) where peripatetic groups would perform songs and sketches – sometimes lascivious and sometimes a little subversive – in a room of a pub.

By the turn of the century the Czechs were confident in their cultural identity. They looked beyond Austria-Hungary to other European countries and even America for contacts and exchanges. In music, the work of Smetana and Dvořák was internationally known; artists such as Alfons Mucha and František Kupka made their name abroad; whilst Czech architects and designers were unique in rethinking cubism as an environment for everyday life. The nationalist cause no longer seemed so critical; and although the literary cabaret came late to Prague, it appealed to the public of the 1900s and 1910s precisely because of its political independence.

Two great directors dominated the Czech theatre in the early twentieth century: Jaroslav Kvapil, who introduced symbolism to the Czech stage; and Karel Hugo Hilar, who introduced just about everything else. Kvapil, himself a poet and dramatist, did not see theatre direction simply as the solving of technical problems, but as the work of an artist, combining the theatrical elements to create a visual and aural experience. Hilar, who seized each new theatrical fashion and made it his own, staged productions which shocked and thrilled Prague audiences. It was under Kvapil and Hilar that Czech playwrights first attracted international attention – František Langer with *The Outskirts of the City* and *A Camel through a Needle's Eye*, and Karel and Josef Čapek with *R.U.R.* and *The Insect Play*.

However, in the years after the First World War the young avant-garde considered even Hilar's expressionist productions at the National Theatre to be old hat. They saw themselves as part of an international movement and created the *Devětsil*, in its early years a left-wing group committed to proletarian art, which drew its members from the fine arts and from architecture, from the theatre and from literature. The *Devětsil* developed the idea of an art derived from popular entertainment and everyday life, an art which would relate to the general public through allusion, invention and metaphor, and to which they gave the name poetism. Poetism – 'a poetry not confined to texts, but of the five senses' – was influenced by cubism, futurism and constructivism, and was a forerunner of surrealism. The sort of theatre envisaged by the *Devětsil* owed more to film than to traditional theatre; its material was to be drawn from the world around – from fairs, carnivals and street events. The Liberated Theatre, founded in 1926, staged Apollinaire and Marinetti and Jarry's *Ubu roi*, as well as the young Czech writers of the avant-garde. But it was two student performers who caught the popular audience: Jiří Voskovec and Jan Werich who, with the composer Jaroslav Ježek, presented topical revues full of satirical repartee and improvised word play, hot jazz and slow blues. In their early revues V + W showed little interest in politics; but as the power of Hitler and Mussolini increased, they began to take their themes from contemporary events: the Spanish Civil War, the annexation of Austria, Hitler's demands for the Sudetenland.

Another member of the *Devětsil*, E.F. Burian, dreamed of his own left-wing, avant-garde theatre, which he founded in 1933. In Burian's hands a text became a scenario, raw material from which he could fashion a 'many-voiced' drama. His stage was small, with few technical facilities, and economy was a necessity; the acting area was expanded by the dynamic use of different stage levels and of lighting, film and projection. The productions were assembled like musical compositions; music, dialogue and action flowed like a well-written score. Burian's most innovative productions were adaptations – Wedekind's *Spring Awakening*, Pushkin's *Eugene Onegin*. In *War*, a montage of voiceband and dance, Burian used Bohemian folk songs presented in an unfamiliar way to show that the strength and hope of the nation was in its ordinary people. But when the Zhdanov doctrine became the official cultural policy of Communism, Burian's powerfully individual work was condemned by the left-wing critics.

During the 1930s, the Czech theatre became source-material for the Prague structuralists, whose research covered a broad field – linguistics, literature, aesthetics, sociology. In the theatre the structuralists analysed the individual elements which make up a performance, and how they relate to each other and to the audience. The Prague theatre, from the National Theatre to the avant-garde, gave ample illustration of ways in which information could be transferred from one element to another, could be conveyed by setting or by speech, by gesture or by sound.

The Czech lands were occupied by the Nazis in 1939. Voskovec and Werich were already in exile in America, whilst E.F. Burian spent the war in the concentration camps. Although the theatres – unlike the universities – remained open, they were restricted to an increasingly circumscribed repertoire. After the war those who returned from exile and imprisonment threw themselves into a renewed and hectic artistic life.

But the world had changed. It was the start of the cold war, and in February 1948 Czechoslovakia came under Communist control. In the 1920s socialism had offered the artists 'a whirligig, a dazzling fairground, a kaleidoscope of thoughts, a celebration of new understandings, manifestos and struggles'. But in the 1950s culture was too dangerous a weapon to be left in the hands of the artists. The daring avant-garde of the pre-war period now endeavoured to

conform to the dictates of their lords and masters, and the years
which followed the victory of Communism were the most sterile
known in the Czech theatre. It was argued that as progressive ideas
could now be presented on the main stages, there was no need for
satirical or experimental theatre. New plays were expected to deal
with the contemporary themes showing the building of socialism,
the fight against bourgeois morality, and the salvation of the
'positive hero'. 'Formalism' was the great enemy, so much so that
theatre directors were afraid of showing any sign of originality in
their productions and adopted the most conventional
interpretation. Numerous playwrights, critics, directors and other
theatre workers were forced to leave their profession, or chose to
leave the country.

And yet, in 1955, from a small cellar bar in the centre of Prague
could be heard the sounds of rock-n-roll – 'a daring word, and at
that time pronounced in the same breath as the word
"imperialism". By some oversight on the part of the authorities, an
amateur group had begun to draw a popular following to the
Reduta bar, reopened after its closure as a place of ill-repute. The
original bass player of the group was a young poet and artist called
Jiří Suchý, who dreamt of a topical theatre like that of Voskovec
and Werich. He formed a partnership with the writer and
performer Ivan Vyskočil, creator of the 'text-appeal', and it was the
enthusiasm of their audience which led to the founding in 1958 of
the Divadlo Na zábradlí (Theatre on the Balustrade).

Round about the same time, in 1957, the actor-director Otomar
Krejča had been appointed to head the drama company at the
National Theatre. Krejča aimed at a theatre very different from the
approved optimism of socialist realism. With the dramaturge Karel
Kraus and the designer Josef Svoboda, he created something like a
studio within the National Theatre, a place where writers and
actors could try out new ideas and ways of working. Krejča and
Kraus sat down with three writers, two of them inexperienced in
the theatre: the older František Hrubín, and Milan Kundera, whose
Owners of the Keys (whilst still conventional in content) caused
widespread admiration in 1962 for the originality of its form. The
third writer, Josef Topol had been a colleague of Krejča in E.F.
Burian's theatre, where *Midnight Wind,* a historical drama, had
been produced. Now they collaborated on two plays which took a
broad view of contemporary life. *Their Day* (1959) shows the
passage of twenty-four hours in the community of a small Czech
town, where the aspirations of youth struggle against provincial
narrow-mindedness. *The End of the Carnival* (1963) is set at the time
of the traditional shrovetide festival in a Czech village where, as
throughout the country in the 1950s, privately-owned land had
been subsumed into a co-operative. It was a familiar setting in
socialist realist drama, but the treatment by Topol and Krejča, their
portrayal of complex layers of relationships and reactions, was

anything but conventional. Both plays used all the resources of a large company and a stage equipped with Svoboda's sophisticated technology.

At the Theatre on the Balustrade, Jiří Suchý's co-founder, Ivan Vyskočil, had engaged a young stage-hand who had been working for a season with Jan Werich. Václav Havel had ambitions to be a playwright, and with Vyskočil co-authored a hit, *Hitch-hike*, based on the cabaret traditions of the small theatres. The series of satirical sketches spoke of contemporary man's dependency on material objects, and of the risks and challenges of a free life. *Hitch-hike* was too popular to go unnoticed by the authorities, who forced Vyskočil's resignation (and kept him under surveillance for the next three decades). In 1962 Jan Grossman was appointed director of the Theatre on the Balustrade, and Václav Havel became his dramaturge. Grossman had been a critic and author who in the 1950s had been banned from publishing. He turned instead to theatre direction, developing his idea of a theatre which did not offer solutions, but which put questions to the audience and challenged them to respond. The repertoire included Czechoslovak premières of Beckett and Ionesco, adaptations of Jarry's *Ubu roi* and Kafka's *Trial*, as well as plays by contemporary Czech authors. In 1963 Grossman invited Otomar Krejča to direct Havel's *Garden Party*, and in 1965 himself directed Havel's *Memorandum*. If the authorities had been upset by *Hitch-hike*, there was more to disturb them in these two plays. Havel presented onstage a microworld which, in its parade of hypocritical corruption, was only too painfully familiar. In *The Garden Party*, characters control and manipulate each other by the use of linguistic conventions; in *The Memorandum*, the audience was reminded of Alfred Jarry's pataphysical machines, structures whose only purpose is to prolong their own activity.

In the mid-1960s Otomar Krejča founded his own company, Divadlo Za branou (Theatre Beyond the Gate). Krejča's earlier experiments with productions using film and stage-machinery now interested him less than long and arduous rehearsal with the group of actors which had followed him from the National Theatre (one of the complaints levelled against Krejča was that he worked too hard, took theatre too seriously, and expected other people to take it seriously too). The leading actors in the company were Jan Tříska and Marie Tomášová, who had been Krejča's Romeo and Juliet at the National Theatre; and it was they for whom the central roles in Josef Topol's *Cat on the Rails*, the play which opened the Theatre Beyond the Gate, were written.

Cat on the Rails is essentially a two-hander, which suited Krejča's wish to work closely with the performers. It was also, in the context of Czech drama, a movement away from the analysis of social themes to a more inward-looking, Chekhovian theatre (Chekhov is a key dramatist in Krejča's theatre). Évi and Véna are a recognisably ordinary couple from Prague on a day's ramble which loses them somewhere near a country railway station, from which they hope to make it back to Prague. Interrupted only by a boy in flight from a local vendetta and his two pursuers, they pass the time with games and reminiscences, until they touch on Evi's longing – the desire for a settled life, for a peace shared with Véna, for a family hearth. But for Véna such peace is no peace at all. The 'hearth' reminds him of an old woman he knew, who destroyed a magnificent historic fireplace to have somewhere to put her cupboard: 'From that time on, "hearth" is a hollow term – like a great many heartwarming words. In due time, they will be joined by "love" when love will have been totally wiped out.' A few days before the première of *Cat on the Rails*, Krejča said of Topol in an interview: '. . . he is convinced that the protagonist of contemporary drama is one who does not swim with the time, who is full of doubt and uncertainty, who is always seeking.'

Following the Russian invasion in 1968, *Cat on the Rails*, like the rest of Topol's plays, was not seen on the Czech stage for twenty years. Topol, like his protagonist, did not 'swim with the time'. For a while he made a living as a translator, until, after he signed Charter 77, that too was forbidden. An English translation of *Cat on the Rails* made in 1966 by Jiří Voskovec (of the famous 1930s' Liberated Theatre) who had been living in America since 1948.

The power struggle taking place in Czechoslovak politics in the mid-1960s was reflected in the energy of Czechoslovak writers and artists. In the wake of the Theatre on the Balustrade and Semafor several new professional theatre companies had started up, and even the established theatres were performing the work of new writers. But these activities came to an end after the invasion of 1968 and the 'normalisation' of the subsequent months. It was comparatively easy to deal with playwrights and critics. Theatres were simply not granted permission to stage any play by any writer on the black list, domestic or foreign, whilst the specialist theatre magazines were closed down in the spring of 1970. The dynamic activity of the theatre was more difficult to control; the nadir was reached in 1978, when a new Theatre Law made it impossible to set up a new theatre company, or even to close down an existing one.

But unlike the post-1948 period, this was not a time of stagnation in the theatre. In the old days some artists and writers had believed that Communism was the way forward, and efforts were made to conform to the Zhdanov doctrine. Now, even the reform Communists, the 'sixty-eighters' had turned dissident, and were for the most part replaced by bureaucrats who – opportunistically or pragmatically – promoted Communism as the only viable form of government for Czechoslovakia. Whereas in the 1950s artists like Burian had tried to conform to socialist realist principles, in the 1970s and 1980s the 'lords and masters' were forced to suppress or contain the subversive artistic spirit. The Theatre Beyond the Gate was closed and Krejča, after a brief period in a suburban theatre, could only find work abroad. Topol worked as a labourer on the restoration of the Charles Bridge. Grossman was banished to the border town of Cheb. Havel put himself beyond the pale by open protest. Many other talented directors, dramaturges and actors were forbidden to work in Prague (a policy which greatly improved artistic standards in the provinces).

Amongst the writers forbidden to publish was the essayist, novelist and dramatist Ivan Klíma. Two of Klíma's plays had been staged in Prague in the 1960s: *The Castle* at the Divadlo Československé armády (Czechoslovak Army Theatre) and *The Jury* at the Komorní divadlo (Chamber Theatre). In both cases critics pointed to the obvious influence of Franz Kafka, whose work had recently been allowed to reappear; but dramatically, a stronger influence was that of Friedrich Dürrenmatt, an author not yet published in Czechoslovakia. *Games*, which Klíma wrote in 1973, was translated into German and performed in Vienna in 1975. It is an early example of the genre which became extensive over the next fifteen years – samizdat: writing which could not be published officially, was typed in editions of increasingly illegible carbon copies, and discussed in small, private groups.

The setting of *Games* is a party which is a microcosm of the society in which Klíma lived during the early 1970s; a society not as conveniently divided into 'Communists' and 'dissidents' as the West might have imagined, but in which any individual might find that the most mundane decision faced him (or her) with a political or moral dilemma. 'Life forces us to assume certain roles, to fulfil other people's expectations,' wrote Klíma in the programme note to the first production in Vienna. 'In games we fake seriousness. And for a while they allow us to avoid confronting our fate. But finally our true nature glimmers through, and, for a moment, we see our real selves. Sometimes this takes us by surprise, for the nature we catch a glimpse of seems totally unknown to us. Or we notice, to our astonishment, that our true nature doesn't exist any more; our role has absorbed us, transformed us, we have already become a function of it . . .' Later in the decade, as people grew more skilful at dissimulation, their responses became increasingly cynical. The characters in *Games* are still inexperienced, surprised most of all by their own emotional responses. Irena, who has planned the party, anticipates it as an evening of escapism – a retreat to a lost innocence. But there is an ugly event which cannot quite be put out of mind – the murder of a young girl whose body was disposed of in a refuse cart. There is no bridge back to lost innocence; the games only strip the characters of the conventions which have so far sustained civilised behaviour.

Games was the last play Klíma wrote under the conditions prevailing in totalitarian Czechoslovakia; after that he concentrated on prose and novel-writing. This translation was made in 1989 for

Midnight Theatre Company, and directed at the Gate Theatre, London, by Derek Wax in the summer of 1990.

Klíma was one of those who had already made their names before the August of 1968, and who remained on the blacklist unless they publicly recanted. Younger writers were dealt with more subtly by the authorities; there was always the hope that they might prefer the considerable privileges of being an officially approved writer, and avoid the humiliation experienced by their older colleagues. One of the younger writers was Karel Steigerwald, whose tetralogy of plays about the Czech experience (*Period Dances, The Tartar Fète, The Neapolitan Disease* and *Foxtrot*) were capriciously banned and released throughout the inconsistent 1980s. Another was Daniela Fischerová, daughter of the composer Jan Fischer, and in 1968 only twenty years old. Fischerová studied at the Film Academy, and subsequently wrote a number of radio and film scripts. In 1979 her first stage play, *Dog and Wolf*, was staged at the Realist Theatre in Prague; after four performances, orders came from the City Council that the play was unsuitable for public performance and should close forthwith. In 1984 Fischerová wrote *Princess T* (Turandot) staged in 1986 in the mining town of Ostrava. In 1987 she completed *Legend* (started in 1981), a version of the Pied Piper story, also staged initially in Ostrava.

Fischerová's three plays belong to a genre typical of the Czech theatre of the 1980s; the historical allegory, the adapting of familiar stories to deal with contemporary moral problems. The action is set against a mythical background – seventeenth-century France, ancient China, medieval Hamelin – overlaid with transparent layers of Central European metaphor. But the themes which run through all three plays – themes of betrayal and of free will – are presented in realistic terms. The characters are faced with concrete situations, which they have to resolve by their own judgement.

The Czech title, literally translated as *The Hour Between Dog and Wolf*, has a double meaning; the hour between dog and wolf is the twilight hour, a time of change and transience, of mutability between one state and another. In the context of the play it is also Villon's choice between the antisocial, lawless existence of the artist and conformity with the establishment. Fischerová takes several moments in time and weaves them onstage into a single 'now', so that at Villon's trial we find present both the murdered victim, as the counsel for the prosecution, and present-day reporters with all their technological apparatus. Towards the end of the final scene, Régnier de Montigny (the Wolf) demands freedom for Villon. Bishop d'Aussigny laughs quietly. 'Freedom? There is no freedom. I thought you knew that. Freedom is only a mask for necessity, and our task is to serve that necessity.' At the end the trial is not terminated but adjourned: 'Here and now!' exclaims de Montigny. *Dog and Wolf* was given its British première by the Rose Bruford College in June 1993, in a production by the young director Petr

Palouš from the northern Bohemian town of Ústí-nad-Labem.

It was the topicality, the 'here and now!', which was the particular quality of Czech theatre in the 1980s. As Petr Oslzlý described, the theatres became almost like 'sacred circles' within a state of unfreedom – ' . . . from time to time, even in the big conventional theatres, an echo could be heard, maybe in just a brief allusion, or in a single appearance, or even a whole performance . . .'. Oslzlý's Theatre on a String in Brno, surviving in an ill-equipped room of the city art gallery, became the leading avant-garde theatre of the decade. Very often it was only the company's international reputation and its appearance at European festivals which saved it from being absorbed into the State Theatre. Paradoxically, one principle of the company's experimental work was commitment to past traditions; believing that the history of Czech theatre had been distorted by communist ideology, the company deliberately drew on original sources of nineteenth- and early twentieth-century Czech theatre. It also adapted texts of modern European classics which otherwise were inaccessible to their young audience, and made links with writers banned from publishing, such as Ludvík Kundera and Milan Uhde. As well as drawing large audiences of young people – who loved the informal surroundings, extravagant language and acting, slapstick comedy and lavish use of fire and fireworks – the company also put on unofficial extra-mural events: concerts, readings, art exhibitions combined with performance. In the summer of 1987 they even held a three-week festival in the Episcopal Gardens in the centre of Brno. Collaboration with other theatre groups, both local and international, was important, and it was out of these co-operative, creative activities that an opposition movement was born. It became a game – a serious game – to see how far back the boundaries could be pushed. Alliances formed, far more intricately linked than the secret police ever realised.

It was one of these alliances that led to the writing of *Tomorrow!*, commissioned by Petr Oslzlý for a specific occasion – the seventieth anniversary of the founding of Czechoslovakia on 28 October 1988. For the last forty of those seventy years the Communist régime had presented their own lacklustre version of how it came about; giving some marginal credit to Tomáš Masaryk (who became the first President, but who spent the war years in exile) and the Czech National Committee abroad, but none to their colleagues who handled the takeover of power in Prague. Havel and Oslzlý worked on a script which would explain in clear terms what exactly happened in Prague on 28 October 1918, and who were the main players. It was told from the point of view of Alois Rašín, who subsequently became Minister of Finance, and whose policies helped to make Czechoslovakia one of the most stable countries in Europe in the inter-war period.

Tomorrow was both didactic and prophetic. Scarcely more than a year later Havel, Oslzlý and their colleagues found themselves acting it out in real life. Many of the elements of the velvet revolution of November 1989 – the meticulous advance planning, the anticipation of the dying régime's reactions, the precautions to ensure calm among the population – are already there in the text of *Tomorrow!* Rašín's dialogue with his wife in the final scene reflects subsequent political problems: the relationship of Czechs and Germans, the break-up of the 'South Slav conglomerate', the low morale of a nation which had always relied on the state to look after its needs. There was a personal note in Karla Rašínová's reference to the Quay that was named after her husband, 'but not for long'; Havel lived in his family house on what was at that time Engels Quay, but which was soon to become Rašín Quay again.

When the Czech theatre co-existed so closely with real life, where could it go next? When the scenes acted on stage were re-enacted in the streets, what could follow on stage? Petr Oslzlý answered: 'In Czechoslovakia in the last twenty years the theatres had taken over those activities which were absent from ordinary life – free speech, free discussion, political debate. And now the theatres had become again only theatres and no more. The activities which the theatres had taken over returned where they belonged; to parliament, to the press, to television, to political conferences, to the privatisation auctions. It is in these arenas that the great dramas are being played out which will transform our society from totalitarianism to democracy. These have become the Theatrum mundi, the setting for the great dramatic contest between totalitarianism and humanity.'

In 1992, the Alfréd Radok Prize was instituted, as a joint initiative of the Czech and Slovak theatre communities. (Alfréd Radok [1914-1976], a highly original theatre director from Burian's school, was marginalised and belittled by the Communists. In spite of the limitations imposed on him, he had a great influence on the work of Otomar Krejča and Jan Grossman.) When the awards were made in 1993, there was no outright winner in the section for new plays. But among the ten highly commended entries (writers entered their work anonymously) were two by Daniela Fischerová and one, *The Innocent are Innocent*, by a student of dramaturgy at the Prague Academy of Performing Arts, the twenty-one-year-old Tomáš Rychetsky. There is a line of succession in the Czech theatre which was not destroyed either by the Nazi occupation or by forty years of Communist totalitarianism; it will survive and surely thrive in the new state which is now the Czech Republic.

Barbara Day
3 July 1993

TOMORROW! ■ VÁCLAV HAVEL

A Historical Meditation in Five Acts
Translated by BARBARA DAY

VÁCLAV HAVEL, born in 1936, had problems in gaining entry to
higher education in the 1950s because of the Communist Party's
objections to his 'bourgeois' background. In 1959 he was employed
by the Theatre on the Balustrade in Prague where his first
professionally-produced work for the stage was written in
collaboration with the writer and director, Ivan Vyskočil. In the
mid-60s, working with Jan Grossman at the same theatre, Havel
wrote *The Garden Party, The Memorandum* and *The Increased Difficulty
of Concentration.* After 1968 publishers and theatres in
Czechoslovakia were not allowed to publish or perform Havel's
work. Havel wrote a number of plays which were published and
performed abroad and a series of shorter ones – the 'Vaněk Plays'–
for performance by his own friends. He became closely, but in
secret, associated with the new avant-garde in the Czech theatre. In
1988 he wrote *Tomorrow! (Zítra to spustíme)* for one of these
companies; it was premièred in October 1988 in a production
celebrating the founding of the Czechoslovak state in 1918. In
November 1989 Václav Havel led the 'velvet revolution' which over-
threw the Communist régime in Czechoslovakia; in January 1990
he became President of Czechoslovakia, and in January 1993 of the
newly-separated Czech Republic.

Characters

RAŠÍN
MRS RAŠÍN
TUSAR
TELEPHONIST
PENÍŽEK
SCHEINER
BENEŠ
ČVANČARA
GEISTLICH
KOPECKÝ
ACTOR A
ACTRESS A
ACTOR B
ACTRESS B
ACTOR C
ACTRESS C
ACTRESS D
CROWD

ACT ONE

Darkness. A telephone suddenly starts ringing. The lights gradually come up. Centre stage are a desk and desk chair, on the desk lots of papers and a telephone; near the desk is an easy chair with a small table next to it, on which is another telephone. All the actors are present, but none of them yet in the acting area; they are sitting round the edge of the set, some of them possibly in the auditorium. The telephone rings for a while, then the actor who will play RAŠÍN *approaches the desk, sits down and lifts the receiver.*

RAŠÍN (*into receiver*). Rašín –

One of the actors takes a receiver from somewhere or other and plays TUSAR.

TUSAR (*into receiver*). Tusar here –

RAŠÍN (*into receiver*). Greetings, friend! So what's going on? Tell me –

ACTOR A (*to the audience*). That's how Rašín recollected it – but it seems he was mistaken; there's enough evidence to show that it wasn't Tusar who called Rašín, but Rašín Tusar –

ACTRESS A (*to the audience*). In those days telephone calls from Vienna to Prague were all intercepted, but not those from Prague to Vienna –

ACTOR A (*to the audience*). So that was why Tusar is said to have made use of an apparently casual conversation with Hodač to ask him to get hold of Švehla or Rašín as quickly as possible and to tell them to ring him – Tusar, that is – immediately. Hodač caught Rašín at home, gave him the message, and the conversation more probably went like this –

RAŠÍN *puts the phone down, but picks it up immediately and dials a number. One of the actresses takes the receiver from* TUSAR *and plays the telephonist.*

TELEPHONIST (*into receiver*). Switchboard –

RAŠÍN (*into receiver*). Connect me with Vienna immediately, please. This is Rašín –.

TELEPHONIST (*into receiver*). Oh, it's Dr Tusar you want, isn't it?

RAŠÍN (*into receiver*). Yes please –

TELEPHONIST (*into receiver*). He should still be in his office, Dr Hodač was just on the phone to him –

RAŠÍN (*into receiver*). I know –

TELEPHONIST (*into receiver*)). I'll get through as fast as I can. When's the big moment?

RAŠÍN (*into receiver*). Wait and see –

RAŠÍN *holds the receiver and waits. The actress who is going to play* MRS RAŠÍN *comes and sits in the easy chair; in her own time picks up the receiver of the second telephone and waits.*

ACTRESS A (*to the audience*). Mrs Karla Rašín wrote in her recollections that she listened to this conversation – as to all her husband's important conversations – on the second telephone –

ACTOR A (*to the audience*). As the more informed amongst you will already have realised, we're trying to reconstruct what took place in the flat of Dr Alois Rašín on the night of 27th to 28th October 1918. We will of course supplement the historical reconstruction with inventions of our own, but don't worry about us confusing your knowledge of history; we'll always make it clear what really did happen and what we made up –

THE TELEPHONIST *quickly passes the receiver to* TUSAR.

TUSAR (*into receiver*). Hier Reichsrat, Tusar am Apparat –

RAŠÍN (*into receiver*). Rašín here –

TUSAR (*into receiver*). It's wonderful you've called, my friend. There's great things afoot!

RAŠÍN (*into receiver*). Tell me!

TUSAR (*into receiver*). This afternoon I had a visit from Colonel Ronge of the general staff –

RAŠÍN (*into receiver*). Ronge? The same Ronge who acted as 'militärwissenschaftlicher Sachverständiger' in our trial?

ACTOR A (*to the audience*). He's referring to the trial of Dr Kramář and his companions in 1916, in which Rašín was sentenced to death –

TUSAR (*into receiver*). The same!

RAŠÍN (*into receiver*). Well, he's nothing but Friedrich's henchman, our sworn enemy!

TUSAR (*into receiver*). I know that. Well, it was this Ronge who – with the full knowledge of the Emperor – asked me to get the Czech deputies to go to the front and talk to the soldiers to get them to hold the front line just a few days longer. He said it's a question of saving military equipment worth several billion. Soldiers are leaving the battlefield *en masse*, defying orders, and apparently it's only the Czech deputies who still carry any moral weight. The war is lost, he said, peace will be declared, it's a matter of a few days.

RAŠÍN (*into receiver*). That's fantastic! If a man like that is begging the Czech deputies for help, then our moment's just around the corner. What did you say to him?

TUSAR·(*into receiver*). I told him what we agreed; that we would be willing to help during the military retreat, but only after Austria had capitulated –

RAŠÍN (*into receiver*). That's right! I think the capitulation will come in a few hours.

TUSAR (*into receiver*). It's quite likely, because whilst Ronge was still with me, another officer of the general staff ran in with the news that it had to be carried out immediately, it's not even a question of days, but of hours, the army is more and more demoralised –

RAŠÍN (*into receiver*). Many thanks for the news, we'll act accordingly!

TUSAR (*into receiver*). Ronge took my reply to the Emperor, he may turn up here again –

RAŠÍN (*into receiver*). Call me any time you want, I won't be going to bed tonight –

TUSAR (*into receiver*). Don't forget it may be a long day tomorrow!

RAŠÍN (*into receiver*). Don't worry, we'll cope! So long!

TUSAR (*into receiver*). So long!

The actor playing TUSAR *puts down his receiver somewhere,* RAŠÍN *and his wife do the same, look at each other, jump up with excitement, run to each other and embrace.*

RAŠÍN. Karlinka, my own!

MRS RAŠÍN. Oh, Lojza, Lojza –

ACTOR A (*to the audience*). We don't have any historical proof that Mrs Karla Rašín did call her husband 'Lojza' in private instead of Alois – in fact , in those days among people of their social standing it's really quite unlikely – but we've taken this poetic licence to convey the joy of the couple as it would be demonstrated nowadays –

ACTRESS A (*to the audience*). Mrs Rašín did indeed write in her recollections: both my husband and I were so excited that sleep was out of the question –

ACTOR A (*to the audience*). Indeed: and everything we've managed to establish concerning that night of 27th October makes it absolutely clear that the Rašíns really did not sleep. And we know another thing for sure, that during his conversation with Tusar, Dr Rašín uttered a very important sentence.

RAŠÍN (*exclaims*). Tomorrow's the day!

The actors turn into the CROWD, *which rapidly fills the stage, and thronging around sings the patriotic song 'Hej Slované'.*

ACT TWO

The stage has emptied and the actors are occupying their original places.
MR *and* MRS RAŠÍN *are embracing each other, then step apart.*

ACTRESS A (*to the audience*). Dr Alois Rašín was at that time the real driving force behind the work of the presidium of the National Committee. And it was his evening conversation with Tusar which convinced him that the following day – that is, the 28th October – Austro-Hungary would capitulate and the same day the National Committee must take into its own hands supreme power in an independent Czechoslovak state; that's to say, proclaim that state on home ground; take over all the public administration and turn into reality that which shortly before had been accomplished *de jure* – when the allied powers had recognised the Czechoslovak National Council in Paris as the legitimate representative of a future Czechoslovak State –

ACTOR B (*to the audience.*). How did Rašín actually envisage the founding of the state at that moment? What did he intend to do on the 28th October?

ACTRESS A (*to the audience*). It's a pity we don't know what Rašín and his wife talked about that night. However, let us speculate!

MRS RAŠÍN. Alois –

ACTOR B (*to the audience*). The first shock of joy being over, we're now going back to the more likely form of address –

RAŠÍN. What?

MRS RAŠÍN. What are you actually going to do? Do you have a plan?

RAŠÍN. Karlinka, this is a revolution! Do you imagine one can have precise plans for a revolution?

MRS RAŠÍN. I know, but all the same –

RAŠÍN. I'll ring Scheiner first of all and tell him to mobilise the members of Sokol during the night. When people come out and see them patrolling the streets – in their Sokol uniforms again after all this time – they'll realise immediately what's going on. And at the same time it'll be a guarantee of public order. We don't want any unnecessary violence or undignified behaviour. Right from the very first day we've got to show the world that we deserve the freedom for which Masaryk and his legionaries fought –

ACTRESS A (*to the audience*). In fact, this speech isn't just something we've invented. Not only did Rašín really use those words at various times and in various contexts, but the truth of his words can be confirmed: the role played by the Sokol members really did contribute to the dignified transfer of power on the 28th October –

MRS RAŠÍN. But the Sokols being there in the street still isn't going to establish the state –

RAŠÍN. Of course not. I'm just saying what I'll do first. In any case, I'll try ringing Scheiner at once –

RAŠÍN *goes to his desk, lifts the receiver and dials a number. No one responds;* RAŠÍN *puts the receiver down again.*

MRS RAŠÍN. And what next?

RAŠÍN. I'll call a meeting of the presidium of the National Council at Švehla's for eight in the morning. I'll tell them what I heard from Tusar and propose we start taking over the state administration –

MRS RAŠÍN. Won't Švehla want to wait until the capitulation really has been announced? You know how careful he is –

RAŠÍN. Stříbrný and Soukup will agree immediately, they'd look ridiculous now if they wanted to wait when a fortnight ago they wanted to get going. As for Švehla, I trust his nose for these things. He's sure to sniff that the time is right –

ACTOR B (*to the audience*). However, it's also possible that Rašín said something quite different. Such as –

RAŠÍN. If any difficulties crop up, I'll do a bit of bluffing. I'll simply say that Austria has already capitulated and that this will be general knowledge in a few hours time –

ACTRESS A (*to the audience*). We don't know what really happened at the morning meeting of the presidium; later on the four national leaders who were its members were not very forthcoming on certain matters. And years later there was still a lot of speculation and debate about their course of action. One thing *is* certain; that straight after their short morning meeting they began to behave as though the capitulation of Austria – following which they wanted to proclaim the state – had already happened. Whether it had been necessary at that morning meeting for Rašín to win this agreement by one means or another, or whether, as Soukup maintains, they did all agree on it from the first, we don't know and probably never will –

MRS RAŠÍN. And if they all agree, what then? What will you actually do?

RAŠÍN. At nine, Švehla and Soukup will go and take over the War Department Supplies Office. They'll go there and just make a minor change in the administration; they won't take it over in the name of the National Committee according to some Austrian directive concerning the participation of national committees in organising food supplies, or some agreement with Vienna or the military. They'll simply take it over in the name of the new state, and they'll get a pledge of the transfer there and then. After all, those who get their hands on the food supplies have one hell of a lot of power! Not even soldiers can stand against us if they've nothing to eat!

ACTRESS A (*to the audience*). As is confirmed by several eye-witnesses, at nine in the morning on the 28th October Švehla and Soukup really did take over the War Department Supplies Office in the name of the new state.

ACTOR B (*to the audience*). At nine in the morning, no one had yet publicly proclaimed the new state, but the taking of the Supplies Office under its administration was the first important manifestation of the state coming into existence –

MRS RAŠÍN. And what are *you* going to do?

RAŠÍN. I shall go to the offices of *Národní listy*, where I'll wait for the news from Vienna, give whatsoever instructions are necessary and hold talks with Scheiner – ah Scheiner! yes.

RAŠÍN *goes again to his desk, picks up the receiver and dials a number. No one responds;* RAŠÍN *puts the receiver down again.*

Where's he got to?

MRS RAŠÍN. And then?

RAŠÍN. Well, as I see it, some time about half past ten the whole presidium will have joined up again at the *Obecní dům*, from which we'll go to see the Vice-Regent and to find Schönborn. We'll inform both of them that from this moment the National Committee is the leading authority of the independent Czechoslovak state and we'll ask them to take the vow of allegiance and to subordinate themselves completely to us, or else to leave their posts –

ACTRESS A (*to the audience*). And that is more or less what did happen on the 28th October. At about quarter past nine Rašín, in the office of *Národní listy*, heard about Andrássy's note—

ACTOR B (*to the audience*). If you don't know what that is, don't worry; we'll explain it when the time comes –

ACTRESS A (*to the audience*). Rašín later said to Penižek, *Národní listy* correspondent in Vienna –

RAŠÍN (*to the actor playing Penižek*). Do you realise, Penižek, that it was you who gave the final push for the take-over?

PENIŽEK. How's that?

RAŠÍN. When you rang the editorial office after nine o'clock about Andrássy's note, I happened to be there myself and that information – which I had been expecting – that information was the final signal for the start –

ACTRESS A (*to the audience*). In one sense Rašín was right because he really had been expecting that 'final signal' and he had prepared everything for its imminent arrival. However, in another sense he wasn't being quite exact; because by the time he learnt about the note the take-over of the Supplies Office in the name of the new state had already begun; so they were really off before the starting signal. What would have happened later – if it hadn't been for Andrássy's note – is difficult to say; maybe the leaders would have gone to the Vice-Regent's Office, maybe they wouldn't. Certainly, without the note there wouldn't have been the spontaneous mass demonstration which formed the background to the next steps taken by the leaders –

RAŠÍN. I began to telephone immediately –

ACTOR B (*to the audience*). And Mrs Rašín later wrote –

MRS RAŠÍN. Some time after nine o'clock our telephone rang –

The telephone rings; MRS RAŠÍN *lifts the receiver.*

(*Into the telephone*). Karla Rašín.

RAŠÍN (*into the receiver of his telephone*). Austria has capitulated; you're the first person to be told. I must hurry. We're going to take over the Vice-Regent's Offices –

MRS RAŠÍN (*into the telephone*). This is the most important thing that's happened in the history of this country for three hundred years! I'm so thrilled you're a part of it!

Both of them put down the receivers.

I remember that conversation very well, because it was and still is a source of great pride to me that I was the first person to hear about it from my husband –

ACTRESS A (*to the audience*). Many books have been written about what happened on the 28th October, countless testimonies have been published and great debates unleashed; but fortunately it's not our aim here to reconstruct what happened on that day. Let's go back now to the evening before, or to be more exact, to the night before. Rašín obviously had in his head a relatively precise plan of action – for he must have been thinking about it for months, if not years – and his wife's curiosity must certainly have been satisfied. However, he put aside her natural concern about his way of life.

MRS RAŠÍN. Don't you think, Alois, that this is rather a risky business? For you, for you all, for the whole population. Don't forget that the Austrians still have a garrison in Prague –

RAŠÍN. I've never kept it a secret from you, Karla, that I'm putting my life at risk. But when it's a question of the nation, individual safety doesn't come into it. We have a historic challenge before us, which we must find the courage to accept – despite the fact we don't and can't have a guarantee of instant success, and must be prepared for sacrifices. As far as the army is concerned, I'm relying on Scheiner – ah Scheiner! yes.

RAŠÍN *returns to his desk, lifts the receiver and dials a number. The actor who will play* SCHEINER *takes a receiver from somewhere and answers.*

SCHEINER (*into the receiver*). Scheiner –

RAŠÍN (*into the receiver*). At last!

SCHEINER (*into the receiver*). I'm sorry, I've only just got back from the National Committee! Have you had any news from Vienna yet?

RAŠÍN (*into the receiver*). Yes, the decision went in our favour, all President Wilson's proposals have been accepted! We're free!

ACTOR B (*to the audience*). That is how Scheiner described his phone conversation with Rašín, but we're rather doubtful as to whether on that Sunday evening Rašín would have declared so confidently to Scheiner that Austria had already capitulated. Let's attribute this version to a flight of fancy by Scheiner the Sokol and put more faith in the version which comes from Rašín's recollections –

RAŠÍN (*into the receiver*). I've spoken to Tusar and it seems that in a few hours' time Austria will have capitulated. Get the Sokols ready, have them out patrolling the streets and let everything go according to the plan we worked out –

SCHEINER (*into the receiver*). I understand, I'll see to it at once!

RAŠÍN (*into the receiver*). I'm relying on you and I'm not worried about what will happen in the streets. But what will we do if the government or the Germans or the Communists stand against us and it comes to a clash? Have you the resources for armed resistance?

SCHEINER (*into the receiver*). We don't have much at the moment in the way of weapons. But we are prepared to seize the military stores and munitions straightaway –

RAŠÍN (*into the receiver*). Maybe we should go and speak to the generals as well tomorrow and explain to them what a waste it would be for any more blood to flow at this time. If you think of anything else, I won't be going to bed tonight. I'll see you in the editorial office tomorrow at nine –

SCHEINER (*into the receiver*). You know what I regret?

RAŠÍN (*into the receiver*). What?

SCHEINER (*into the receiver*). That old Franz Joseph never lived to see the day!

Both of them start laughing; the actor who played SCHEINER *puts his receiver down;* RAŠÍN *puts his down as well. A pause.*

MRS RAŠÍN. Shouldn't you try and get some sleep? I can listen out for the telephone –

RAŠÍN. It's nice of you, but I've still got work to do –

MRS RAŠÍN.What work?

RAŠÍN. I've got to write a law for the establishment of the state –

The actors change into the CROWD. *They quickly fill the stage, singing and joyfully thronging around.*

CROWD (*singing*). The Czech state is born at last,
    Let us all rejoice,
    Austrian majesty is past,
    Let us raise our voice–

ACT THREE

The stage empties and the actors return to their original places. RAŠÍN
*remains alone in the middle of the acting area. He sits at his desk correcting
something.*

ACTOR B (*to the audience*). On the initiative of the 'Mafia' a secret
   commission had already spent some time on the preparation of
   a constitution and the first laws of the new state. Rašín had
   been one of its members and when on the eve of the 28th
   October he wrote the first law of the new state he could rely on
   the texts which the commission had prepared, especially drafts
   produced by Dr Ferdinand Pantuček, privy councillor to the
   supreme court in Vienna –

MRS RAŠÍN *comes in bringing a cup of tea for* RAŠÍN.

RAŠÍN. Thanks –

MRS RAŠÍN. How are you getting on?

RAŠÍN. It's more or less there, I think –

MRS RAŠÍN. What? So quickly?

RAŠÍN. I read through Pantuček's working papers and a couple of
   other things and decided in the end to keep it as brief as
   possible –

RAŠÍN *shows* MRS RAŠÍN *the paper he has in front of him.*

MRS RAŠÍN. That's it?

RAŠÍN. I think so –

MRS RAŠÍN. I would never have thought you could found a state
   on half a sheet of writing paper!

RAŠÍN. You can do anything when there's a revolution on. Shall I
   read it to you?

MRS RAŠÍN. Of course.

RAŠÍN (*reads*). The independent Czechoslovak state has come into
   being. In order for there to be continuity with the previously-
   existing legal order, for there to be no confusion and for the
   transition to the new statehood to be orderly, the National
   Committee in the name of the Czechoslovak nation as the

exponent of state sovereignty directs: Article I. The form of
state of the Czechoslovak State will be determined by the
National Assembly in agreement with the Czechoslovak
National Council in Paris as organs of the unanimous will of the
nation. Before this happens, state sovereignty will be exercised
by the National Committee. Article II. All the existing
provincial and imperial laws will for the present remain in
force. Article III. All local, state, and county offices, the state
provincial, regional, county and municipal institutions are
subordinate to the National Committee and will for the time
being function and act according to the laws and directives
currently in force. Article IV. This law becomes effective as of
today. Article V. The presidium of the National Committee is
enjoined to ensure that this law is implemented. Prague, 28th
October, 1918.

ACTOR B (*to the audience*). Rašín read his proposal in the early
evening of the 28th October at the plenary sitting of the
National Committee in the *Obecní dům*, which approved it
unanimously –

ACTRESS B (*to the audience*). After some minor textual changes –

ACTOR B (*to the audience*). And issued it as the first law of the
Czechoslovak State. The independent state was thus officially
announced in Prague on the evening of the 28th October;
nevertheless at the moment of its announcement it already had
behind it an important piece of history, made up of the wealth
of events which had taken place during the first day of its
existence –

MRS RAŠÍN. Why doesn't it say that it will be a republic?

RAŠÍN. Until Kramář's delegation in Geneva reaches an agreement
with Beneš, we here in Prague can't determine what form the
state will take! The state is coming into being thanks to its
recognition by the victorious allied powers and thanks to the
recognition of its own government abroad – without that
government or before it acts or without agreement with it no
one can decide what form the state will take. Obviously it *is*
going to be a republic, but we simply don't have the right to
declare it, if we did we might undermine Masaryk. Not only
from the point of view of competence, but possibly even
materially; what if those abroad have given some kind of
undertaking for a constitutional monarchy?

ACTOR B (*to the audience*). This is how – in total agreement – all
the domestic political leaders would have answered Mrs Rašín's
question. And yet, ten days previously, the famous Washington
declaration had been published, in which Czechoslovakia was

declared a republic and in which a number of the constitutional principles of the republic were specified. So the question arises: why did no one know of this in Prague? Or did they know, but preferred for some reason to wait for the outcome of the negotiations of the National Committee in Geneva? Or was there some other matter involved? Maybe the fear that premature expression of the word 'republic' might still provoke some military resistance on the part of the collapsing monarchy?

ACTRESS B (*to the audience*). We admit we haven't found a satisfactory answer to this question in any of the historical sources. It seems to us that the most likely explanation is that the text of the Washington declaration simply wasn't known to anyone in Prague on the 28th October –

The telephone rings. RAŠÍN *quickly reaches it and picks up the receiver; at the same time* MRS RAŠÍN *picks up the receiver of her telephone.*

RAŠÍN (*into the receiver*). Rašín –

The actor playing TUSAR *takes a receiver from somewhere and speaks.*

TUSAR (*into the receiver*). Tusar here. I'm calling so as not to disturb you later on. No one came, it seems that they've blocked up that hole again –

RAŠÍN (*into the receiver*). On the contrary, I think they understood the futility of any such enterprise. I've set all the preparations here in motion, I'm certain tomorrow's our moment –

ACTOR B (*to the audience*). Tusar was ringing from Vienna, so the telephone was tapped. Tusar was taking precautions while Rašín obviously thought that these were already unnecessary.

RAŠÍN (*into the receiver*). I've no intention of going to bed, ring whenever you like if you hear something –

TUSAR (*into the receiver*). Very well. I'll keep my fingers crossed!

RAŠÍN (*into the receiver*). Thanks. Good bye –

The actor who played TUSAR *puts his receiver down.* MR *and* MRS RAŠÍN *put down theirs. A pause.*

MRS RAŠÍN. Alois –

RAŠÍN. Hm–

MRS RAŠÍN. Can I ask you something?

RAŠÍN. Of course –

MRS RAŠÍN. Hand on heart –

RAŠÍN. There already –

MRS RAŠÍN. Aren't you really rather pleased the old man's in
  Geneva just now?

RAŠÍN. Karlinka, please –

MRS RAŠÍN. Don't say you're not!

ACTRESS B (*to the audience*). We invented that question for Mrs
  Rašín. But we had our reasons: it's not inconceivable that some
  of the younger leaders of the political parties represented in
  the presidium – notably Stříbrný and Rašín – had been quite
  pleased to send their revered elders – namely Kramář and
  Klofáč – to Geneva. Maybe not so much because they were
  longing for the credit which would otherwise have been reaped
  by the main party leaders, but simply because the ever-changing
  stage called for more dynamic actors than the older men. For
  obvious reasons we've refrained from putting into Rašín's
  mouth any answer to his wife's question –

MRS RAŠÍN. I know you don't have any personal ambitions, I'd
  never suspect you of that! And in any case – I'm very proud of
  you! One day our grandchildren will call you the man of the
  28th October!

  RAŠÍN *laughs, goes across to* MRS RAŠÍN *and hugs her. The actors
  change into the* CROWD. *They quickly fill the stage, singing the song
  'By the strength of the lion, by the flight of the falcon', merrily thronging
  around.*

ACT FOUR

The stage empties and the actors resume their former places. MR *and* MRS RAŠÍN *are embracing each other centre stage. After a while they step apart.*

ACTRESS B (*to the audience*). From our reconstruction of the events so far, you might have got the impression that the 28th October was turned into a revolution just by the national leaders present in Prague – that is, Švehla, Rašín, Soukup and Stříbrný – who simply decided (justifiably anticipating the Austrian capitulation) to carry out the revolution that day. However, we wouldn't be true to the facts of the case if we didn't mention, briefly at least, the other makers of the revolution: that is, the people. Later on, in dramatic discussions about who really brought about the revolution of 28th October, another opinion emerged and to put that to you we have to skip forward again several hours from the night with which we've been concerned. According to this view –

ACTOR C (*to the audience*). Put forward, for example, by the director of the *Národní politika* printing house, Geistlich –

ACTRESS B (*to the audience*). The revolution of the 28th October occurred completely independently of any planning or organisation, being in part due to chance, in part the result of misunderstanding, but mostly as the expression of the irresistible need of the people, that happened to find the right men in the right place at the right time –

ACTOR C (*to the audience*). By which of course is meant men other than the political leaders. According to this the politicians merely improvised around the spontaneous decision of the citizens, acted as it were under pressure from the street –

ACTRESS B (*to the audience*). In that case, who were the 'right men in the right place'?

Three of the actors step forward and play Beneš, Čvančara and Geistlich.

ČVANČARA. Us, for example!

BENEŠ. I'm Václav Beneš, editor of *Národní politika*; this is Čvančara, the secretary of our paper, and this is the director of our printing house, Geistlich. At 10.20 on the 28th October

Andrássy's note reached our editorial office –

MRS RAŠÍN. By that time my husband and his colleagues were already taking over the Vice-Regent's Office!

ACTOR C (*to the audience*). Count Andrássy was the Foreign Minister of Austro-Hungary –

ACTRESS B (*to the audience*). This note, if you don't know already, was written in a curiously ambiguous manner: in it, Austria agreed with all the conditions which President Wilson attached to any sort of armistice talks, but, at the same time, nowhere did Austria in so many words actually capitulate. She simply indicated that she was competent to hold armistice talks, and accordingly to discuss the contents of President Wilson's demands, including the provision whereby the Czechoslovaks were to determine the manner of their future statehood. Basing itself on Emperor Charles's manifesto of federalisation, Austria apparently meant by this that, with the states of the Entente – as their genuine although defeated partner – and at the same time with her own national minorities she would discuss the establishment of national states, of whose constitutions she would in some manner be patron – doubtless in the unspoken hope that the monarchy would thereby survive at least in the form of a sort of symbolic umbrella which would shelter the newly emerged states. However, what the note meant to say was less important than how it was understood –

GEISTLICH. When Beneš read it he ran immediately to Čvančara and said –

BENEŠ (*to* ČVANČARA). So this is an end of it all, there's an armistice!

GEISTLICH. I remembered immediately that for two years I'd been hiding a sign with the word 'Armistice' in big red letters. I told Čvančara and he exclaimed –

ČVANČARA (*exclaims*). Put it up on the signboard at once! And get them to hang red-and-white flags from the window!

ACTRESS B (*to the audience*). In other words, these gentlemen, like the rest of the nation including its leaders, chose to interpret Andrássy's note as the final defeat of Austria, the end of the war, and freedom for the Czechs and Slovaks. But at the same time they imagined that it was thanks to their signboard and their flags that the nation took this to be the meaning of the note. From one point of view they were, as we shall see, quite right. On the other hand, we can hardly credit that even without their signboard the nation wouldn't have realised the significance of Andrássy's note.

During this, BENEŠ, ČVANČARA *and* GEISTLICH *hang the sign 'Armistice' over the stage and red-and-white flags around the stage.*

BENEŠ. So Geistlich's sign was put up immediately and flags – the very first that day – fluttered on the building of *Národní politika,* by which *de facto* the fuse was lit –

GEISTLICH. And then it all took off!

ČVANČARA. Obviously the passers-by stopped to look – reading the sign again and again – debating it among themselves – waiting around for more details – the news quickly spread – excitement grew – more and more people gathered – the handful soon became a crowd –

The actors gradually gather on the acting area, looking at the notice, debating among themselves, the excitement grows, they become the CROWD. *After a while one actor, who will play* KOPECKÝ, *emerges from the crowd. He moves forward and addresses himself to everyone present.*

KOPECKÝ. And at that moment, if you'll allow me to say so, it was I who played an irreplaceable role. We can't be certain whether without my intervention the notice on the *Národní politika* building would have had the far-reaching historical significance it did have, and for which the gentlemen from *Národní politika* naturally wish to take the credit. But allow me to present myself: František Kopecký, greengrocer, from the Old Town in Prague. On the 28th October at about 10 o'clock I left my home in Havelská Street and crossed Wenceslas Square to the Franz Joseph Railway Station – now Wilson Station –

ACTOR C (*to the audience*). Today Main Station –

KOPECKÝ. Because I was travelling on business to Nový Bydžov. That's why I was armed with a walking stick, which unexpectedly came in handy as a conductor's baton –

ACTRESS B (*to the audience*). We weren't able to establish why greengrocers travelling on business to Nový Bydžov in those days should arm themselves with walking sticks –

KOPECKÝ. Happening to pass by the building of *Národní politika,* I saw a group of people gathered; I approached them, and read that sign saying 'Armistice'. And suddenly it hit me: we're free! In the stress of the moment I shouted it out loud. (*He shouts.*) We're free! Everyone stared at me –

The crowd stares in astonishment, then begins to be convinced.

CROWD. Yes! It is true! We're free!

KOPECKÝ *begins to shout slogans, waving his walking stick; the*

CROWD *joins in.*

KOPECKÝ and the CROWD (*shouting*). We're free! We're free! We're free! Independence! Independence! Independence! Down with Austria! Down with Austria! Down with Austria! Away with the Habsburgs! Away with the Habsburgs! Away with the Habsburgs! Long live Masaryk! Long live Masaryk! Long live Masaryk! Long live Wilson! Long live Wilson! Long live Wilson! We're free! We're free! We're free!

The CROWD *grows quieter, forms itself into a procession and led by* KOPECKÝ *circles the stage.*

KOPECKÝ. The news spread quickly and Wenceslas Square was soon packed with people. I led the main procession and all that day I controlled its direction and its slogans, I conducted it, so to speak. I didn't return home until late that evening, when my young wife was extremely upset and I'd completely lost my voice. So it was the people really, whom I'd roused to it, who made the revolution. All the leaders had to do was to confirm officially what we, the ordinary man in the street, had proclaimed. But we didn't get any streets or embankments named after us –

MRS RAŠÍN. You can leave the embankment out of it, Mr Kopecký! If you die a martyr's death like my husband, then you might have something named after you. Only it didn't stay named after him for long. But that's not the point at the moment. I have evidence –

The CROWD *stands in a circle round* MRS RAŠÍN *and listens to her.*

– that the political steps which were taken by my husband and his friends on the 28th October and which led to the establishment of the state, were well-prepared and thought out in advance, and that even the 28th October as the day of the revolution had been decided before the people rose at the news of Andrássy's note. The leaders had been expecting the note and were counting on the reaction it would provoke among the people. Why else, for example, would they have mobilised the Sokols during the night? Why else would my husband have spent the night writing the law about the establishment of the state? Why would the presidium have already gone to the Vice-Regent's Office long before the time Mr Kopecký was reading the signboard outside *Národní politika*?

CROWD (*chanting*). Long Live Rašín! Long Live Rašín! Long Live Rašín!

ACTOR C (*to the audience*). Mrs Rašín – although obviously not in those words and certainly not in personal polemics with Mr

Kopecký – many years later did rise to the defence of the political leaders when their credentials were called into question. The gentlemen from *Národní politika* and Mr Kopecký likewise spoke out in public debate about the 28th October, even though they didn't emphasise their contributions – Mr Kopecký in particular – quite so pointedly as, for dramatic reasons, we have presented them here –

ACTRESS B (*to the audience*). The more memorable the day of 28th October became in public awareness, the more people claimed recognition of their own contributions and protested that the contributions of others were over-rated; year by year as the anniversary approached, new witnesses, new actors, new analysts emerged. We'll close this whole diversion with a relatively simple but – in our opinion – most likely hypothesis: as ever in history, the truth was somewhere in between: the people would have been nothing without the leaders and the leaders nothing without the people; both sides obviously made their own contributions; the unforeseen and spontaneous action of the people was, in that moment, the chief support for the political acts of the leaders in Prague, and the political acts of the leaders were the only thing which could at that moment have changed the will of the people into the political reality of an independent Czechoslovakia –

KOPECKÝ (*begins to sing the National Anthem*). Where is my home, where is my home –

The CROWD *joins in with* KOPECKÝ, *solemnly standing and singing the National Anthem.*

ACT FIVE

*When the actors have finished singing the Anthem they quickly clear the
acting area and resume their original places. MR and MRS RAŠÍN
remain centre stage. He is sitting in an easy chair; she on the ground at his
feet, head resting on his lap; both gazing thoughtfully in front of them.*

ACTOR C (*to the audience*). The morning of the 28th October is
   slowly drawing near. Mr Kopecký is still sleeping the sweet sleep
   of a respectable citizen of the Austro-Hungarian Empire; he has
   not yet lost his voice and he has no inkling of what will prevent
   him from travelling on business to Nový Bydžov tomorrow
   morning. Dr Rašín has explained to his wife what he has in
   mind to do the next day and has written the first law of the new
   state. He and his lady wife have stayed awake. What are they
   thinking about?

MRS RAŠÍN. What are you thinking about?

RAŠÍN. This will surprise you; I was thinking about you –

MRS RAŠÍN. About me? Now?

RAŠÍN. I was remembering the first time you visited me in
   Möllersdorf prison and how upset you were by my wretched
   condition –

MRS RAŠÍN. You looked dreadful! But whatever made you think of
   that now?

RAŠÍN. I've no idea –

ACTOR C (*to the audience*). It's very likely that during that long
   night, perhaps the most important of his life, Rašín thought
   back at least once to some of the important moments of his life,
   one way and another linked with his life in politics – as for
   example the trial long ago with *Omladina,* when the courtroom
   was completely filled by police with bayonets; or the death
   sentence at his trial with Kramář; or his encounter with hunger
   and death in Möllersdorf prison. He must have been aware that
   he was about to embark on the fulfilment of the idea upon
   which he had set his whole life, and for which he had sacrificed
   so much –

ACTRESS C (*to the audience*). And it's most likely that at the same time he must have been aware of what a loyal and valuable support his wife had always been –

ACTOR C (*to the audience*). He was naturally a very reserved man when it came to expressing his own feelings, which is why we have supposed that he is unlikely to have said aloud to his wife any more on these lines than he said a moment ago. And apart from this he was always more inclined towards the future than the past; and how much more the future must have occupied his thoughts that particular night.

ACTRESS C (*to the audience*). What was he hoping for and what did he fear? What historic opportunities, alternatives and dangers did he see facing the state that was just coming into being?

ACTOR C (*to the audience*). We know nothing of all this and so are forced to enter the realm of pure guesswork. Let us ask ourselves: could he for example have been thinking along the following lines?

RAŠÍN. It's not an easy matter, to found a new state. It's even more difficult to make sure it keeps going –

MRS RAŠÍN. Do you think that the new republic might not keep going?

RAŠÍN. It will be a small state with enormous minorities, in effect multinational; and what is more, geopolitically in an exceptionally exposed position – supposing Germany gets back on her feet again?

MRS RAŠÍN. Oh, I think the peace conference will make sure that nothing like that could happen –

RAŠÍN. Karla, Karla! The tougher the conditions the conference imposes on Germany, the more dangerous will be the consequences! What if they turn bolshevik? And can you imagine what it would mean for us if we had some sort of expansionist Germany as our neighbour, when we've got such a powerful German minority within our borders?

MRS RAŠÍN. I think everything will be different after this war!

RAŠÍN. Many things will be different, that's for sure. America has become a world power with a grasp of its responsibility for the rest of the world, Czechoslovakia will have guarantees from the allied powers, not only those which result from the peace conference, but others – Edvard Beneš will certainly make sure that we have a good network of military treaties –

MRS RAŠÍN. There you are then –

RAŠÍN. But it's still not enough! Up to a short time ago they didn't

even know that we existed, and they can hardly be expected –
should God forbid things turn ugly again – to shed their blood
for us just like that! Treaties are one thing, reality another –

MRS RAŠÍN. With our geographical position, they'd be sawing the
branch from under them should they ever give us up to
anyone's tender mercies –

RAŠÍN. We know that, but do they? It's not going to be easy to fill
the vacuum Austria will leave in Central Europe! Austria may
have been a rotten Colossus, that's why she had to perish, but
there must have been some logic in having such a Colossus in
that position: it meant that between Germany and Russia – and
Russia will get back on its feet under one ruler or another –
something existed which couldn't easily become a playground
for such a variety of expansionist ideas as may now threaten,
with all at once a small group of new, inexperienced states
variously squabbling with one another! If we could at least rely
on the others – but how do we know how things are going to
turn out? The Hungarians aren't going to change overnight,
the Poles are already arguing among themselves and however
some south Slav conglomerate is going to hold together God
only knows!

MRS RAŠÍN. You're frightening me a bit! Whatever has this doom-
mongering got into you now for? Šmeral would love to hear
you –

RAŠÍN. I'm not doom-mongering. I'm only saying it all to show
what an enormous responsibility we're taking on for future
generations and what a difficult challenge lies ahead. And
anyway, what worries me more than the Germans, the Russians
and the Hungarians put together are the Czechs –

MRS RAŠÍN. The Czechs?

RAŠÍN. The country's in ruins, there's been no investment in it for
years – just look at the condition our railways are in! – during
the war people forgot how to work, now they'll expect to get
everything from the state – 'since it's ours, let it look after us' –
the socialists will want to parcel out the country estates, the only
things that are still more or less functioning – it won't be
possible to keep the currency stable and to ensure economic
progress without unpopular measures and sacrifices – and
that's the last thing our people are interested in! Long ago they
forgot that the first prerequisite and criterion of freedom is
responsibility! Up to now we were united against a common
enemy, but once that's gone and we've got to go from pulling
down to building up, it'll be a different story. I must own up to
you, sometimes when I look at certain colleagues on the

National Committee and imagine what they're going to be like in government, it does makes me shiver a bit!

MRS RAŠÍN. But your fiscal policy is beautifully worked out! Once you get that through –

RAŠÍN. That's just the question! It's certainly not going to be popular and it's going to be difficult for our party to get it through on its own; we're only small and under the new election law we'll lose a lot of influence. People will find Klofáč's demagogy more straightforward, we're more the sort of type that appeals to university professors –

ACTRESS C (*to the audience*). Let me explain: Rašín was a member of the constitutional democratic party, which after the revolution changed its name to national democratic –

ACTOR C (*to the audience*). And another thing it would be appropriate to mention at this point: Dr Alois Rašín – before his assassination on 5th January 1923 by a young political opponent – did, as the first Czechoslovak Minister of Finance, succeed in getting his ambitious fiscal and economic plan adopted and implemented, thanks to which Czechoslovakia – almost as a solitary island in the midst of general inflationary chaos – ensured for itself a firm and permanently self-stabilising currency and soon achieved some major economic successes. Rašín's fiscal policy met with the admiration of all Europe –

RAŠÍN. You know, Karlinka, it is quite complicated: because where poverty threatens, then there's the danger of socialism; and where socialism threatens, there's the danger of poverty!

Pause.

MRS RAŠÍN. Lojza –

RAŠÍN. Mm?

MRS RAŠÍN. Please, my dear, don't think about those sort of things! You know what a lot you've got to do tomorrow! Wouldn't it be better if you took a little nap?

RAŠÍN (*looks at his pocket watch*). In an hour I must ring Soukup about the early-morning meeting of the presidium – but maybe I could switch off for a little while –

MRS RAŠÍN. It's the most sensible thing you could do!

RAŠÍN *stretches out comfortably in the easy chair and half-closes his eyes.* MRS RAŠÍN *brings out a tartan rug from somewhere, gently covers him, strokes his head and crosses to his desk.* RAŠÍN *dozes off;* MRS RAŠÍN *carefully picks up the paper with the draft of the first law and, moved, gazes at it for a long time. Without drawing attention to*

*themselves, the remaining actors begin to move towards the centre of the
stage, but without filling it, only creating a sort of circle around* MR
and MRS RAŠÍN. *At the same time music from Smetana's* Libuše *can
be heard very faintly. As it gradually gets louder,* MRS RAŠÍN *slowly
puts the paper down on the desk, gazes into the auditorium, and then to
the accompaniment of the orchestra begins to sing Libuše's closing
prophecy. There are, in the manner of a sound collage, inserted into her
singing recorded excerpts from authentic speeches by various Czech and
Slovak statesmen which seek to mirror both bad and hopeful times, and
the important historical turning points which Czechoslovakia has
experienced from her foundation until the present day. A variant could
be that the fragments from the speeches are reproduced in Rašín's voice –
it is, after all, his dream. At the moment when the collage of Libuše's
prophecy and the historical quotations have reached their climax and
come to an end, there is a tomb-like silence. Everyone stands there
motionless and looks at* RAŠÍN. *He wakes up, rubs his eyes and looks
around in confusion.*

ACTOR C (*to the audience*). We can provide no historical proof that
in the early hours of the 28th October 1918 Dr Alois Rašín
dropped off to sleep for a few moments. And still less do we
have proof that he dreamed such a dream!

ACTRESS D (*exclaims*). Then who did dream it?

Blackout.

GAMES ■ IVAN KLÍMA

Translated by BARBARA DAY

Playwright, novelist and essayist, Ivan Klíma was born in Prague in 1931. Being half-Jewish, he was incarcerated for three years during the Second World War in Terezín. After the war he graduated in Czech and Literature at the Philosophical Faculty of Prague's Charles University. From 1959–63 he was an editor at the Czechoslovak Writers Publishing House and from 1964–69 he was an editor of the leading Czech literary weekly, *Literární listy*. The paper was banned following the invasion. In 1969 he was Visiting Professor at the University of Michigan, later returning to Prague. For the next 20 years Klíma was prevented from publishing his work in the State-run publishing houses and official media. He wrote for publication abroad and in the thriving Prague samizdat, which circulated typescript copies of banned authors' works. In 1989, together with Václav Havel, Klíma re-formed the Czech PEN Club, of which he is now President. Since November 1989 his work has been produced and published in Czechoslovakia. In Britain, several of his novels have been published, including *My First Loves*, *A Summer Affair* and *Love and Garbage*. His plays include *The Castle*, *The Master*, *The Jury*, *Klára and the Two Gentlemen*, *Café Myriam*, *A Bridegroom for Marcela*, *A Room for Two*, *Thundering* and *The Minister and the Angel*. *Games (Hry)* was premièred in 1975 at the Josefstadt Theater in Vienna.

Characters

PETR, a physicist. SOVA's friend. IRENA's brother. 35 years old.
IRENA, a designer. Petr's older sister.
FILIP, a judge. Irena's husband. 40 years old.
KAMIL SOVA, a sociologist. Petr's contemporary and friend.
JAKUB, a sportsman, Filip's nephew. 27 years old.
JOSEF DEML, an architect. About 45 years old.
EVA, his mistress. A singer. About 25 years old.
BAUER, in his fifties.

The action takes place in a spacious room, with a ceiling made up of massive old beams. A flight of stairs leads up out of the room, which is furnished in the baroque style with an armchair, table, writing desk, cupboard and other items. Antique pictures, maps and weapons hang on the walls. There is a coat-rack.
Because every scene is at the same time an independent play, it would be appropriate for the titles to be made a part of the staging, whether by projection, mime, or a placard.

Games was first performed in Britain by the Midnight Theatre
Company at the Gate Theatre Club, London, on 19 July, 1990. The
cast was as follows:

IRENA	Joan Blackham
KAMIL SOVA	Bill Britten
JOSEF DEML	Hugh Simon
EVA	Erika Hoffman
JENIK BAUER	Michael Medwin
FILIP	Nick Kemp
JAKUB	David Pullan
PETR	John Moreno

Directed by Derek Wax
Produced by Rebecca Wolman
Designed by Rebecca Janaway & Jennifer Siley
Lighting by Martin Hazlewood
Stage management by David Caron, Kun Ma, Liselle Terret, Collette
Ive, Weronika Wasniewska, Kenny Wax & Lonnie Zarum

Setting – Irena and Filip's flat in Prague, 1973

ACT ONE

Game One

Little Cooks

IRENA *brings bowls of salad to the table and arranges them. Tastes them. Makes a satisfied face and then frowns, runs off, returns with a chopping board, onions and a long knife. The doorbell rings. Carrying the chopping board, she goes to let someone in; halfway there she puts it down on the armchair. She opens the door.*

SOVA. Good evening. Do you know who I am?

IRENA. Yes of course, you're Kamil. Petr's always talking about you. He calls you 'Tenzing'.

SOVA. They used to call me that, in the old days. I was usually known as the 'Red Rhino'. I never understood why I was the 'Rhino', nor 'Red' if it comes to that. (*He laughs.*) I'm delighted you still remember me. But I ought to warn you. I've never really been good at games.

IRENA. That doesn't matter, I'm just glad you've come. Petr's looking forward to seeing you. Do you know, I got hold of your book not long ago? Now they say it's been taken off the library shelves. Why? There are such wonderful, inspiring ideas in it. Filip – my husband – was as enthusiastic as I was. You know, I'd like to understand sociology. I've even remembered some lines from your book: (*She quotes with pathos.*) Even the freest head is stuck on a trunk whose hands are tied. (*She corrects herself.*) Well, it may not be quite right, but that's what inspired me. I haven't offended you, have I, I'm sorry that Filip isn't here yet. He had to write some report on prisons, it's a lot of work for him. He'd like to help those wretches, but I keep telling him, once someone's in prison, then it's already too late. People shouldn't let themselves sink so low, it's not as though they're bad from birth. Someone ought to have a word with them in time. You know, I believe terribly in the power of the word, like it says in the Bible; people can understand each other, what do you think, Kamil?

SOVA. Certainly – in principle. Although there have to be two to

make a conversation: one to speak and one to listen. Petr won't
be here today?

IRENA. Oh yes, my brother is sure to be here. He's gone for some
wine. I don't know a thing about drink.

SOVA (*reviving*). Of course, I have looked into the theory of games.
Would you believe it, one can actually come across quite
interesting puns or even stories? For example: a guest is
expected for lunch, but the servant doesn't know exactly who is
coming. He only knows that it may be Mr A, who only drinks
red wine or sherry, or Mrs B, who only drinks gin or brandy, or
Mr C, who only drinks red wine, brandy or sherry. The servant
looks in the cellar and finds there only whisky, gin and sherry.
Now, careful. The question is: can the servant be sure that he is
able to satisfy the expected guest? (*A moment of awkward silence.
He goes to sit in the armchair where* IRENA *put down the board with
the chopped onions.*)

IRENA (*rescuing the chopping board at the last moment*). I'm sorry, I'm
just a bit nervous. I've never held an evening like this before.
But it struck me it would be fun to get people together for once
and instead of talking about politics and nasty things like that, if
we just played together. You know, forget we're grown up and
burdened with all the cares of this terrible world on our
shoulders. Like what happened here, less than a month ago, a
student was strangled in the Castle Gardens. And her body
wasn't even found, they say the dustbin men took it away.

SOVA. It's a splendid idea, Irena. Can I help you in some way?
Cooking is my hobby nowadays.

IRENA. They've got a new dustcart now, orange, open at the back
with these rotating blades inside. And they say they threw the
poor girl into it. Everyone knows, but what can you do with
them! Someone has to carry the rubbish away. Do you really
enjoy cooking, Kamil?

SOVA. I resolved to go into it for fundamental reasons. One has to
be independent in something as essential as the preparation of
food. I don't deny it was difficult to start with. I nearly poisoned
myself once when I misread the recipe and mixed four
tablespoons of bicarbonate of soda into the pastry instead of a
quarter of a teaspoon. But now I can even make you a
Neapolitan Salad!

IRENA. Oh, a salad from Naples! I knew I'd hear about something
exceptionally interesting from you. You know, salad for me is
something like a symbol. If you ask for some salad in a pub,
they'll bring you a few slivers of preserved beetroot, or at best, a
few withered lettuce leaves drowned in watery vinegar. Don't you

think that's really humiliating and undignified? You must let me have your recipe. I'll let you have a recipe for marrow salad in return. – And I don't know if you get that restful feeling as well, when you slice an onion or chop a marrow into cubes. I forget everything that's happened to me, everything horrible in my life. Perhaps you don't know that my second husband also . . . (*She stops herself.*) I've got a hundred and eleven salad recipes: Salad with Truffles, and Banana Salad, and Bosnian Salad, and Hot Cucumber Salad, and Cheese Salad with Crab, and Fennel Salad, and Hanák Salad, Miami Salad, Greek Salad and . . .

SOVA. I'll try and get it together. Yes. First of all I'll acquaint you with the basic material. That is cooked macaroni. Next I shall introduce the necessary raw vegetables. These are green peppers, sweet capsicums, garlic and spring onions. Now for the spices: pepper, vinegar, salt. Unfortunately I have a funny feeling I've forgotten something. I'm not very good at explaining recipes.

IRENA. No, no! You're telling it wonderfully. I'll boast about having had that recipe from you.

SOVA. Now I have it! Hard cheese!

IRENA. And what are the measures?

SOVA. The measures? Yes. The problem is, I always decide on the measures according to the mood I'm in. That's the part of it I enjoy most. Finding the right measures for a given moment. I realised that not long ago. When I was young I had the opposite idea, that the optimal measures could be discovered exactly once and for all. I even thought I knew them. I don't know if you follow me?

IRENA. I follow you very well. When we were girls we used to play a game we called Little Cooks.

SOVA. Then I realised that the optimal measures can't hold for anything for always. You can't decide on the right measures of the smell and bitterness of tea any more than you can the freedom and rights of the citizen. You can only determine the measurements of a flag or a uniform.

IRENA (*exclaims*). Good heavens, I promised you that recipe for Marrow Salad. And there'll be people here any moment. Have you a piece of paper?

SOVA *looks through his pockets, then pulls out a thick notebook.*

IRENA. I'm going to have stage fright. Dictating a recipe to you, of all people. Filip's never been interested in cooking. May I start? First of all you must peel the marrow and scrape out the soft inside ... (*notices that* SOVA *is not writing but looking for something in his pockets.*) Don't be cross, maybe it is obvious, but ...

The sound of a car arriving and then a ring at the door.

SOVA. But I'm not at all cross. On the contrary. Your introduction concerning the marrow was perfectly appropriate.

DEML *enters with* EVA *and* BAUER, *rushes up to* IRENA *and kisses her hand.*

DEML. I hope we've not missed the beginning. What a marvellous idea, Irenka, games! (*To* EVA.) What do you say to this, darling? Fantastic, isn't it? An oasis of quiet and peace.

IRENA. That's thanks to you as well. (*To* SOVA.) Josef Deml, architect. He helped us design the flat. (*She looks at* EVA *with some awkwardness.*)

DEML. That was ages ago. I was still a romantic in those days. And this is Eva!

EVA (*puts down the guitar she was carrying, and approaches* SOVA *rather coquettishly*). But we already know each other from somewhere.

DEML (*hurriedly*). And this is – Jeník Bauer.

SOVA (*with embarrassment*). I'm not too sure. Would it have been at the Faculty? But that would have to be at least three years ago. I don't do any more lecturing!

EVA. Oh yes, I used to sing there. Don't you play the percussion somewhere, by any chance?

SOVA. I'm afraid not. I started to learn the piano as a boy, but then, times changed – nothing but meetings, politics, no time for anything else.

EVA. I just had the feeling I'd seen you play the drums somewhere.

BAUER (*stops in front of a large canvas*). Quite nice, though I'm no expert on modern art. (*Notices the pistol on the wall.*) My God, a real colt, an original Hartford, I'd say early fifties. (*Goes to lift it down.*)

IRENA. Be careful, it's loaded!

BAUER. Ah. Is it!

IRENA. My husband doesn't like it, but that's what my brother wants. He's a bit of an eccentric. (*Gestures towards the weapons.*) They're all loaded. He says they won't go off on their own, but it's exciting to be led into temptation all the time.

BAUER. Of course, if-you'll-allow-me-to-say-so-dear-lady, it's worth quite a bit nowadays. Inlaid with mother-of-pearl.

DEML. Jeník helps me with interior decoration. I don't have time for it any more.

EVA (*to* IRENA). He's is frightfully busy, aren't you, pet? He's not only divorcing, but also building the longest tunnel under the sun.

DEML (*irritated*). Bridge. How many times do I have to tell you, sweetheart, it's a bridge and not a tunnel.

EVA. There's not much of a difference.

DEML (*to the others*). We're trying to solve the traffic situation on a grand scale. You know that in our vicinity there are more than a hundred thousand villas and weekend cottages that are only used a few weeks a year? And that's at a time when we're talking about a housing crisis! And you know why? The transport system is hopelessly inadequate. People wouldn't be able to get to work. I discussed it with the minister himself not long ago. The average time for getting to work would be seventy-eight minutes. Those are the hard realities.

IRENA (*to* EVA). He always was a man of action.

DEML. That's all in the past. (*Glances at* EVA.) I'd rather chuck it all in and have some private life. (*Importantly.*) But what can one do? Take our young people, one has to feel for them. (*To* SOVA.) You know, my friend, that the housing crisis can be blamed for thirty-six percent of marriage breakdowns? And we haven't even started counting the couples who for these very reasons don't embark on marriage. One cannot remain indifferent to this situation. (*To* EVA.) That's my nature. I feel other people's hardships and misfortunes as my own!

BAUER (*approaches another painting*). And this pony, if it were slightly more blue, one would say it's a Chagall. I've seen a similar painting in his studio in Paris. As I was looking round there I stopped in front of one of his typical ponies and said to him: Mr Chagall, I'm no expert on modern art, but I'd take that one at any price. He smiled and said: you think you don't understand art, Jean? Three hours ago Ford of Detroit offered me three hundred thousand for that pony. Then Chagall said to me: it's yours, if you can find me something like this. And he drew for me on a piece of paper (*He rummages through his pockets, pulls out a piece of paper and thrusts it towards* SOVA.) this house. In fact, as you can see, more of a small château, by a lake. The roof glazed over to make a studio. And then, as you see, Chagall painted a few trees on the shore and said: Jean, you'll get me such a villa. I don't ask for more than ten rooms and absolute quiet. No phones and no bugging equipment of any kind, no cars outside, not even any water skiing. (*Helps himself to a sandwich.*)

IRENA. And did you get it for him?

BAUER (*delighted by the attention*). I'm telling you, ma'am, it was no joke. Try and find a quiet place anywhere today. What's more, I was only on a fourteen-day tourist visa. But in the end I did find just the place and just the villa in Switzerland by that lake – hell – it's on the tip of my tongue, in one of these rundown cantons. A baroque tusculum belonging to some impoverished German baroness. Four million, she said. But I said to her: Gnädige Gräfin, take a look at your beams, there's mould in the antlers and dry rot in the walls. She said her solicitor would be in touch. That kind of impoverished aristocracy do care terribly about proper form. Why, when I was in the labour camp in the fifties, by chance I had the next bunk to a Count Schwarzenberg, of the Krumlov line . . .

DEML *a meaningful cough.*

IRENA (*to* SOVA). How interesting it must be to sit next to you at dinner. Most men are barbarians at the table. Do you know, Filip refuses to eat meat? (*With satisfaction.*) And he doesn't drink either!

BAUER. Fifteen years, he got. For high treason, sedition, sabotage, in fact they accused him of all anti-state activities except terrorism. And he wasn't anything but a radio ham.

From outside, the sound of an approaching car. FILIP *enters with* JAKUB.

FILIP. My love. (*Kisses* IRENA.) I'm sorry we're a bit late. (*To* SOVA.) I don't think we know each other?

IRENA. This is Kamil, Filip.

FILIP. Oh yes. (*Shakes* SOVA*'s hand.*) We often talk about you. Irena reads your books. I've read that one of yours they suppressed. Most interesting. The problem of freedom, is that it? (*Quotes.*) The freest brains are stuck . . . are stuck on heads with hands . . . never mind, never mind, allow me, this is my nephew Jakub. Now he is terribly good at games. Fair play. He's a sportsman.

JAKUB (*– who has been staing at* EVA *– bows and hands* IRENA *a native mask*). Hi, Irena, I brought this for you from Tananariva.

SOVA. Do you study African ethnology?

FILIP. Oh no! He's started to study . . . what exactly have you started to study?

JAKUB. Nothing. (*Looks at* EVA.) You know that very well, Uncle
    Filip!

FILIP. Well, he had to break off his studies because of his
    swimming.

JAKUB. Rowing, Uncle. (*To* EVA.) Uncle Filip's not really into
    sport. But I'm sure that nowadays it's the only field where a
    bloke can achieve something and get real satisfaction out of it.
    (*Plucks up courage and moves nearer to* EVA.) I've seen you a lot
    on television. Last time was that hit of yours about Christopher
    Columbus, that was great.

EVA. I feel as though I know you from somewhere as well. I think
    I've seen your photo in a magazine. Didn't you win some
    swimming competition recently?

JAKUB. But I row.

EVA. That's what I mean. Do you row a canoe or a kayak?

JAKUB. Skiff.

EVA. Yes, I knew I knew you from somewhere. So we can be on first
    name terms. Call me Eva!

JAKUB. Thank you. It's an honour for me. I've been a great
    admirer of yours for a long time.

EVA. Do you know where I sang for the first time? At a school
    party. About a froggie, that would a-wooing go. People clapped
    an awful lot, and I was given a bag of toffees. I didn't think
    then, what a drudge it would turn out to be. They made me
    study everything under the sun: geometry, history. And at the
    same time you get people who think that a singer doesn't do a
    stroke of work.

JAKUB. That's just envy. It's the same with us sportsmen, people
    spread malicious gossip around that we don't need to know
    how to do anything else. And yet it's been scientifically proved
    that an Olympic rower – for example – to cover the two-
    kilometre course has to expend three times as much energy as
    Einstein did in discovering his theory.

IRENA (*to* SOVA, *quietly*). You see, when Filip was starting, he went
    through such terrible things. Since then he's not been able to
    bear any killing, even animals.

FILIP. That's enough. There's no connection, you know that.
    Animals are innocent and helpless – just like children.

IRENA (*nervously*). I think I can hear my brother.

PETR (*comes in, looks round, nods to* SOVA, *bows*). Welcome, dear friends. Although I can't say I know everyone here. I beg the pardon of any potential enemies.

DEML (*gestures towards* BAUER *and* EVA). They're with me . . .

PETR. No introductions, please. We'll get to know each other in the course of our actions. I think my dear little sister has decided to organise an evening of games. She thinks she'll return us to the age of our innocence. She doesn't realise that at every moment games only reveal what we are and not what we were in childhood. (*Sits down.*) Why so silent? Why no flow of ideas, stories and meaningful pronouncements? (*To* DEML.) Some of your impressive statistics? Isn't it worth mentioning that the Moscow underground carries five million passengers daily and that not far from Warsaw they've erected a television mast six hundred and thirty four metres high, whilst the centre span of Tancarville bridge measures six hundred and eight metres, which is twice the length of the centre span of the bridge in Rio de Niteroi? Isn't it all splendid evidence that reason hastens towards ever higher goals, and that we can spend this evening without worries. Why aren't you rejoicing?

BAUER. I would like, if your honours would permit, to proceed towards the organising of the entertainment. I would like (*To* FILIP.) to propose one game, which you, as Public Prosecutor, might particularly enjoy.

SOVA (*to* IRENA). But we should let the lady's wishes take precedence.

IRENA (*frightened*). You think I ought to propose a game? I'm not sure. I did have a game ready – but it's one we used to play as girls, it might not suit you at all! Look, there are ten dishes of salad on the table. You're blindfolded, and you have to guess what's in each dish.

FILIP. Why did you have to choose that game? (*Forcibly.*) You know I can't bear people being blindfolded!

IRENA (*desperately*). I'd forgotten all about that. I just thought – with blindfolds it's difficult to guess, it means everyone has to use their sense of taste and smell only.

BAUER. It's a splendid game, my dear lady, it reminds me of a Jewish joke: Kohn was travelling by train and Abeles was sitting opposite him, chopping a carrot onto a chopping board on his knee.

IRENA (*takes a napkin from the table*). Who'll go first?

FILIP (*to the others*). I don't like people to be blindfolded. It's inhuman.

EVA. Why should it be? It wouldn't worry me. (*Takes the napkin from* IRENA.)

BAUER (*to* PETR *who's the only person listening to him*). When Abeles cuts up the carrot, he opens the window and throws it out. Then he cuts up some potatoes and throws them out of the window. Kohn is puzzled: may I ask you what you're doing? I'm making potato salad, Mr Kohn. And may I ask why you're throwing all the ingredients out of the window? What else can I do with them, Mr Kohn, when I don't eat salad? (*He laughs.*)

PETR *gazes at* BAUER *with an impassive face.*

BAUER. I'm sorry if I'm boring you, Professor.

PETR. On the contrary, it's an excellent anecdote! Please go on! Or is that all? That's the trouble with anecdotes. They don't go on. On the other hand, the thing about the universe is that it does go on. Even though Einstein said: the world is finite in space. That holds good, if the central density of weighable matter in the universe doesn't equal zero. But this alternative shouldn't worry you. (*Suddenly points at* EVA.) Or you think it should? Does it worry you?

EVA (*confused*). No, no certainly not!

PETR. Then why are you silent? So young and lovely.

EVA (*hurriedly ties the napkin round her eyes*). Now pass me the dish. (*Takes a dish of salad from* IRENA, *sniffs it.*) Onion.

IRENA. Excellent!

EVA. I always used to eat masses of salad on tour. Peppers, of course!

IRENA. Very good. You're really very good.

BAUER *meanwhile makes his way to the wall; he can't stop himself; he takes down one of the guns and looks at it.*

FILIP (*notices him*). Put that gun down at once.

EVA. Vinegar, and I think I would say a little bit of ginger.

BAUER *hurriedly hangs the gun up again.*

FILIP. And take that blindfold off! (*He goes up to* EVA *and tears the napkin off. Hysterically.*) I can't bear this comedy with blindfolds and guns and all that . . .

JAKUB. Then think of another game if you hate this one so much!

BAUER. Yes, that's a good idea. I'd like to suggest . . .

EVA. After the show we sometimes used to play charades, if you know it.

IRENA. Yes, that would be nice. (*To* SOVA.) I still haven't dictated that recipe to you.

SOVA. I don't want you to trouble yourself over it.

IRENA. It's no trouble.

EVA. We'll divide into two groups. (*She shows everyone which side they have to go. She takes* FILIP *herself and pulls* IRENA *and* SOVA *to join them.*)

IRENA. I'll write it out for you myself. (*Grabs* SOVA*'s notebook: something catches her eye.*) But you've got a recipe written out here already. And with the measures. (*Reads.*) We must take measure of it as precisely as we can. The transcendental reduction binds me to the current of my pure perceptions of consciousness, and to the units construed on the basis of their topicality and potentiality. . . Oh Kamil, I'm sorry, that sounds rather peculiar. Perhaps I shouldn't have read it. Shall I turn over?

SOVA. You can write underneath.

IRENA (*writing, reciting half aloud*). Now: get rid of the centre of the peeled marrow gourd and chop it up. Meanwhile fry some red peppers in hot oil . . .

Game Two

Charades

FILIP, IRENA, SOVA *and* EVA *have left the stage. Those remaining are obviously enjoying themselves.*

DEML (*nervously*). Why don't they come?(*Looks at his watch.*) It's more than ten minutes. Why do they take so long?

JAKUB. It's all part of the game. You have to be patient. Take a boat race – you have to wait for ages and then it's over in two minutes.

DEML. I'm afraid I'm not a racing man. I have to work for a living.

FILIP (*enters, putting on a good humoured face*). I must admit that I didn't really pay enough attention. I don't know if I'm quite clear about the rules. (*About to take a glass of wine.*)

IRENA. Filip!

JAKUB. We'll read you that sentence. (*Reads from the piece of paper.*) 'Liberty was violated by laws.'

FILIP. Well, what about it?

BAUER. It's like this, my learned friend, you have to act that sentence, as the young lady explained to you at the start.

FILIP. Act that sentence? Why?

JAKUB. So that the others can guess it.

FILIP. Show it to me! (*He takes the piece of paper from* JAKUB, *reads under his voice.*) 'Liberty was. . .' I ask you, how does one act 'liberty'?

JAKUB. That's your problem, Uncle Filip!

DEML (*impatiently*). Well, couldn't you act the Statue of Liberty?

JAKUB. Don't help him!

FILIP (*conceding*). All right. But how do I act: 'was'?

JAKUB. You don't act 'was' on its own. You act 'was violated'.

FILIP. Well. . . all right. (*Stops himself.*) Exactly, how can I act: 'was violated'? In any case, I don't agree with the content of that sentence.

JAKUB. But Uncle, I told you, the content doesn't matter. It can be nonsense.

FILIP. But that sentence isn't nonsensical – it's false! It throws doubt on the meaning of equity and justice.

PETR. No sentence can throw doubt on the meaning of justice, as long as you don't doubt it yourself.

FILIP. Are you hinting at something? Something to do with me? Well let me tell you, I never. . .

JAKUB *calls the others from the next room.*

FILIP. I don't like it all. All my life I've worked to make justice serve truth and liberty . . . (*Takes off his jacket and pulls his shirt out of his trousers, rolls up his sleeves, ties a handkerchief round his forehead, sticks a pencil, pen and fork in the handkerchief.*) Of course, no freedom has any meaning without well-founded material guarantees. . .

IRENA *enters with* SOVA *and* EVA, *who sit next to her, whilst* FILIP *freezes in the position of the Statue of Liberty.*

IRENA. Go on, act something for us! Show us! (*To* EVA.) You'll have to help us. We don't know how to play this game!

FILIP *motionless.*

EVA. He might be acting already. You've got to put more into it, you need to let yourself go a bit.

IRENA. Well, have you started acting?

FILIP *nods.*

IRENA. What are you acting?

EVA. You can't ask that! You have to ask: Are you . . . well, are you an ostrich?

SOVA. Is it an object?

FILIP *shrugs his shoulders.*

IRENA. He doesn't know if it is an object. What can it be, when even he doesn't know what it is?

SOVA. We don't know that he doesn't know. Perhaps we asked him the wrong way?

IRENA. He's obviously pretending to be something. Are you an ostrich? (*She shoots questions at him;* FILIP *shakes his head to each one.*) A ploughman? A tramp, a beggar? A vagabond? (*Triumphantly.*) I've got it: an idiot! A lunatic? A moron? (*Wavers.*) An exhibitionist?

SOVA. Hold on a minute, his right arm is up in the air. It must mean something.

FILIP *nods agreement.*

SOVA. You're a Nazi?

IRENA. Then what *are* you? (*Sudden inspiration.*) I know! An Indian! A savage!

FILIP *comes to a decision, moves a chair under the chandelier, removes a light bulb, tosses it from hand to hand for a moment till it cools, then holds it in his right hand and takes up his previous pose.*

EVA. He's holding a light bulb. Excellent, Filip! You're a lighting man? A cameraman? A photographer? Or are you Edison?

IRENA. Perhaps he's acting in *Gaslight.* Is that it?

SOVA. What's he trying to show us? Is it really a light bulb he's holding? (*Begins lecturing.*) What I find interesting about this game is that fact that nothing means itself, everything, as far as I understand, is just a symbol of some other substance, which is why we have to question everything again and again.

IRENA. Isn't your arm aching? Does your hand hurt? Is the bulb still hot? This is getting me so worked up.

SOVA. I think we should be more systematic in our questioning. We should try to narrow the field of possible associations. Do you represent something in any way concrete?

FILIP *shakes his head.*

SOVA. Something abstract?

FILIP *shrugs his shoulders, then nods uncertainly.*

SOVA. So it's something symbolic?

FILIP *agrees.*

SOVA. Let's be more exact: you symbolise something abstract!

IRENA (*to* SOVA, *in wonderment*). You ask such fascinating questions!

SOVA. Not at all, I just apply the basic principles of formal logic. (*Begins to expand.*) Carroll demonstrated that there are only three types of statement: 'Some fresh cakes are tasty', 'No fresh cakes are not tasty' and 'All fresh cakes are tasty'. Do you follow me?

IRENA. Of course I do, although I would say that fresh cakes always . . . Excuse my saying so – give me wind.

FILIP *thumps his fist on the table.*

EVA. Don't be cross, and act something. Why are you standing there like a statue?

FILIP *enthusiastic agreement.*

IRENA (*amazed*). So you're a statue, are you, my darling?

SOVA. That's it . . . you're the Statue of Liberty.

FILIP *relieved agreement.*

IRENA. Are you? (*To* SOVA.) How did you get that straightaway?

SOVA. Well – liberty – freedom. (*To* IRENA.) Note what a diabolical term. (*Begins an exposition.*) There is nothing more difficult to define and to demonstrate than freedom. Consider that contemporary man in order to be man must make full use not only of most of his own skills, beginning with speech but also of stereotypes and established values. He even has to automatise his physical and mental acts. The question is, where is the boundary . . .

FILIP *hammers on the table.*

SOVA. I am sorry! What are you acting now?

FILIP *lifts three fingers.*

IRENA. Is that three you're showing?

FILIP *agrees.*

IRENA. Why three? Because there are three of us? Three brethren? Three kings?

SOVA (*helping her*). A triad? The Holy Trinity?

EVA. A trio? Or a tricot?

IRENA. Three Weird Sisters? Three Graces? Three Musketeers? Three R's?

SOVA. A triptych? The Triple Alliance? The Three Estates? A trident?

FILIP (*screaming*). I'll murder you! I'm showing you the third word!

EVA. Don't get so cross. It's only a game.

SOVA. We'll have to be more systematic. What sort of part of speech is it now? A verb?

FILIP *nods, but hesitantly.*

SOVA. Liberty is doing something?

FILIP *indicates that it is the other way round.*

SOVA. Something is being done to liberty?

FILIP *agrees.*

IRENA (*to* SOVA). You're wonderful, I'm so pleased I'm in your team . . .

FILIP *goes to the light switches, turns some of them off. Pretends to be a girl – a few carefree steps. Suddenly he/she sees someone in front of him/her and freezes in terror. He/she is assaulted, fights, is apparently knocked down, bites, scratches, is left lying down.*

SOVA. Now what's all that about? Some kind of esoteric way of bringing enlightenment or revelation?

IRENA. More like running amuck. Or were you brawling with someone?

FILIP *gets up, confirms this with reservations.*

IRENA. Were you overcome? Overwhelmed? Overthrown? Molested? Murdered?

SOVA. Mugged? Manhandled? Frisked? Interrogated?

FILIP *makes a decision. Takes a knife from the table, sticks it in his belt, approaches* EVA *and persuades her to get up and walk round the room as he did before. Then he hoots like an owl and hides behind an armchair.* DEML *jumps up, but* BAUER *holds on to him. As* EVA *passes* FILIP, *he jumps up and, knife in hand, flings himself on her.*

EVA *shrieks involuntarily.*

FILIP *knocks her down into the armchair.*

DEML (*wrests himself away from* BAUER, *grabs* FILIP *by the shoulder and drags him off* EVA). You . . . you . . . brute, stop molesting her, the game's over.

FILIP (*tries to behave with a superior calm*). What do you think you're doing? Tell me then, how do you expect me to act it?

DEML. Why didn't you pick your wife to act it with?

FILIP. I'll tell you why. Because I would have put you on the wrong track.

EVA (*recovering*). He acted it very well.

DEML. Acted? I've nothing against acting, but I can't stand violence.

FILIP (*annoyed*). It wasn't me who thought up that sentence.

PETR. At the Roman circuses they carried the Christians around in giant saucepans and submerged them up to the waist in boiling oil.

IRENA. But those weren't proper games.

PETR. On the contrary, my dear little sister. If you define a game as a human activity bound by agreed rules but having no goal other than its own end, accompanied by a sensation of release from everyday life – you'll find that it was a game like any other.

DEML. Not for those in the saucepans.

PETR. They were merely an insignificant minority.

DEML (*to* PETR). You're a cynic. I won't play any more. I don't find amusement or release in such improper behaviour.

EVA. Oh, but I noticed how you were laughing when he was acting that statue, that . . . liberty.

DEML. That was quite different. When he pulled out his shirt, it reminded me . . . (*Giggles.*) At our school, there was this seedy little Jew – later on they gassed him – he always had his shirt poking out. One day we smeared his shirt tail with glue, and as we were standing in the canteen queue (*Choking with laughter.*) – he got himself stuck to that fatty, she was studying chemistry, well, he got himself stuck to her skirt and they couldn't separate them.

JAKUB. Let's play another game.

PETR. Of course! Change is essential. Even when you don't know
what for. But change as such always helps; even when it's a
change from bad to worse. Who said that? (*Gestures towards*
SOVA.) Doesn't he know how to change the world for the
better?

SOVA (*exasperated*). I gave up wanting that kind of thing long ago.
Let the world stay as it is.

JAKUB. Well, we used to play a game – don't be put off by the title
– we called it Murder. These are the rules. The referee gives out
pieces of paper. They're all blank but two. On the first one is
the word: 'detective' and on the second: 'murderer'. That's
how you all know what to play. Then the referee turns the lights
out and everyone tries to hide from the murderer. At the same
time the unknown murderer stalks his chosen victim (*Looks
round to see who he can demonstrate on, approaches* EVA.) and
squeezes her throat with his hands. (*Demonstrates.*)

EVA *screams.*

JAKUB. That's it. The victim screams and falls. From then on she's
obviously not allowed to speak. The detective turns the lights
on as quickly as possible, shouts for everyone to stand where
they are and begins the investigation. Everyone has to tell the
truth about what they heard and what they noticed in the dark.
Only the murderer is allowed to lie.

DEML. I most certainly can't agree to this.

EVA. What if he murders the detective?

DEML (*emphatically*). I'm having nothing to do with this game.
How can you be sure it's the throat the murderer finds in the
dark? And that he really wants to kill? I see through this game
of yours! Putting all the lights out!

JAKUB. It's impossible to play games with you. (*To* EVA.) The
detective shouldn't scream, so the murderer knows he's got to
find another victim. (*Tears some pages out of his notebook and
writes.*)

SOVA. Well, this could turn out to be quite an interesting game.
Sudden darkness. And we know that death is lying in wait for
us.

FILIP (*to* SOVA). You seemed to be fascinated by death!

SOVA. I have been thinking about it lately. I don't want it to take
me unawares.

FILIP (*categorically*). I don't like people playing with death. It isn't funny. It's not the right subject for a game.

IRENA (*to* SOVA). When Filip was younger . . .

FILIP. Shut up!

JAKUB. But this isn't about murder, in fact it is about investigation.

BAUER. If I may, I'd like to propose a game you'd all like.

JAKUB. I'm getting the papers ready.

DEML (*even though everyone has forgotten about him*). All right. I give in. On condition I play the role of the murderer.

JAKUB. But that would . . . The whole point of the game is to discover the unknown murderer.

DEML. It's a stupid game. (*He looks offended.*)

BAUER (*to* FILIP). As we've got together, my dear doctor, I've got a little question for you. It's about some business with antique furniture. What it is, a few items were slipped over the border – nothing precious, on the contrary, the country would benefit from the hard currency, but the permit was overlooked and there was a bit of a hitch on the border. You know the sort of thing. A criminal offence. I just wondered whether it couldn't be arranged for the file to get lost.

FILIP. Out of the question, dear sir.

BAUER. Obviously the risk involved would be adequately rewarded. (*Takes him by the arm and leads him aside.*) Shall we say: fifty grand? (*He misunderstands* FILIP's *silence.*) Sixty? You could get yourself a decent place in the country with that, and hang everything else. There's an old water mill I could put you onto, first-rate property for conversion. Fantastic. Waterwheel in working order.

FILIP. I'm sorry, but this is simply preposterous. What do you take me for?

BAUER. Well, come on . . . I wouldn't go so far as to say . . .

JAKUB *hands out the bits of paper.*

DEML (*examines his paper and says in a grand voice*). My piece of paper is completely blank!

JAKUB (*in astonishment*). But that's what I've been explaining, it's only the detective and the murderer have anything written on their papers.

DEML (*peremptorily*). It's a stupid game. You can play it if you want, but without me!

SOVA. My dear friend, I admit there are games we find revolting, but I should say that only if we overcome our revulsion can we cleanse ourselves . . .

JAKUB. You've all looked at your papers? I can turn the light out? (*Switches it off.*)

Darkness, footsteps, people running around. The sound of a blow and someone falling. A shriek. Then another shriek. Another blow. A series of hysterical shrieks. A door creaking, someone falls.

FILIP (*nervously*). Why doesn't someone put the light on?

SOVA. Someone pushed me, I can't find the switch.

Eventually the light goes on. EVA, FILIP and JAKUB are lying in the middle of the room. PETR is sitting in the armchair reading. BAUER is sitting on the cupboard. DEML is hopping around on one foot, the other is bare. He's obviously looking for his shoe.

SOVA (*unsure of himself*). Stay where you are! I am the detective! But . . . I thought there would only be one victim. Or two at the most.

FILIP (*lying on the ground*). I don't want to spoil the game, but where is Irena?

SOVA. You're right, she's not here!

PETR (*scarcely raising his eyes from his book*). They've probably murdered her for real. It's occurred to me many times that according to the law of polarity depraved and repulsive individuals are attracted to each other.

FILIP (*offended*). I strongly object to such statements.

SOVA. Then I'll start. (*To* PETR.) What were you doing at the moment when . . . when you heard the shriek?

PETR. Which one?

SOVA (*unsure*). The first one.

PETR. I was concentrating on my own problems. To be more exact: on the function of the wave length which transforms itself on the basis of the irreducible representation of the group D6h.

FILIP (*jumps up*). But she couldn't have vanished. We must look for her.

DEML. Someone had his hand in my pocket here – (*Shows them.*) I hit him with my shoe, but then I dropped it.

IRENA *stifled cry.*

FILIP (*hysterically*). She's being strangled! Strangled! Do something! (*Runs around the room.*)

PETR *gets up, goes to the cupboard and opens it.*

IRENA (*almost tumbling out, sobbing*). Someone, someone put his hand here. (*Points to her throat.*) That was what must have happened to that poor girl they carried off in the dustcart. I was terribly frightened, so I opened the door (*Shows them the cupboard.*) but then someone closed it again, and there was something strange and warm inside. And it was smelly.

DEML. Here it is! (*Throws himself in the cupboard and pulls his shoe out.*) I said it was a stupid game.

IRENA. Don't be cross! I don't think we should have been playing something so rough and cruel. Life may be like that, but I don't think people are. So why should we act as though we were. Please, get up!

FILIP. I insist myself that we change the game. Why all this blindfolding? This violating, this strangling?

SOVA. But nevertheless, games must follow each other – there must be continuity. I believe that what we lack most is the sense of continuity. We are always making a new start and the result is that we are uprooted, unsure and prone to violence.

BAUER (*makes an announcement from the top of the cupboard*). I'd like to suggest a marvellous game.

SOVA. And where do our discontinuity and our inclination to violence and our unconscious desire for death lead? To revolution. I am sure of it. I also wanted to change history by force and I was so attracted by death that I used to dream about it. I imagined being led to the scaffold. I saw the well-pressed trousers of the executioner, I heard the flags flapping in the wind and I shouted: Long live freedom! Long live revolution! You can't imagine my satisfaction. But when I finally lived through the revolution I began to understand the value of the continuity of life. The message and warning of history.

BAUER (*from the cupboard*). I'd like to suggest a game that would correspond famously to this sense of continuity! Execution!

FILIP. What?

BAUER. Execution. It's not very demanding. There's the hangman, his henchman and the condemned.

FILIP. You've gone right off your head.

JAKUB. At least let's hear him.

BAUER. You have to draw lots for the judge and the priest. You put up the gallows and the hangman starts his work. The game goes on till someone says: 'That's enough!' Then the one who said 'That's enough' has to play the condemned.

IRENA. That sounds . . . that sounds horrible.

FILIP. I don't understand how you even dare suggest something like that in this house – the house of a judge – and after what I've told you a minute ago.

BAUER. But it would be a game.

FILIP. No one will ever play anything like that in this house. There'll be no executions here!

BAUER. I'm sorry, Mr Prosecutor, if I offended you.

FILIP (*shouts*). And don't call me 'Mr Prosecutor', I keep telling you I've always been no more than a judge, even in the hard times in the past.

PETR. It's in hard times that people really reveal their true nature.

FILIP. What do you mean by that? Are you insinuating something?

PETR. As in a game. A game resembles hard times, for it continually forces new decisions from us. Who's got a new game for us? Innocent, if possible. No blindfolds, no evocation of the past, and no turning off the lights!

DEML. Good. I've got one.

Game Three

Hostages

EVA, IRENA *and* FILIP *are sitting in armchairs which can be arranged one behind the other as in an aeroplane.* PETR *gets an old Austro-Hungarian army helmet and sabre out of the cupboard.* DEML *is sitting behind the table, smoking.*

IRENA (*clearly nervous. Gets up, sits down again*). What's it like outside? Don't you think the wind's picking up?

EVA (*looks out of the window*). I can't tell, it's dark. Are you nervous?

IRENA. Well, I can't help it. I've been through too much in my life. I'm always frightened of that silence before the door opens. My father – they came for him – we were only children. Then my first husband . . . Don't be cross with me, I know this isn't the same thing.

JAKUB (*enters. He should be wearing something which in some way or other looks like a pilot's uniform*). Ladies and gentlemen, I have to inform you that we are forced to land. I must ask you to remain calm, as the aeroplane is under the control of armed gangsters.

IRENA. Oh no, I don't believe it!

BAUER (*comes in with* SOVA, *a shotgun in his hand*). I'm sorry, my dear lady, but you'd better believe it!

JAKUB *exits*.

SOVA (*he may be wearing a coloured sash or tricolour round his chest*). We are not gangsters. We are members of a revolutionary army . . .

FILIP (*to* BAUER).Where did you get that gun?

BAUER *shrugs his shoulders*.

FILIP. Put that gun down immediately. It's loaded. (*Shouts.*) Didn't you hear me?

BAUER (*doesn't move*). But Mr Prosecutor, they made me . . .

DEML. Let him have it. It's only a game. And it heightens the effect. They'd have no chance unarmed.

FILIP. The chances are the same, with arms or without. I assume they don't intend to use it.

EVA. But I like it with the gun. It's more realistic.

FILIP. I don't intend to play staring down the barrels of loaded guns!

PETR (*butting in*). You've played like that lots of times!

FILIP. What do you mean?

PETR. Or maybe those weren't games? All those poor farmers and alleged spies who went to their deaths because you sentenced them, because that was what was required?

FILIP. I . . ., I . . . but that's outrageous!

IRENA. Petr, please, how can you . . . At that time everyone . . . And now he's the very opposite.

FILIP (*forcing himself to calm down*). None of that was my game at all. You know that very well. But unfortunately there are times in one's life when one must do what one doesn't want to do, or even what one disagrees with. (*To* BAUER.) But not now, and not here!

IRENA. So please do put that gun down. My husband can't bear it.

SOVA (*with resolution*). Only when you give in to our demands.

IRENA. Are you serious, Kamil? Petr, talk to him!

PETR. I've not been alerted yet. You still have to negotiate with him yourselves.

DEML. That's right! And your job is to persuade the assailants to back down from their demands. Or at least to moderate them. You have to keep them talking till the police arrive.

IRENA (*to* SOVA). What are your demands?

SOVA. A hundred million!

IRENA. A hundred million! But we've not got that much!

SOVA. We're not demanding it from you. You are only our hostages.

IRENA. And who is going to give it to you?

SOVA. The airline. The Government. The United Nations. There must be somebody.

IRENA. And when there is nobody?

SOVA. We'll blow you to pieces. One or two useless people more or less don't matter. Do you know how many are dying of hunger every day?

IRENA. You can't be serious. We've not done anything wrong.

BAUER. That's life, madam.

IRENA. What about my children? They get back from holiday in two days time. I have to be there to meet them!

SOVA. Millions of children have no opportunity to go on holiday!

IRENA. I know. I am against it too.

EVA. How long have we got?

SOVA (*looks at his watch*). Your captain is radioing our conditions. We gave him sixty minutes.

EVA. You're certainly a man of action.

SOVA. I serve my cause.

EVA (*stands up and walks towards him*). I bet you're a real man. I've always wanted to meet a real man.

DEML *coughs.*

SOVA. Stay where you are.

BAUER *aims the gun at her.*

IRENA. For goodness sake, sit down!

JAKUB (*enters*). Your conditions have been communicated.

SOVA. Is there an answer?

JAKUB. They said you'd gone mad.

SOVA. It's the world that's mad.

JAKUB. You're asking a lot.

SOVA. We're asking little. A small instalment on a large debt.

EVA. How long have we got?

SOVA (*looks at his watch*). Fifty-two minutes.

EVA. And then?

SOVA. Finish!

EVA. Even for me?

SOVA. We make no exceptions.

EVA. What will you get out of killing me?

SOVA. Me? Nothing.

EVA. Then why don't you make an exception?

SOVA. Our cause will get something out of it. Next time people will
    pay up when they see we don't make exceptions. We need
    money. To buy weapons, to print books, to influence public
    opinion worldwide.

IRENA. You write books as well?

SOVA. I've written one.

IRENA (*with pleasure*). Oh, but I've read it. I even remember . . .
    (*She quotes.*) 'The freest head sits on a trunk whose hands are
    tied.'

SOVA (*drily*). I never wrote anything like that. We're not interested
    in free heads, but in justice.

IRENA (*confused*). But I mean . . . Do you think it would be just to
    kill us?

SOVA. Through your deaths the just cause will succeed.

IRENA. But – you can't mean that seriously. (*Shocked.*) That would
    be murder!

FILIP (*with resolution*). Look here my man, I'm a lawyer.

Representative of a big business dealing in petroleum and . . . and . . . (*He can't think how to carry on.*) Petroleum!

SOVA. A rich bastard, in other words!

FILIP. You're wrong! I grew up without any privileges. And in any case – I'm a pensioner! Let me introduce myself. (*He is unable to invent any name.*) Filip. What can I call you?

SOVA. My name does not matter.

FILIP. Look here, you've chosen us and you want to sacrifice us for a cause you think is noble, but I've got the nerve to persuade you . . .

SOVA. You won't persuade me!

FILIP. You've chosen the wrong people to sacrifice. Take me, for example: I'm working on a major study of the reform of prisons. And before that, yes, I gave away all my goods to help the wretched prisoners, you ought to be understanding about that.

SOVA. I know your sort. You're not really concerned wth prisoners. What you're trying to do is get rid of some sort of guilt.

FILIP (*coming out of role*). That's going a bit far, I'll ask you in this house not to . . . (*Stops himself short.*) What do you mean?

SOVA. Some people have the idea they can save themselves. But it's no use. We all carry our guilt inside ourselves.

FILIP *thumps his fist on the table.*

BAUER (*butting in*). Correct. My count use to say: The worst clowns are the reformed sinners, and they're also the most dangerous.

FILIP. I don't know who's 'reformed' and who's not 'reformed'! (*Gains control over himself and gets back into role.*) What do you really want? People like you always set this merry-go-round of violence going, and no one can stop it. What are you waiting for? Sooner or later they'll catch you and put you on trial.

SOVA. No! *We* will put *you* on trial.

BAUER. Quite right. My count used to say: the one who gets there first will be first to judge. And then he'd say . . .

FILIP. You can bloody well shut up about your count!

BAUER (*won't be put down*). Guilt will always out.

FILIP. And what if the police get you first?

SOVA. They won't get me alive.

IRENA (*astonished*). Aren't you even afraid of death?

SOVA. Not if I die in the struggle for a better world!

FILIP. You, you're a fanatic!

SOVA. I'm not a fanatic, I know that the truth is on my side.

FILIP (*to the others*). How long do we have to listen to this blethering? (*Pulls himself together.*) And what's more, why aren't the police here yet? An aircraft is highjacked, decent people are threatened and police are off somewhere harrassing some innocent victim . . . (*He waves his hands.*)

PETR (*approaches* DEML *and salutes him*). Colonel, we have just been informed that flight number 289 from Colombo . . .

DEML (*with pleasure*). Hijacked?

PETR. They're asking for twenty million. Dollars.

DEML. They're mad, they're going beyond the bounds.

PETR. Thanks to them we can yet be of service to some sort of starlet. (*He looks at* EVA.*)

DEML. What starlet? (*He understands.*) We're not here to be of service to anyone special, we're here to serve people! What's the deadline?

PETR. Only an hour, Colonel.

DEML. Extend the deadline. As usual.

PETR. I'm not so sure. The leader of the hijackers is an unusually tough fanatic. (*Confidentially.*) As it happens, I know him. We were students together. He never had any luck with women – that's why he joined the revolutionaries.

SOVA *turns round indignantly, ready to protest, then remembers that it wouldn't be appropriate and resumes his former stance.*

DEML. Do you think he could be enticed by some sort of – sexy girl?

PETR. Too late! He wouldn't know what to do with her!

SOVA *about to make another gesture of protest, again he overcomes it.*

DEML. If we were to pay up, we would only be encouraging him.

PETR. There are people on board.

DEML. And him as well. He knows what would happen to him if he took his demands to the extreme.

PETR. It's all the same to him. He knows he's nothing else

to look forward to.

DEML. So what do you propose?

PETR. Pay up.

DEML. Out of the question.

IRENA (*to* SOVA, *hurriedly*). And it didn't occur to you that maybe your wife or girl friend, someone you love, could be in such a . . . could be like us?

SOVA. I have none.

IRENA. You have no what?

EVA. Don't you have a woman at all? Why don't you find one?

SOVA. Not me!

EVA (*stands up, starts to undo the buttons of her blouse*). How about me? Don't you fancy me? (*Undoes some more buttons.*)

DEML (*runs towards her*). Eva, stop it, you're going too far.

BAUER (*holds on to him*). Stay where you are, Colonel!

EVA (*to* SOVA). Want to know who I am?

DEML. You're a whore! (*He spits.*)

SOVA. As far as I'm concerned, you're a hostage! (*He nods to* BAUER, *who levels his gun at* DEML *and forces him to retreat a few steps.*)

EVA. Don't you know I'm a singer?

SOVA. I don't have time for that.

EVA. You don't have time to sing?

SOVA. To listen to pop singers..

EVA. Won't you let me sing to you?

SOVA. It's up to you what you do with your last twenty-nine minutes.

EVA. Very well. (*She gets her guitar.*)

IRENA. I don't know, I'm not sure it's appropriate . . .

FILIP. Leave her alone! Why shouldn't we sing? It'd be better than this stupid game!

EVA *sings the song about Columbus.*

JAKUB *applauds at the end of the song.*

EVA (*carries on with the game*). Wouldn't you like that better?

SOVA. What do you mean?

EVA. Isn't it better to listen to a song than to do what you're doing?

SOVA. It has no meaning. Listening to pop songs doesn't have any higher meaning.

EVA (*undoes the last button on her blouse*). To experience what those songs are about! We could travel away somewhere together . . .

DEML *again tries to run to* EVA.

PETR. Just a moment, Colonel. It's too late now for you to intervene personally. (*He pulls out a white handkerchief, ties it to a stick and waves it.*)

BAUER. Stay where you are!

IRENA. At last! Help is on the way!

SOVA. I warn you that if you try to attack us, we'll blow up the aeroplane before the deadline expires.

PETR. Why should we want to attack you?

PETR. They'd say you'd sent the people in the aeroplane to their deaths.

DEML. No. We mustn't think just about the fate of those on board, but about the fate of all the others. When it comes to it, we can't pay criminals. It makes sense, everyone would understand . . .

PETR. Not those on board.

DEML. There's no war without victims. And in any case, we can't start giving away money that belongs to everyone.

PETR. But think about your starlet, Colonel! She ought to be yours and yours alone.

DEML. Very well. Go away and think something up. Something (*He points.*) that would get those out of this.

PETR. I see. As ever, the subordinates have to shoulder the responsibility.

BAUER (*to* SOVA). Beg to report, there's a copper coming this way.

SOVA. Prepare hand grenades!

EVA. And is this what you get your pleasure out of – out of killing people?

SOVA. It's not a question of pleasure, it's a question of duty. It's my task.

FILIP. And who laid that task on you?

SOVA. My conscience.

FILIP. He's a fanatic. They're the worst. They can't be bought off
and they can't be intimidated. When they were blindfolded . . .
(*He stops short in fear.*)

SOVA. Because you're the police. At a certain stage of the meta-
organisation of society . . . (*Stops short.*) The police always
defend the interests of property owners and the ruling
authorities.

PETR. You're wrong there. For some time past, the police have had
their own interests.

SOVA. That's an idea worth some attention . . . (*Stops himself.*) I'm
not interested in the interests of the police.

PETR. I realise that (*Quietly.*) They could be your interests as well.

SOVA. Your interests and ours are fortunately irreconcilable.

PETR. You think so? (*Reprovingly.*) Every revolution begins with a
struggle against the police and ends by putting power into the
hands of its own police.

SOVA. Fortunately I won't live to suffer such disgrace.

BAUER (*a question to* SOVA). Shall I sting him? Our count used to
say: When the deer comes out to pasture, I don't delay.

PETR (*ignores him*). What can you do against us? You know yourself,
there is no power could conquer the world. Against your little
bombs we have megatons of explosives, not to mention much
more subtle weapons which we can use against you.

SOVA. There are situations in which you are powerless. (*His acting
has become increasingly convincing, and now he speaks as himself or at
least from his own memories.*) And those occur when you come
into conflict with genuine resolve.

PETR. You are mistaken. We may be powerless, so long as it's only a
single incident. But I thought that you were concerned with
more than this. I thought that you were concerned with the fate
of the world. With us behind you, you would be able to
determine history. You would be all-seeing, ever-present and all-
hearing. And at the same time invisible. You would dispose,
propose and compose. You would invent what has not
happened and deny what has happened. You would prosecute,
delegate and execute. Isn't that a more attractive prospect than
trudging round the world with your little bombs?

SOVA (*with passion*). Your speech is only able to convince me that truth and the future are on my side.

PETR. You are making a mistake.

SOVA. It is you who are making the mistake. (*Looks at his watch.*) In place of your revolting litany, your celebration of monstrous power, you should be thinking up some words of comfort for these people. They have less than twenty minutes left!

IRENA. My goodness, that's true . . . I'll begin . . . (*She jumps up and runs to the table, where she picks up the plate of sandwiches.*) No one's having anything to eat!

BAUER *points the gun at her.*

FILIP (*in fury*). I've had enough of this! You'll put an end to it at once. Can't you see how upset she is?

BAUER (*quietly*). I'm sorry Procurator, but it's up to you. You could try to help us. Persuade them to pay the ransom.

FILIP. And don't call me Procurator! I've explained to you already!

BAUER. Why does it matter to you so much?

FILIP. I . . . (*in fury.*) I don't have to answer that!

BAUER. No, you don't. You've said enough.

FILIP. What do you mean by that?

BAUER. That you're a little bit frightened!

FILIP. I'm frightened of you? It's you who should be frightened of me!

IRENA (*offers them the plate of sandwiches*). Come on, have a sandwich!

BAUER. Begging your pardon, dear lady. (*Takes a sandwich to FILIP.*) I'm not frightened, I've been around in my life, I've seen what goes on.

FILIP. And you think I haven't?

BAUER. Maybe – but from the other side.

FILIP. I've had enough of these insinuations. Of this whole comedy. As if there weren't enough excitement in the world. I'm getting out of this. (*He tries to leave.*)

BAUER. Not a step further! (*He raises the gun and fires into the air.*)

FILIP *clutches his heart and falls into a chair.*

IRENA. Filip, oh my god!

BAUER (*moderately surprised.*) It really was loaded. Don't get upset, dear lady, it was only lead shot. (*To* FILIP.) I don't like it when someone talks down to me. (*To* IRENA.) But if you think . . . (*He hangs the gun over his shoulder.*)

FILIP. It's a bit too much. In my own home. With our own gun.

PETR (*laughs, to* BAUER). He'd rather you shot at him with your own gun.

IRENA (*to* FILIP). You can calm down, he's put it back over his shoulder.

FILIP (*to* PETR). What you you laughing at? What's funny about it? Take him away. Get the gun off him.

PETR (*approaches* BAUER – *more quietly*). I can see you're a man of principle. But just one question. Are they going to give you any of these millions of dollars? I know what they're like – everything is for the higher cause.

BAUER. I'm not doing business with you. (*Quietly.*) He might hear me!

PETR. Did you listen to me earlier?

BAUER (*guardedly*). I hear when I want to hear and I don't when I don't want to.

PETR. Revolutions. Assassinations. Dreams of million-dollar ransoms and of changing the world. That may suit novices, but not you. (*Quietly.*) A hundred thousand down and a post as my deputy. With a view to advancement!

SOVA (*to* BAUER). Stop talking to him! You're risking everything. Conversation with the police!

PETR. Very well. I'm leaving. Your obstinacy disappoints me. (*To the others.*) An honest police force is impotent when it comes face to face with the Terror. (*He moves to one side.*)

IRENA. What do you mean, you're leaving? You're leaving us here?

EVA. Did you think they were going to launch an attack on the aeroplane? We could've been killed at once!

IRENA. But that means . . . We'll have to do something ourselves. (*To* SOVA.) Won't you lower your demands? (*To* FILIP.) Do something! You can't leave women to act on your behalf.

FILIP (*reluctantly*). We can't offer you the sum you're asking for, you know that. It's obviously a matter for negotiation, we could come to an agreement about a more reasonable sum.

SOVA. We can't change our demands. It's the first retreat that brings defeat.

FILIP. He's a fanatic. There's no sense in him. (*Shouts.*) I don't understand what sense there is in any of this!

EVA. How much time is left? Fifteen minutes?

SOVA. Twenty minutes fifty seconds.

EVA. Won't you extend it a little?

SOVA. I've told you already what a retreat leads to.

EVA. And won't you ask for less?

SOVA. I never compromise.

EVA (*approaches him*). Wouldn't you even compromise with me?

SOVA. Stand back!

EVA. All I want is to be kissed just once by a real man. (*It's not clear whether she is still in role.*) I'm serious. Kiss me.

SOVA. I have no desire to kiss you. You should be thinking of higher things . . . the last ten minutes of your life.

EVA. What a pity. (*Shrugs her shoulders, turns to* JAKUB.) And you, Captain?

JAKUB. Alas, I'm powerless.

EVA. Won't you kiss me at least? We only have ten minutes.

JAKUB. I certainly will. (*Runs to her and kisses her.*) I always knew that we two . . .

DEML (*jumps up.*) I protest, this sort of improvisation could be taken advantage of! It's not part of the game!

EVA. Oh, but it is. The last ten minutes of my life. Whatever else would I have to do?

PETR (*to* DEML). Calm down. Everything is happening just as it should.

IRENA. You think so? I don't know. We should do something. (*To* SOVA.) Please, tell me, what do you actually want? What is the aim of your organisation?

EVA (*extricating herself from* JAKUB*'s embrace*). Aren't you, aren't you sorry to be living such a life?

SOVA (*to* IRENA *and* EVA). It's too late for that. You wouldn't understand anything anyhow.

IRENA. Suppose we believed in the same sort of thing as you? Take me, for example, I've always wanted to live in the sort of society where people didn't think just about themselves, where they gave up everything superfluous of their own free will, and looked for meaning in something higher! Because it should be quite easy for people to understand one another. Tell me, isn't there some kind of task that I could undertake?

SOVA. Your task is ordained. You are hostages.

IRENA (*nearly in tears*). But wouldn't we be more use to you alive than dead? You can't simply murder us without finding out what we want and what we believe in.

SOVA. All the oceans in the world lie between me and you. There is no meeting place for our beliefs. (*To* JAKUB, *who is embracing* EVA.) No news?

JAKUB. Nothing.

SOVA. I fear there are only three minutes left.

IRENA. This is terrible. Perhaps he can't hear me. How can I talk to him, when he can't hear me?

SOVA (*to* BAUER, *who is moving towards the window*). Away from the window, there are marksmen outside!

IRENA. He can't have any pity. How can he understand us, when he can't hear us?

SOVA. Two minutes. Do you want to pray? (*To* EVA.) To sing?

IRENA. Don't you feel any sympathy? Regret? After all, we are all born into the world the same way, and the same fate awaits us all . . . we have so much in common, how can you speak of justice when you don't feel this?

SOVA. Justice is not one; for us and for you.

BAUER. How long is there?

SOVA. One minute.

BAUER. Are we going to be blown up with them?

SOVA. We can't leave. There is at least a battalion of marksmen waiting outside.

BAUER. Aha. (*He approaches* SOVA *from behind and hits him on the head.*)

SOVA *staggers and sinks to the ground.*

IRENA. My God! You're . . . you're one of us? (*Remembers where they are.*) Did you clout him for real?

BAUER. Only partially, my dear lady.

FILIP (*to* SOVA, *maliciously*). That's what you get when you mix up a game with real life.

IRENA. But Filip, Kamil played his part beautifully. (*To* PETR.) You were so nasty to him! And it was only a game, why did you take it so seriously?

SOVA (*gets up, magnanimously*). It's quite all right. A game has to be taken seriously. (*He starts to move to one side.*)

BAUER. No one move! I was promised a reward. I haven't had it yet.

DEML (*to* BAUER). What are you on about, Jeník, what reward? This game has finished. The attackers were overpowered and failed to attain their end. We won. The hostages and the police, that is. Put the gun down, Jeník.

BAUER. Is that so? And what about my reward?

PETR. Correct. And in any case I'm bound to disagree with the previous speaker. The police can never win because their game is never at an end. Thus the police have not only thwarted the criminal plot of the hijackers, but by their unremitting vigilance they have uncovered certain critical circumstances concerning one of those present.

DEML. What are you going on about? This is against the rules. The game has simply finished.

PETR. The duty of the police is to defend society against the criminal in our midst.

DEML. I've told you, it's against the rules.

PETR (*to* BAUER). Understandably, he'll cause trouble once he knows who I'm talking about. I hope that in case of need I can count on you. (*To* DEML.) What rules? We make the rules now! Didn't you see? Didn't you see who it was who held our fate so firmly in his hands? From the moment a man surrenders his self-defence and puts it and his weapons into the hired hands of strangers, there are no rules he can rely on. He lives by the favour of those whom he once created by his favour. Power no longer rests in the hands of the people – only in the hands of gangsters or the police. Now we're going to hold a trial. The evidence we'll present will shock everyone. (*To* BAUER.) Don't allow anyone to leave the house. You will be answerable. I name you my deputy, or representative. I'm sure you know that representatives used to be richly rewarded. And that from time to time, when they broke faith, they were thrown to the executioner.

FILIP. I don't understand anything. (*To* BAUER.) It's all because we let you keep that gun.

EVA (*to* SOVA, *who in the meantime has sat up*). I wanted to tell you: your performance was wonderful. You're a born actor.

SOVA. You think so? But I wasn't acting at all. It was all from memory.

ACT TWO

Game Four

The Trial

The living room as before. BAUER *is on patrol with a gun.* PETR *is wearing a black coat and carrying a file of papers under his arm.*

DEML. I protest at the way he's threatening me with that gun, he should put it away!

EVA. It was you who let him have it in the first place.

DEML. That was different.

PETR. Some of us will play the parts of the prosecution and others the defence. The Judge – that's me – will do the summing up.

DEML. That was a different game. About conspirators.

PETR. A guard has to carry a weapon as well. If the verdict is 'innocent', it means the defence has won. If the verdict is 'guilty', it means the prosecution has won.

DEML. And I'm not going to play this game.

PETR (*silences him with a gesture*). Now let's share out the parts; we know who's in the dock.

DEML. Who? Me? Why me?

PETR (*taps the file*). Because you committed the crime!

DEML. I'm not going to go into the dock. Why don't you accuse someone else – one of these hijackers. At least that would have some continuity.

PETR. I explained just now that hijackers aren't usually put before the court. (*To the others.*) Are you blind? Who lost his nerve when we put in a completely innocent piece of violence? Who got upset at the idea of turning the lights out during the next game? What kind of nightmare would that have brought on? And finally, who voiced his doubts about the chances of the murderer grabbing his throat? Was it not in fact the voice of macabre experience speaking out?

FILIP (*angry*). Don't you think that's overdoing it a bit?

EVA. Sounds interesting enough to me.

DEML. Sweetheart!

PETR. The roles of the judge and the guard are both settled. That leaves the roles of the counsel for the prosecution, the counsel for the defence, and the witnesses.

DEML (*to* EVA). He talks about me as if I were some sort of criminal, and you enjoy it!

EVA. Oh but pet, you really don't know how to play games. You take everything so seriously.

BAUER. If I'm the guard, then I have to be armed. My Count Schwarzenberg, before he died, he said to me: better to be naked with a gun than in the cooler wearing a fur coat.

IRENA. He died there?

BAUER. With respect, dear lady, he wasn't the only one.

PETR (*to* FILIP). You can be the prosecutor!

FILIP. What? You keep pestering me with being a public prosecutor as well? (*Vehemently.*) You're all ganging up against me, I'm beginning to see that now. You're trying to provoke me, trying to force me back to something that finished long ago. Anyway, I'm perfectly calm. I'm not going to be put out as easily as that. Whatever it is you're up to: blindfolding, strangling, blowing up, sentencing and I don't know what else, just please yourselves! Go on playing. After all, you *are* our guests!

PETR. Fine! Who'll be the prosecutor then? (*To* EVA.) You?

EVA. Me? But what am I supposed to accuse him of?

PETR. Here's the documents. (*He gives her the papers.*) All you have to do is read them. That way you'll be just like a real prosecutor. (*To* IRENA.) You can be counsel for the defence!

IRENA. I don't know that I could handle it. I'd get terribly worked up.

PETR (*to* JAKUB). You can be witness for the prosecution!

SOVA. I think it would be better to toss up for the roles!

PETR. Why? I'm casting everyone in the role which suits them best, it's better that way. A moment ago you were such a splendid revolutionary. Yes, of course, and now you think you're someone different. Good, try witness for the defence. And now I must ask the accused to take his place. (*Points.*) The witnesses ought to leave the courtroom, but it will be enough if they stand to one side. Thank you.

DEML. You really do want to play this game? And I – I just can't see what's expected of me. I've had nothing to do with any murder.

JAKUB. Who said anything about murder?

DEML (*offended*). What do you mean by that? Are you suggesting I know something others don't?

FILIP. Don't count on me for anything in this game. At best I'll be (*Joking.*) the usher. (*Amused.*) I often used to envy them. Their independence. Him and the cleaning women. No one ever dared to give them any orders . . .

PETR. Thank you, Counsel for the Prosecution, Counsel for the Defence. Excellent. We declare open the trial of Josef Deml.

DEML. I, I . . . (*He's about to protest.*)

EVA. Don't get cross, pet, it's only a game.

DEML. Well, all right. (*To* EVA.) Just for your sake . . .

IRENA (*to* EVA). Oh dear, it reminds me . . . Do you feel worked up as well?

EVA. No. I'm used to appearing in public.

PETR. Thank you, my learned friend.

EVA (*leafing through her papers*). Now . . . now this really is it. (*Surprised.*) Is this what you invited us for? (*Reads.*) On the 20th July of this year, just twenty-nine days ago, a nineteen-year-old student, Pavla Malá, set out from home to meet her friends at a holiday camp not far from Saint John's. It has been ascertained that she arrived there and stayed till nearly midnight. She then left with the intention of hitching a lift back home in a passing car. When she left she was wearing a light dress of blue cotton and a scarf over her hair, because it was starting to rain. However, she never arrived home. I accuse Josef Deml here present that on the 21st July he enticed her with criminal intent into his car, drove her to the park known as the Castle Park and murdered her there. Further, that in collusion with the crew of the refuse disposal cart CC 27 27 he arranged for his victim's body to be taken away and burnt.

DEML (*looking round at the others, who are listening intently, somewhat embarrassed*). You can't be serious. This sort of stuff.

EVA. And here we have some newspaper cuttings.

PETR. We'll look at those later. Prisoner in the dock, you have heard the charge. Do you accept your guilt?

DEML (*recovering*). It's outrageous. Something as vile as – ugh!

IRENA. But that girl really did, (*She points to the window.*) here in the park, they . . .

FILIP (*to* DEML). You mustn't show your feelings so openly. Just say: no!

DEML. I'm not playing. And I demand an apology!

FILIP. That kind of behaviour won't convince anyone. If you are innocent, it will be proved.

DEML. *If* I am innocent . . . Do you have any doubts about that?

FILIP. We always have to start out believing someone is innocent. Until they're proved guilty! Today it applies just the same.

DEML. What do you mean by that? I have nothing to do with any of it. (*To* EVA.) And you, reading out these outrageous things about me. You know I've got work waiting for me at home and I'm only here for your sake. Because I know you like to enjoy yourself.

EVA. And I am, don't you worry, pet!

PETR. We now move to the cross-examination of the accused. (*To* DEML.) What were you doing twenty-eight days ago between four and five in the morning?

DEML. What a question, do any of you know what you were doing a month ago? What day of the week was it, anyhow?

PETR. The same as today – you know that very well!

DEML. What could I have been doing? I know: I was asleep. (*Tries to make a joke of it.*) It may strike you as unusual, but at that time in the morning I was actually asleep!

EVA. But pet – (*She stops herself.*) I mean, prisoner in the dock, don't you remember!

DEML. Remember what?

EVA. Four weeks ago today!

DEML. It's nobody's business what I was doing. There's no game gives anyone the right to pry into my private life. And that's my final word.

EVA. Come on, tell them!

DEML. No!

EVA. Wasn't that the night we drove back home?

DEML. It's my business whether I was driving back from

somewhere or not.

PETR. Prisoner in the dock, I have to admonish you.

EVA. It was gone midnight when we gave a lift to that hitch-hiker!

DEML. What if I did give her a lift? It was dark, raining, there she was, trying to hitch a lift on a road where she'd be lucky if two cars passed in an hour.

EVA. And you said, that you'd drop me off and give her a lift all the way home.

DEML. So, I gave her a lift!

PETR. Where, you must remember where you took her?

DEML. It's nobody's business where!

FILIP (*over excited*). But you mustn't answer like that. Make something up. People make things up even in front of a real court. If you answer like that you begin to sound really suspicious.

DEML. I don't feel like making anything up. (*Glances at his watch.*) At one in the morning.

PETR. So where did you take her?

DEML. I can't remember.

FILIP. You're not helping yourself!

PETR. Interesting. What did she look like, you should remember that at least!

DEML (*angrily*). I don't need to help myself. I simply gave her a lift!

PETR. Answer the court, prisoner in the dock!

DEML. To hell with your court! Anyway, I'm not going to answer any more questions!

IRENA (*quietly, to* DEML). Perhaps if you . . . perhaps it would be better if you did answer. Otherwise it's going to look as though you really are hiding something!

DEML. Well, I've got the right to hide something if I want. I'm not in the confessional here. And in any case, I don't have anything to hide.

PETR. Can you describe that student for us?

DEML (*shouts*). I don't know if she was a student. I never said she was a student. I never knew her.

EVA. But of course she was. Don't you remember, pet. You asked why she was in such a hurry at that time of night and she said she had to get up for a seven o'clock lecture.

DEML. She said so? I don't remember that at all!

EVA. And you chatted about what she was studying, and she told you how she had a chromatics exam or something of the sort.

DEML. I really don't remember it. I . . . (*Loses control.*) I forbid you to talk about such . . . such nonsense! Besides, our journey was private.

EVA. Was she tall or short? How was she dressed? Did she have black hair?

DEML. I don't remember. She was wearing a scarf. (*Frightened.*) Or maybe she wasn't. I didn't look at her hair.

EVA. She was blonde. What colour was the scarf?

DEML. I don't know!

EVA. Blue. Like her dress.

IRENA. That proves nothing. Lots of women have blue dresses.

PETR. And then it stopped raining?

DEML. When?

PETR. When you were giving the student a lift?

DEML. I didn't give any student a lift!

PETR. You didn't?

EVA (*surprised*). Interesting. Here's a newspaper cutting about the murder. (*Reads from* PETR*'s files.*) Traces of blood were found at the place, together with a scrap of blue silk and some strands of long blonde hair. The analysis proved that they were from the head of a woman aged about twenty . . .

PETR. Did you or didn't you give her a lift?

DEML. I've had enough. I'm not playing. (*To* EVA.) Come on, we're going home.

BAUER (*lifts his hand*). Can I say something?

PETR. No, you're the guard.

BAUER. What a shame! I could tell you something about him. About his character.

IRENA (*to* PETR). It doesn't follow from what has been said so far that my client had a relationship – excuse me, I'm rather upset – that his activity was in any way related to this crime. All he did was simply to give a lift to a girl in a blue dress.

PETR. Did you give her a lift or didn't you?

DEML (*with relief, to* IRENA). Yes of course, I gave a girl a lift. (*Gestures at* EVA.) She knows about it. She was in the car with me and she was chatting with her. She can witness that it's all nonsense.

EVA. You know I can't, I got out first.

DEML. So what? She got out straight after you. I took her to her street and she got out.

EVA. You see, you did give her a lift, why don't you admit it?

DEML. I didn't give anyone a lift! It's all a bloody lie.

PETR. Prisoner in the dock, don't insult the court!

DEML. Don't address me like that: prisoner in the dock! I can remember you when you were leaping about the garden with nothing on.

FILIP. Don't get so upset. All right, you didn't give her a lift. Let's assume you didn't give her a lift.

SOVA (*jumps out of his seat*). Now I understand! There are activities or rituals which should never be demeaned by such undignified comedy. Why do you drag into this a real and tragic incident?

PETR (*to* BAUER). Expel him from the courtroom!

BAUER (*lifting his gun*). Come on!

SOVA. You're playing at justice but at the same time all you show is injustice. I demand that we stop this game!

BAUER. Come on now, get a move on! (*Quietly.*) It may not be a game at all. Maybe he's really done it. I know him better than you do.

SOVA. Aren't you ashamed to speak like that about a friend?

BAUER. What friend? I'm the guard and he's the prisoner in the dock. A short time ago you were threatening to blow them to pieces.

SOVA. This game must stop!

BAUER. Why does it matter to you so much? Are you afraid your turn will come too?

SOVA. How dare you say such a thing?

BAUER. No one's conscience is completely clear. My Count Schwarzenberg used to say: The only difference between the innocent and the guilty is that the innocent hasn't yet been up before the judge. One day everyone will get his own guardian angel . . .

SOVA. Shut your mouth! You brute! It was you who knocked me out just now!

IRENA. Kamil, please, don't get so cross!

SOVA (*to* BAUER). Violence sickens me. But it's practically oozing from you. (*Returns to his seat.*) I'm letting you all know that I'm taking no part.

PETR. Very well, sit and watch. Although it isn't just the wrongdoer who commits injustice, but the man who looks on as well. We will move on to the interrogation of the witness. (*Nods towards* JAKUB.) Who are you?

JAKUB. Jakub Samek.

PETR. You are answerable before this court as a witness. You will speak the truth and nothing but the truth.

JAKUB. Yes.

PETR. Can you recall what you were doing exactly four weeks ago today, early in the morning?

JAKUB. As a matter of fact, I can. I got up at three in the morning.

PETR. As early as that?

JAKUB. I was going off to a sports contest. The plane was due to take off at half past six. And I do have to train in the morning.

PETR. Do you train every morning?

JAKUB. I do fitness training.

EVA (*joining in*). Could you tell us exactly what you do?

JAKUB (*with enthusiasm*). It's in two stages. Based on the Smith-Voronov system.

EVA. Could you give us a demonstration?

JAKUB. With pleasure. But I'd need – well, a piece of rope at least.

PETR (*to* FILIP). Give him the rope!

FILIP *opens a cupboard, throws out of it some junk including a length of red material and a small climbing axe, then pulls out a long piece of rope which he gives to* JAKUB.

JAKUB (*throws the rope over a ceiling beam, climbs up it, does a few exercises*). Four men in our squad tried to follow the three-stage Keiserschad-Kowalski system, but they failed. The muscle

volume increased threefold, but the heart simply gave up. The
last of them died a month ago.

PETR. Carry on. What you did after you'd exercised.

JAKUB. Then I had breakfast. At about four o'clock I left to catch
the bus. (*Lets himself down to the ground.*)

PETR. Where did you leave from, and where did you go to catch
the bus?

JAKUB. Where from? From here, obviously. The bus stop is by the
park. We were off to Madagascar!

IRENA (*astonished*). But that's perfectly true. (*To the others.*) He did
sleep here and he did go off early. (*Hurriedly.*) But that doesn't
mean anything. And the bus stop is quite a distance from the
park!

PETR. Did you see anything interesting or unusual on your way?

JAKUB. Yes, I did. Or rather: first of all I heard something. I heard
a kind of scream.

IRENA. But – but you didn't tell us anything about that.

FILIP. It's only a game, my dear, you mustn't get so worked up!

IRENA. Yes. But it all sounds so strange.

JAKUB. I wasn't sure whether the scream meant anything. And I
was in a hurry.

PETR. Where did it come from?

JAKUB. Where from? From the park, I'd say!

PETR. What sort of a scream was it?

JAKUB. What do you mean?

PETR. Could you make out any words?

JAKUB. It was a person, a woman, I'd say, but stifled. Like when
someone's being strangled, and they scream.

IRENA. Have you . . . Witness, have you ever strangled anyone?

JAKUB. Yep. In fun.

FILIP. This is too much. There's nothing funny about anything
that's been said. (*To* IRENA.) Why don't you make a protest?

IRENA. I protest at this answer.

PETR. Very well. What did you do next?

JAKUB. I got into the bus. If I hadn't caught it, my mates would have left me behind.

PETR. Was that all?

JAKUB. No. I happened to glance into the park and see this dustcart trundling along the path.

PETR. And didn't that strike you as odd?

JAKUB. It did. What were the dustmen doing on a path in the park at half past four in the morning?

PETR. What did it look like?

JAKUB. What? Oh, the dustcart? It was a sort of reddish colour – more of an orange. Almost new, I would say. The number plate was CC 27 27. I remembered that, because I'm actually twenty-seven myself.

PETR. Is that everything?

JAKUB. No, there was something else a bit . . . but I don't know if I ought to mention it, I mean, I don't want to throw any false suspicion.

PETR. Speak out.

JAKUB. This bloke suddenly rushed out of the park, all out of breath. He'd got earth all over him, and I think, actually blood as well. Just then my bus arrived.

PETR. Did he get in the bus?

JAKUB. Him? No – I did. He got in the dustcart. It drove out of the park, they opened a door and he jumped in.

PETR. Do you think you would recognise him again – this man?

JAKUB. I'm pretty sure I would. He was sort of eye-catching. Fat and bald. And he was the only living thing around. (*Looks at* DEML.) He's sitting right there! That's him!

IRENA (*blurts out*). But this is terrible! Why didn't you tell us anything about this?

DEML (*stands up*). This is too much. You little sod, take it back!

FILIP (*wearily.*) Calm down, dear. Remember, you're supposed to defend him!

DEML. Take it all back this minute. He never saw me. Until here, today. He made it all up.

PETR. Prisoner in the dock, silence!

DEML (*approaches* JAKUB). I am going straight home, but I want you to say that you made it all up and apologise!

JAKUB. What are you pushing me like that for? (*Pushes* DEML *so that he practically flies away from him.*)

DEML (*threatening* JAKUB). Take it back, take back all those lies! And apologise!

PETR *rings his bell.*

BAUER. What's that meant to mean?

JAKUB. What lies? I'm a witness for the prosecution!

EVA. Pet, don't get so worked up, it's only a game.

IRENA. But one shouldn't lie – even in a game. Especially when you're playing a witness.

DEML. So you're not going to apologise? I'll show you, you bastard! (*Tries to hit* JAKUB, JAKUB *catches hold of his arm and twists it behind him.*)

BAUER (*to* PETR). Should I intervene?

PETR. What else is there for it, my loyal jailer!

BAUER *throws his gun across his back, quickly grabs one end of the rope which* FILIP *pulled out of the cupboard and throws himself on* DEML.

SOVA. That's enough! (*Tries to hold* BAUER *back.*) We can't have this kind of thing. Don't forget, we all met here as friends!

BAUER *pushes him away.*

IRENA. My God, no, please!

A struggle, angry cries, overthrown chairs.

EVA (*holding* IRENA *back*). Leave them alone, at last they've let themselves go a bit. Do you think I played my part all right? You know, I really do hate making up the words.

Game Five

Kindred Spirits

The struggle is over. DEML *and* SOVA *are not only handcuffed, but each one tied to an arm chair.*

PETR (*rings the bell*). The court is adjourned for fifteen minutes. (*Rises, moves towards the stairs.*) I hope that in the meantime law and order will be restored. The verdict should be delivered in dignified surroundings. (*He sits on the top step, takes a book out of his pocket and reads.*)

FILIP. We can't go on like this. (*To* BAUER.) You've overdone it. Game or no game, I'm the host and I can't allow people to be violated like this.

BAUER (*ignoring* FILIP *until he approaches* SOVA). Stay where you are, don't go near them.

FILIP (*astonished*). What do you mean, don't go near them?

BAUER (*points the gun at him*). This is a court of law!

IRENA. For goodness' sake – get rid of that gun once and for all!

BAUER. He's got to stay away from them and not impede the proceedings.

FILIP (*moves away, bewildered*). Perhaps he's gone mad.

BAUER. I'm only carrying out orders!

DEML. I demand . . . this is simply unheard of! (*To* FILIP.) First of all you invite us here, then you accuse me, insult me, and finally tie me up!

FILIP. It wasn't me who tied you up. You brought that criminal with you yourself!

IRENA. Filip, how can you use such a word. Have you forgotten what you were saying just now?

FILIP. That was all part of the game!

SOVA. Untie him. It is your duty – not to put up with such injustice!

BAUER. Silence, the court is still sitting. First of all you say you're not playing and then you start poking your nose in. People like that are the worst.

DEML. If you don't untie me immediately, I'll shout for help. I'm not going to let myself be treated like some kind of criminal!

JAKUB. And what if you are? We heard some nice things about you!

DEML. You're the criminal! I'll get even with you, you yob! Do you think I haven't noticed how you've been after her the whole evening? (*He manages to jump up a little, taking the chair with him, and kicks* JAKUB *on the shin.*)

JAKUB *shouts with pain, turns round and lifts* DEML *and the chair into the air.*

DEML (*roaring*). Help! Violence! The way you were kissing her, that wasn't in the game at all! Help! He's going to kill me! Murderer!

JAKUB *puts the chair down again, but the other way around, so that* DEML *is sitting facing the wall. He takes off his sweater, wraps it round* DEML's *head and ties the sleeves together.*

FILIP (*to* BAUER). You see, you don't stop *him* getting near.

BAUER. He's a witness for the prosecution.

FILIP. So?

BAUER. He's giving justice a bit of a helping hand.

FILIP (*taking umbrage*). Don't you try to teach me about justice, you, you fraud, you furniture smuggler . . .

BAUER. I think maybe it was in court I heard the phrase 'assisting justice to be done'. You're not telling me you never claimed something of the sort, Mr Prosecutor?

IRENA. Please, come to your senses, all of you! We can't have this kind of violence here.

JAKUB. You don't like us having shaken him up a bit? (*To* EVA.) Don't you like it either?

EVA. Why not? It's all a game. I've played such a lot of games. Once they blindfolded me, put me in the driving seat, and I had to steer where they told me.

IRENA (*with a glance at* FILIP). No, I wouldn't like that. Supposing you'd been killed?

EVA. It's in my horoscope that I'm going to die young.

SOVA. It can't be said that the situation we find ourselves in is altogether outside the framework of a game. For myself, I actually find it quite inspiring. I admit that many times in my imagination I've been brought face to face with my interrogator with my hands bound. And I even felt some kind of satisfaction that only my hands were tied. Perhaps these (*He lifts his hands.*) are not the most terrible bonds. Power, for example, or false beliefs, bind us far more.

DEML *stamps.*

IRENA. I agree, Kamil. But I don't think violence is right in a game. And there's been a lot of it this evening.

BAUER. There's no harm in a little violence, with all due respect, dear lady. I remember my count telling me, how when he was in Turkey in the hands of the Sultan's guard . . .

FILIP. Don't get so upset about it. It wasn't you who started it. It was them who began to play about with a loaded gun.

BAUER. But fortunately he could speak seventeen languages. Once we had reveille at three in the morning as a punishment and he's a bit late getting up and the warder catches him and gets in a fearsome rage. Just as he's at his worst, my count says: 'Que quiere decir el verbo madrugar? El verbo madrugar quiere decir levantarae muy temorano.' And that's the end of that. And during roll call, when we're all standing to attention, he squats down on the ground for no reason, and when they start to blast him, he tells them: 'Kusimama kurefu kunamchokesha mzee.' Which in the negro language means: long waiting tires an old man, only they thought he was going off his trolley, so they sent him to the sick room.

SOVA (to BAUER). Let me just ask you one question. Considering we all met here as friends to play games, doesn't it make you feel awkward that you suddenly start treating us like villains?

BAUER. So why do you play at being villains?

EVA. Never mind. Let's just relax and enjoy ourselves here. There are still some more games we could play, or we could just let ourselves go a bit.

IRENA. But first of all we must let them go.

BAUER. In real life every villain acts innocent and in a game every innocent acts a villain and underneath they're all the same. (To SOVA.) Only you don't see those real connections.

SOVA. Don't you instruct me about connections, you . . . you dilettante.

BAUER. Now, let me just tell you a few names: Lincoln! Heir to the throne Franz Ferdinand, Lenin, Kennedy. Now have you got it?

EVA (to FILIP). It's your turn to suggest a game.

BAUER (to SOVA). The whole world is victim of one big conspiracy, even we are no exception. We're followed at every step!

IRENA. I don't think this is quite the right time to start playing a new game.

EVA. Why·ever not? In fact all this is a game. You've no idea what can be done in a game. Do you think I've never been tied up? And what they did with me then!

DEML stamps.

FILIP (to DEML). So you're blindfolded now, are you? It was

coming to you. I warned you. Now it's got going, I know what it's like. But you just wouldn't hold back.

IRENA. But we never wanted to play these cruel games. It just all happened somehow. (*Draws a chair up to* SOVA.) I'm so upset about all this, Kamil. I was so looking forward to this evening, and I was hoping you'd enjoy it. What terrible knots. (*Tries to undo them.*) I don't think I can undo them at all. You know, I've always wanted to live in some kind of good fellowship. But I never succeeded. So I thought, at least in play, at least we could play at it, at being close. And then I thought, that afterwards, perhaps, after we'd gone our separate ways, after the games had finished, that perhaps you'd remember . . .

SOVA. I assure you, Irena, it has been a most unusually interesting and stimulating experience. It can't be so apparent to you, but I'm beginning to see the world change in front of my eyes. As though I had grasped its precise measures. That one, (*Nods towards* BAUER.) – power. Thick, pitiless, deaf. Like death. The final negation of all our ambitions. Their utter debasement. The swollen confidence of emptiness. Or you, for example. Your longing for harmony, eternal, unattainable and therefore tragic. Me? All at once I feel a friend of so many people, we have a common bond – (*Lifts his bound wrists.*) this. They may not even realise that their hands are tied as well.

FILIP (*to* EVA). Very well then, I'll try to lead you out of the abyss. I know one very simple game. (*To* IRENA.) Everyone has to go into a separate corner or even a separate room and there they have to try to concentrate on one particular person present, whom they feel close to. Then everyone writes down the first words they think of. Sometimes it happens that two people write down words so close that it seems unbelievable. We call them kindred spirits. But of course, after all that's happened you may all find my game too peaceful.

JAKUB. Let's have some paper!

IRENA (*to* SOVA). You know, perhaps I'm under a curse. I've only got to meet someone and like them, or respect them, and something happens to them. Mr first husband, we'd had scarcely a year together, he was called out to a patient one night and he'd had a little bit to drink, it was his only weakness, the roads were icy. I didn't even know he'd gone out, we never said goodbye. My second husband, again . . . (*Stops short.*) I'm sorry, I know it's not the proper time . . . He was such a quiet man, he didn't drink or smoke, and all the same . . . Death doesn't choose, but why is it all around me? I never hurt a soul, and what if something now were to happen to Filip? I couldn't make another fresh start.

FILIP *has found some paper and gives a piece to* JAKUB.

JAKUB (*to* EVA). I'll be thinking of you during this game.

EVA (*takes paper from* FILIP *and goes to* DEML). We're playing another game, do you want to join in, pet?

DEML *stamps.*

IRENA (*refuses to take the paper* FILIP *is offering her*). How can we play a game, when they . . . (*To* BAUER.) Why don't you let them go, we're playing a different game now!

BAUER. I'm under orders.

JAKUB. Can we start?

BAUER. I'm curious what the verdict will be.

EVA (*to* JAKUB). But you'll have to go out somewhere! (*Pushes him in the opposite direction from* BAUER's *patrolling.*) We'll call you. (*Pushes him offstage.*)

IRENA (*to* BAUER, *indecisively*). Very well, I'll untie them myself. (*Appealing to the others.*) They are my . . . they are our guests! (*She looks uncertainly at* FILIP.)

FILIP (*shrugs his shoulders*). That game came to an end as far as I'm concerned. I'm going to concentrate! (*He goes off.*)

EVA (*returns alone, hurriedly tidies her hair, undoes a button on her blouse, and goes below where* PETR *is sitting on the stairs.*) Petr, won't you play with us again? We've got another game now.

PETR. You're tempting me. But I don't feel like it. We've already had too many unfinished games this evening. Why begin another one?

EVA. But you enjoy playing games.

PETR. No – it's just that I realised that the game is really our last refuge when we grow up. I never played games when I was a boy. I wanted to do something serious. To control thermo-nuclear reactions or some quite unknown source of energy. But then I realised there was no point to it. Society is full to bursting point with such activity. There's no reason for discovering anything, no point in looking for a new source of energy or new ideas – in any case someone's found them all before us. Found, formulated, and written them down. What is there left but to play games?

BAUER. Is the verdict ready?

PETR. The verdict? Oh yes. You really do persevere. But it doesn't seem to me to be the right time for a verdict.

BAUER. And what about those? (*He nods towards the two tied-up men.*)

PETR. Be patient. Sometimes we have to wait years for some verdicts. Or even centuries. And that's not to speak of verdicts which are never pronounced. They just hang over us. (*To* EVA.) Did anyone tell you that? (*Answers himself.*) Of course they did!

IRENA (*struggling to untie the knots*). I'll have to take a knife to them. (*She stands up and goes out.*)

BAUER (*shrugs his shoulders*). I don't know then. (*He sits on a chair, holds the gun in his lap, pulls out a pencil and begins to write.*)

EVA (*climbing a few steps*). What's that you're reading? A catalogue?

PETR. Catalogue? Why no – a catalogue of the stars. (*Reads.*) Our galaxy belongs to a great sky which has several thousand members and has a diameter of around fifty million light years. (*Looks up.*) The catalogue is a bit out-of-date. We've already penetrated nearly a billion light years into the distance. In this space there are more than a hundred million constellations similar to our galaxy. From that, as you are about to say, it follows that we often see the light of stars which perished long ago. Two questions arise from this. Firstly: have they really perished, when their light still exists? It's the same question as when we query the after-life of the soul. And the second question: isn't it time to go to bed?

EVA. You understand the stars?

PETR. No one can understand the stars, my lamb. It's just a game, everything we say about them. We play at billions of light years just as we do at eternal friendships, timeless works of art or love beyond the grave. We play in order to forget what wretched creatures we are. But you could put it the other way round. We play at billions of light years because we know just what wretched creatures we are.

JAKUB (*from the next room*). Ready?

EVA. Hold on a sec!

IRENA (*returns with an enormous butcher's knife*). This'll do it! (*Kneels again by* SOVA *and very carefully, even with some horror, tries to cut through his bonds.*)

EVA. I was just wondering perhaps whether you could do my horoscope.

PETR. Now?

EVA (*hesitating*). I could come round to you sometime.

PETR. When were you born?

EVA. September. The nineteenth of September. Early in the morning, they say.

PETR. Virgo. According to the Babylonians your stone is jasper; according to the Byzantines, sapphire: according to the occultists, beryl; and according to the medieval astrologers, chrysolite. As you see, it's all a game that can't be trusted. (*Takes a stone out of his pocket and gives it to her.*) But you can keep this as a souvenir.

EVA. Is it beryl or chrysolite?

PETR. It's a pebble, but it came from the stomach of a goose. It might bring you luck.

JAKUB (*from the next room*). Can I read now?

EVA (*examines the stone*). All right, but stay where you are. Read yours from there!

JAKUB. Who's going to start?

EVA. You can! (*She stands opposite PETR and addresses herself to him.*)

JAKUB (*calls from behind the scenes*). Man.

EVA. Gambler.

BAUER (*startled*). Is it my turn now? Well, what I've got written down, it's the only thing I could think of: beer.

FILIP (*enters and reads*). Morning.

> *In quick succession* FILIP *and* BAUER *read from their papers.* EVA *has no paper and addresses herself to* PETR; *but* JAKUB *assumes that her words are meant for him.*

JAKUB. Moonlight on water.

EVA. Stars.

BAUER. Dumpling.

FILIP. Winter. Frost. Footsteps.

JAKUB. Fate.

EVA (*to* PETR). Horoscope.

BAUER. Plate.

FILIP. Paper.

JAKUB. Aeroplane.

EVA. Miami.

BAUER. And then all at once I've got gambling den. And why isn't everyone reading?

FILIP. Courtyard. Stone flags. Footsteps – but I've read that already.

JAKUB. Beauty,

EVA. Virgo.

BAUER (*surprised at himself*). I've got Alan written down here. But perhaps it could be alarm.

FILIP. Vodka.

JAKUB. It's amazing, I never expected it to be possible. Such coincidences. Love.

EVA. Waiting, telephone.

BAUER. Lager. Or is it larder?

FILIP. Beam.

JAKUB. All I've got left is night. And a kiss.

EVA. Evening. Tomorrow.

BAUER. Handcuffs. And because everyone's played two words, I'll have cufflinks as well.

FILIP. Rope. (*Vehemently.*) I know that can't be right, but I couldn't concentrate. (*Shouts.*) How can one concentrate? It's bedlam in here. You spend your whole life trying to concentrate. There's always someone talking. You're always listening to someone you don't want to hear.

BAUER. Damn, now I've thought of a really good word.

JAKUB. I've not got any more. But I don't need any, we don't have to go on playing. We're obviously kindred spirits. Come out here with me. There's a splendid couch.

BAUER (*regretfully*). It's a pity it's come so late. And it's such a lovely word.

JAKUB. Come on, I'm waiting for you!

BAUER. Casemate.

EVA (*to* PETR). Shall I?

PETR. Why shouldn't you. After all, you can come back whenever you like. And in any case it's all only a game – it too must end.

IRENA. There we are, Kamil! (*Throws the bonds to the ground.*)

PETR (*to* SOVA). Congratulations, it must be a splendid feeling, if only for a fleeting moment, to have the freest head on your shoulders.

EVA. I'll go, then.

BAUER (*comes to himself, jumps up, grasping his gun*). No one's going anywhere!

IRENA. And now you too ... (*Undoes the sweater which is wound round* DEML's *mouth.*)

JAKUB (*peeping inside*). Come on then, come on!

DEML (*shrieks*). I can hear everything you say, I heard everything you said. You bastards, I'd like to see you all hanged. (*To* EVA.) You drunken whore, I hate you!

IRENA. For goodness sake, please don't start squabbling now, we don't want to part bad friends!

DEML. I'll kill you all, you shits!

BAUER (*to* EVA). Stay where you are! No one is to go anywhere!

PETR (*in disgust*). Let me inform you that the games in which I gave you the role of the guard, or even my deputy, finished long ago. Kindly put down that pop gun! (*Goes towards* BAUER *as though he were about to struggle with him.*)

BAUER. Exactly, they are finished. You can't order me around any more.

IRENA. Stop it for goodness sake! (*Hysterically.*) I'm beginning to be frightened!

BAUER (*bows*). With all due respect, dear lady, the time is ripe for my game!

Game Six

The Execution

DEML (*to* BAUER). And you think that I'm going to play with you again? That I'm ever going to speak to you again?

EVA. He's quite right, I still want to play his game.

FILIP. Perhaps I may enquire what kind of game it is?

BAUER (*having put the gun down at last*). I've described it already, haven't I? Execution.

PETR. Something else you and your count used to play at together?

BAUER. Something we used to play when we were kids. The condemned man is chosen by lot, but anyone can volunteer to be hangman. Who's volunteering then?

IRENA. Why do we have to play at executions? Please don't, I've had enough! It's all been too much already.

PETR. Follow him, little sister, you must follow him, he's just invited you back to the domain of his childhood.

FILIP. I knew it, it had to happen. (*Vehemently.*) And do you really think that here in this house you'll find a volunteer hangman?

BAUER (*knots the rope, which has been hanging there since they played at The Trial, into a noose*). It's the perfect game to finish with. Because unlike most of your games, with due respect, dear lady, it has to come to an end. It comes to an end if someone says 'Stop'; and it comes to an end if they don't. If the condemned man holds out to the last second, then he's won and changes place with the hangman.

FILIP. I'm warning you for the last time. All of you!

DEML. All right then. I will!

FILIP. You will what?

DEML. I'll volunteer as hangman!

EVA. You, pet?

DEML. Don't you speak to me, you . . . you whore!

JAKUB. Strange, though, isn't it – first we had a gangster, then we put someone quite different on trial, and now we're going to hang a third person . . .

BAUER. Why? This is a completely different game.

PETR (*to* JAKUB). Objections like that aren't going to take you far in life.

JAKUB. All right, we have to hang an innocent man, but why?

PETR. Because such is the fate of the innocent. Fortunately their numbers are declining.

JAKUB. I don't understand, I really don't. I don't like it.

BAUER *tries out the strength of the noose and then goes to get a stool.*

SOVA. I should like to express my opinion at this point, if I may. I can't conceal my fear that this game may appeal to our basest instincts. But on the other hand . . . (*He paces back and forth in excitement.*) It struck me when I was a boy, how much I'd like to speak to a condemned man on the eve of his execution. I even got hold of a few books on the subject, but they didn't satisfy me. Either the authors hadn't taken the trouble to visit the condemned cell or if they had, they hadn't asked the right questions. What I want to know is: does a man change his gauge of time and values the moment he feels the noose around his neck? Does he hate the world, abandon it, love it; or on the contrary, does he stop caring about it? (*To* JAKUB.) And you spoke of the innocent man! That would embody the human predicament to an even greater extent!

BAUER (*takes a box of matches out of his pocket*). We'll draw lots for the condemned man!

EVA (*draws the first match. To* DEML). Would you hang me too?

DEML. With pleasure!

BAUER *offers a match to* PETR, *to* JAKUB, *and then to* IRENA.

IRENA. My match is broken. (*Horrified.*) Does that mean . . .?

BAUER. Unfortunately, with all due respect, dear lady!

IRENA. But it's so horrible, that you should – that I . . .(*Gazes at the noose.*)

EVA. Don't worry, someone is sure to give in and say 'Stop!'

IRENA. But what do you want . . . what do you want to do with me?

SOVA. I volunteer!

FILIP. What? To be the condemned man?

IRENA. No Kamil, I would never ask that of you. It wouldn't be right. Why don't we agree not to play this game?

SOVA (*takes his jacket off*). There is some sense in this game. For me at least. (*Unfastens the top button of his shirt.*) I'm ready!

BAUER. Not so fast. (*Indicating* DEML.) The hangman has to have his helper. Then there has to be someone who reads out the sentence. And someone to be the priest!

IRENA. No, stop it! I'm telling you, stop!

BAUER. You can't say 'Stop' yet, my dear lady, as the game hasn't yet started. (*To* FILIP.) You can read out the sentence.

FILIP. I told you before, I don't want to play.

BAUER. It's only the sentence! You do it with such style! (*To* IRENA.) You can be the priest!

IRENA. Me? The priest? But I can't be the priest! I . . . I'm not sure I have enough faith!

EVA. You don't have to have faith. I don't believe in everything I sing about.

BAUER (*to* JAKUB). You can do the dirty work.

JAKUB. Leave off insulting me.

BAUER. You can assist the hangman, I mean.

JAKUB. I'm doing no dirty work. I've had enough.

DEML. Can we start now?

FILIP. Very well! (*He fills a glass and drains it down.*)

IRENA. No, Filip, no, you promised me, never again!

EVA. Could a woman play the hangman's assistant?

BAUER. Anyone can play anything!

JAKUB. You're not going to play that part, are you!

EVA. Why not?

JAKUB. It doesn't suit you.

EVA. I'll wear a mask! (*She picks up the mask* JAKUB *brought for* IRENA, *then pours a glass of wine and offers it to* SOVA.) Have a drink for the last time!

SOVA. Thank you, no. I want all my senses to be clear to register what is going to happen to me, what my feelings are.

EVA. What use will that be to you? (*She drinks.*)

DEML (*wraps the red material round himself*). Let's start! (*To* SOVA.)

Come and stand on this stool.

BAUER. Wait a minute! Not so fast. We have to have the sentence first. (*To* FILIP.) Carry out your function!

FILIP *empties the glass that* EVA *has poured out for him.*

IRENA. Filip! You know you're not used to it. (*To* PETR.) Petr, please do something. We mustn't go on with this game!

FILIP. There are lots of things one isn't used to. For instance, I'm not used to talking about myself. However, now I am going to utter a few words about myself.

BAUER. All you have to utter is the sentence.

PETR. Dear friends; I think the time has come for me to say thank you and good night. My little sister thought she would return us to the age of innocence, but now she can see for herself that one can no longer return there, or even that there was no age of innocence. And so now she is asking you to bring this evening of games to an unceremonious conclusion.

EVA (*about* FILIP). Why don't you leave him alone? Let him talk. You be glad too, that he's letting himself go.

PETR (*irritated*). He doesn't know what he's doing. None of you know any longer! (*He tries to get hold of* FILIP, *who is climbing onto the table, but* FILIP *pushes him away.*)

SOVA. I am innocent!

PETR *climbs the stairs, opens a book and begins to read.*

FILIP (*climbs on the table*). I'm going to make a speech about myself, about law and justice.

IRENA. Filip, please, please . . .

FILIP. Dear friends, what is the law? When I was a student I was inspired by the age-old saying: 'In ius est ars boni et aequi.' To do right is the art of truth and justice. That is why, quite seriously, I had this saying set in brass letters and hung over my table. At the age of twenty-five I entered the district court of law.

IRENA. Filip!

FILIP. Silence. My predecessor was serving his final year. He had been trained in the Austrian school and lived through six regimes; he could tell splendid anecdotes, knew the Napoleonic code through and through and would often say to me: My boy, the law is nothing but a legalised form of lawlessness, since from the beginning it serves power rather than justice. I, who have judged the guilty and the innocent now for twenty years, can, if you will allow me, confirm that that is how it is.

BAUER. This is beside the point. We're wasting time.

FILIP (*silences him with a gesture*). And allow me, dear friends, to inform you that the innocent are always punished more harshly than the real criminals. Since to punish the innocent at all, you have let slip the dogs of unreason – and unreason is never ashamed to pronounce a heavier sentence. Dear friends, please don't laugh at me, even though I do admit I'm a little drunk. I declare what I have known for a long time: that whenever I don my judge's robes I become an actor who's only reading someone else's text. It would come to the same thing if instead of: 'In the name of the law, hear the sentence pronounced,' I said, (*To* BAUER.) 'Kusimama kurefu kunamchokesha mzee,' or broke into song, (*To* EVA.) 'Oh let me fly, fly, fly stony water,

Oh let me walk around the miles of rolling sea . . .'

EVA. He has let himself go! Bravo, Filip!

FILIP. It makes no difference because I am not justice, I don't give
the law, I live in fear myself, yes my friends, all my life I've been
thinking about all those, so many they won't even cram into my
brain, who I've no idea who they all are, but who lived at the
same time as I lived, and who were sentenced under the same
song and under the same senseless mumbling by my renowned
colleagues to exile, to the galleys, to the gas chambers, to the
gallows, to the axe, to the labour camps, to pits where their
bones rot. (*Sings.*) Oh let me fly, fly fly stony water . . .

EVA. He's fantastic! (*She takes her guitar and accompanies* FILIP.)

FILIP (*sings drunkenly*). Oh let me walk around the miles of rolling
sea, Oh let me run, run run around the great infernal land . . .
These bones rot in pits, I tell you, and when I close my eyes I
can see them, the bones coming together, bone to bone, and
the flesh covering them, and the flesh clothed in rags, creating
an army, a huge army, a gigantic army, which fills the whole
land and starts moving towards me, against me, and I know that
for me there is only one possibility, dear friends, to judge them,
to judge them once more, to condemn the innocent once
more, because they are the ones who call for justice more
passionately than anyone else, and there is no justice, there
never has been and there never will be, for justice is
unattainable.

BAUER. Get to the point, we're in a hurry!

FILIP. I had to make this speech in order to explain that it is not in
my power to change the sentence which is about to be carried
out, even when I know that it will punish the innocent.

SOVA. What you have just said is the most passionate defence of
contemptible servitude and·of servile contemptibility that I have
ever heard.

IRENA. Kamil, no, you're unjust. Filip is an honourable man. Every
injustice makes him suffer. His only wish is to live in a better
world. Just like me.

BAUER. Get to the point!

FILIP. Justice is unattainable, and I realise that from a certain
viewpoint the innocent are the most dangerous. For it is they
who simply by their existence show up the imperfection of our
actions. (*To* BAUER.) You want me to sentence him. He has
been sentenced. He's sentenced himself!

BAUER. I don't know if that's enough.

FILIP. Kusimama kurefu kunemchokesha mzee. Kupotea njia
ndiko kupua njia. Enough?

EVA *applauds.*

BAUER. Does it mean the rope?

FILIP. More or less.

BAUER. Does it mean that there is no appeal against the sentence?

FILIP. Whether there is or not must be decided by a higher
authority. Which, basically, is him (*Points to* DEML.)

DEML. Me?

FILIP. You're the hangman! It's you who now have to execute your
duty! My compliments, ladies and gentlemen. (*He jumps off the
table.*)

EVA. You were great. I'd no idea you could sing so well.

FILIP. We often used to sing when the hearing was over. What else
was left for us to do?

DEML. Maybe we can put him on the stool now!

SOVA (*opens the neck of his shirt*). I am innocent!

BAUER. Now for the priest!

IRENA. I can't, I can't, I'm too upset. Petr!

PETR *carries on reading.*

EVA. Go on. (*Pushes her towards* SOVA.)

IRENA. I don't know what . . . (*To* SOVA.) Dear son . . . no, that's
not right. Kamil, you know what I'm trying to say, that I believe
that one day people will create a society like I described to you,
and that they will become close to each other. Do you believe
that too?

SOVA. No! Once I used to believe that too. Now I know for certain
that it's not so. My life has been one great mistake.

IRENA. But Kamil, that's terrible, what you're saying. You must
believe. Why else do we live? (*Notices that* FILIP *is drinking.*)
Filip, leave that alone! (*Seems to be about to snatch the glass out of
his hand, then stops herself.*)

SOVA. It's all the same to me. It's all the same to me now, why you
live.

IRENA. No you mustn't get bitter like that. (*Turns again to* FILIP.)
You must find peace in yourself. (*To* SOVA.) I don't know
whether you believe in God, but think about him. Think about

something good. Or imagine something from your childhood.

SOVA (*closes his eyes*). Yes, thank you.

IRENA. Think about him. Can you see him?

SOVA. I can see flags. A great forest of flags. You can go now!

IRENA (*turns away, sobbing*). That's enough. This has all upset me terribly.

SOVA. No, carry on. I'm ready

DEML (*to* EVA). Bind him!

SOVA. No, there's no need for that. (*But he allows* EVA *to bind his hands.*) I am innocent!

DEML. Now stand on this stool.

SOVA (*climbs on the stool*). My friends! Where are you? Are you going to allow the innocent to fall into the hands of the hangman! Will you forsake me now?

IRENA (*goes to the bottom of the stairs, upset*). Can't you hear him? He's calling for you!

PETR (*looks up from his book*). He's excellent, at last he's found his role!

IRENA. But he's calling for you!

PETR. Unfortunately, they didn't remember to include a part for the friend in this game. It's up to you to comfort him.

IRENA (*runs to* SOVA). Kamil, they're not here. They can't hear you, but if they could they would come, they would certainly save you. But I'm here, Kamil. You must believe. In people. In a better world. In the good that will prevail. Peace on your soul, Kamil!

DEML (*takes hold of the noose*). Someone ought to say something now, some sort of formula. (*To* FILIP.) Isn't there something one's supposed to say while it's going on?

FILIP. And another is to be added to the huge army. I see already how he arrays himself, how he is set against me!

DEML. And then he's got the right to his last wish.

SOVA. There's no need. My only wish is to leave this world of yours as quickly as possible. I can see it now. I can see you. There is no hope nor love in you. There is no will to live, only to have a good life style. And hence the devastation. You can't see your own lives, you can't see yourselves. You have covered the mirrors with all those flags!

DEML. It's up to you! (*Puts the noose round his neck.*)

IRENA. I can't go on! (*Goes to* JAKUB.) Could we have a drink together?

JAKUB. A drink together? But you know I don't drink!

IRENA (*takes* EVA *by the elbow and leads her aside*). I'm sorry, but could we have a drink together?

EVA (*takes off the mask*). Sure, why not? Haven't you had a drink yet? I'm always ready for a drink. (*Takes a glass and pours one for* IRENA.) Pretty good, aren't they, eh? I'd never have thought they could let themselves go like that.

SOVA. Flags, flags! There are more flags than people. More than mice! More than thoughts. More than words. (*He laughs.*) They're suffocating me. They will suffocate us all.

JAKUB (*to* EVA). There's no sense to these games. I'd rather give you a demonstration.

IRENA. I don't understand them anymore. They're behaving as though they really want to hang him. (*She drinks.*) Tell me, do you like to cook as well?

EVA. Me? Never. I always get a take-away if I'm at home. But usually I'm on tour.

SOVA. I am innocent!

JAKUB (*takes the small table over next to* SOVA *and takes off his sweater.*) I'll show you something, something you could never have seen before!

IRENA. I don't like cooking either! Just salads, I enjoy making. I have a hundred and eleven recipes.

JAKUB (*catches hold of the beam and starts to exercise.*) This is the Keiserschad-Kowalsky booster!

EVA (*steps back, goes to the bottom of the stairs to* PETR). It's going to be over soon, you know!

PETR (*glances up*). Just as well. And tomorrow evening you will ring me. And I'll have to get your horoscope ready. But I'll disappoint you. I don't know how to do horoscopes and the telephone is out of order. I could of course meet you somewhere at that time, but after all, it was all only a game.

EVA *remains standing for a moment at the bottom of the stairs, then puts the mask on again and returns to* DEML.

JAKUB (*out of breath*). And now I'm going into five of the most difficult Ho-Fu-tun movements.

SOVA. He should get down, it's not dignified!

PETR (*more or less to himself*). Though the telephone is likely to be repaired in a few days. (*Glances at* EVA.) We'll see . . .

IRENA (*hasn't noticed that* EVA *isn't still standing next to her*). For example, Salad with Truffles and Hot Cucumber Salad and Cheese Salad with Crab. And Bosnian Salad and Hanák Salad and Miami Salad and Greek Salad . . . You know, when I start chopping cabbage or pumpkin into little pieces, I can forget about everything else . . . (*She takes a knife from the table and begins to slice some cheese.*) Only I have to go over the measurements in my head, so I don't get them wrong.

BAUER. I'll count to three. Then we both pull at the same time. One!

JAKUB (*finishing out of breath*). That . . . that's what I call something! That's the only way I can . . .

BAUER. Two!

SOVA (*loudly*). I am innocent!

JAKUB (*hanging by the arms next to him, tongue stuck out, breathing heavily*). . . . can feel really find some satisfaction!

SOVA (*quietly*). No . . . not dignified at all.·

Curtain.

CAT ON THE RAILS ■ JOSEF TOPOL
Translated by GEORGE and CHRISTINE VOSKOVEC

JOSEF TOPOL was born in a small town near Prague in 1935, and came to Prague at the age of eighteen to work in the theatre directed by E.F. Burian, the great Czech director of the inter-war period. His first play, *Midnight Wind* was an historical drama written for this theatre. In the late fifties Topol was encouraged by the director Otomar Krejča to write for the new regíme he had created at the National Theatre, where Topol's plays *Their Day* and *The End of the Carnival* marked a new wave in playwriting in Czechoslovakia. He also worked as a translator, particularly of Shakespeare and Chekhov. *Cat on the Rails* (*Kočka na kolejích*) was written in 1965 for the opening of Krejča's new venture, The Theatre Beyond the Gate which was closed during the 'normalisation' of the early seventies. Topol continued to work as a translator until 1977 when, having signed Charter 77, he was forbidden to do any other than manual work. During this period he wrote *Goodbye Socrates!* and *The Voices of Birds*; the former was produced at the Theatre of the Estates in 1990, the latter at the Vinohrady Theatre as early as June 1989.

Characters

ÉVI
VÉNA
THE BOY
FIRST YOUNG MAN
SECOND YOUNG MAN

The action takes place at a whistle stop of a railway branch line, not far from Prague.

The scene is a whistle stop of a railway branch line. Shadows of the spread-out branches of a large tree fall on a wooden shed, the type found at whistle stops the world over. A single track runs alongside the proscenium. Upstage and parallel to it, a footpath, between the track and the shed. A little distance from the shed, a bench.

It is night.

Situation One

THE BOY *enters running along the path. He is wearing a white shirt with an open collar and carries his jacket under his arm. He is out of breath. He stops for a moment, then runs into the shed. An irritated male voice is heard from inside:* 'Hey!' THE BOY *backs out of the shed, throwing the jacket over his shoulders.*

VÉNA *enters from shed, rubbing his forehead.*

VÉNA. You out of your mind, idiot! (*He stuffs his shirt tails into his trousers.*)

THE BOY. How could I . . .

VÉNA *steps threateningly towards him.* THE BOY, *backing away, lifts his hands to protect his face; the jacket slips off his shoulders, he trips over it and sits on the bench,* VÉNA *towering over him.*

VÉNA. How could you what?

THE BOY (*bursts out*). It's a waiting room . . .

ÉVI *appears in the door of the shed.*

ÉVI. He calls it a waiting room? This hedgehog nest?

BOY *grabs his jacket, starts off, but* VÉNA *gets hold of a sleeve. The jacket is stretched taut between them.*

VÉNA (*giving the sleeve a jerk*). Let's have it: 'I didn't know you were having such a good time . . .'

BOY (*sarcastically*). I didn't know you were having such a good time . . .

VÉNA (*prompting*). 'I could kick myself.'

BOY. I sure could kick you. (*He tries to jerk the jacket free but* VÉNA *pulls him back and twists his arm.*)

VÉNA. Good. Let's see you try.

ÉVI. Let him go, Véna. (*To* BOY.) What's your name?

BOY. Ivan.

ÉVI. That's better, Ivan. Got a match?

BOY (*making a face.*) Nyeh! (*A hiss of pain as* VÉNA *twists his arm.*) . . . Sorry.

VÉNA (*letting him go*). No match but some cheek.

ÉVI. We'll never get a smoke. (*To* BOY.) Can you strike a flint?

VÉNA. The peasantry has lost the art of flint striking.

> *A distant sound of running feet is heard on the tracks, off.* BOY *gets fidgety.* VÉNA *notices it, drapes* BOY's *jacket over his own shoulders.*
>
> You in a hurry? Sit down. (*Sits down on bench and ties his shoe laces.*)

BOY. You crud.

VÉNA. What have you done? Well?

> BOY *stand helplessly, peering into the night.*

ÉVI. You can tell *me.* I'm an outlaw too.

VÉNA. Kind of a wildcat.

ÉVI. Kind of your unlawful wife.

VÉNA. Sure.

> *Someone is heard whistling, off.*

BOY. So what? They're after me.

ÉVI (*to* VÉNA). He set fire to the pub.

VÉNA. Him? He's got hot pants, that's all. Bet you there's a woman. (*Feeling the jacket's pockets.*) No matches. (*Tossing the jacket to the* BOY.) Good boy. Tells no lies.

> BOY *catches jacket, looks around in alarm and darts off behind the shed.*

BOY (*as he runs off*). You can both go and . . .

VÉNA. Mind your language. (*Picks up a stone and throws it after the* BOY.)

ÉVI. What if you'd hit him?

VÉNA. I didn't, did I?

ÉVI. You always play the fool. (*Pours broken pieces of glass out of her handbag.*) You were lying on my mirror.

More whistling, off.

VÉNA. Seven years' bad luck.

ÉVI. Already, with you. (*Begins to make up.*)

VÉNA (*feeling his forehead*). The bastard. I got a lump.

ÉVI. Such a useful little mirror.

VÉNA (*crushing the fragments with his heel*). And unto dust it shall return . . .

ÉVI. How am I going to see myself now?

VÉNA *offers his face for a mirror.*

Vandal (*Almost tenderly.*) It was for me you were showing off, wasn't it?

VÉNA. Showing off?

ÉVI. That act you put on. Trying to scare him. (*Paints his face with her eyebrow pencil.*)

VÉNA. What're you doing to me?

ÉVI. A moustache. It won't come off. I made it a defiant one.

Two figures, unseen by the couple, enter from the darkness.

VÉNA (*sticking out his chest*). Ho-ho!

The two figures approach. They are TWO YOUNG MEN.

FIRST YOUNG MAN (*grabbing* VÉNA *from behind*). Got him!

SECOND YOUNG MAN (*grabbing* ÉVI *almost simultaneously*). Got him!

ÉVI *kicks his shins; he hurriedly lets go of her.*

Sorry . . .

VÉNA (*throws* FIRST YOUNG MAN *off*). What's this?

ÉVI. Playing cops and robbers?

FIRST YOUNG MAN (*picking himself up, to* VÉNA). Seen a kid – about like so?

VÉNA. Mm. Seen a few about like so –

FIRST YOUNG MAN (*angry*). Did you or didn't you?!

ÉVI (*Pointing at herself*). *She* did.

FIRST YOUNG MAN. Where'd she go?

VÉNA (*with irony*). What she do to you?

FIRST YOUNG MAN (*screams*). Where'd he go!

SECOND YOUNG MAN. Easy!

(*To* VÉNA). You know what a vendetta is? If you don't, shut up.

FIRST YOUNG MAN. Speak up, dammit, speak up!

SECOND YOUNG MAN.We're going to kick his teeth in. Right?

VÉNA. The kid's, that is.

FIRST YOUNG MAN *starts taking a swing at* VÉNA.

SECOND YOUNG MAN (*backs away*). He can't be far. His train will be here any minute.

FIRST YOUNG MAN (*exploding*). I'm gonna kick his teeth in! (*He runs towards the shed.*)

ÉVI. Look at the sky – It's so low . . . If it weren't for the shed it would collapse.

FIRST YOUNG MAN (*stopping*). That funny?

ÉVI. Isn't it though?

FIRST YOUNG MAN *starts towards the shed again.*

VÉNA. Suppose he's got a catapult –

FIRST YOUNG MAN *turns to* VÉNA *angrily.*

SECOND YOUNG MAN. A stone would do –

FIRST YOUNG MAN *gives* SECOND *a dirty look. He reaches the shed, dodges sideways.*

FIRST YOUNG MAN (*banging the shed wall with both fists*). Come on out! Come on out! Let's have a look at you.

Silence. FIRST YOUNG MAN *grabs a flashlight from* SECOND*'s hand and directs the beam inside the shed.*

SECOND YOUNG MAN (*peering in*). Some mess.

FIRST YOUNG MAN (*stupidly*). Where'd all the eggshells come from?

VÉNA. From the bright ideas we hatched.

SECOND YOUNG MAN (*to* FIRST). C'mon, let's go home. You'd need a police dog.

FIRST YOUNG MAN (*stops*). I once had a dog. Smart. Could he point!

SECOND YOUNG MAN. A train ran him over.

FIRST YOUNG MAN. Sonofabitch train.

ÉVI. Poor thing.

FIRST YOUNG MAN (*shouts into the night*). Go fish in your own waters, you stinker! Hear me?

SECOND YOUNG MAN (*to* ÉVI). The kid's after his sister.

ÉVI. That against the law?

SECOND YOUNG MAN. Only I was going out with her first!

FIRST YOUNG MAN (*shouting*). Go fish in your own waters, I swear to you! C'mon and get one in the teeth! Come on out!

Silence.

He hid in the rye. Betcha he's in the rye. (*Starts off, stops.*) Hear him rustling? (*He goes.*)

SECOND YOUNG MAN. I can hear him. (*Stumbles after* FIRST. *They are gone.*)

ÉVI. What about the matches?

VÉNA (*calling after them*). Hey, fellas – wait! Got a match?

Silence.

ÉVI. We're just never ever going to smoke again. I know it.

VÉNA. Morons.

ÉVI. Wind's getting up.

VÉNA. Live, they say. Be full of life. What for?

ÉVI. For a girl – Not you.

VÉNA. I'm not a stag in October.

ÉVI. Next thing I know you'll be saying love is only for beasts.

VÉNA. You bet. I could use a drink.

ÉVI. Whatever in the world we talk about – you always wind up with 'I could use a drink.'

VÉNA (*laughs*). Come on, cat. What's the matter? (*Sits on the bench.*) So, the kid's after the moron's sister. That makes sense to you?

ÉVI. Maybe she's his step-sister.

VÉNA. What a fuss for a Suzy.

ÉVI. Everything revolves around us.

VÉNA (*pacing up and down the path, preaching*). That's why darkness prevails. If it weren't for Suzies, the world would revolve around the sun.

ÉVI (*watching him*). Hey, are you putting on weight?

VÉNA (*stops*). Me? – Well, that ought to make me good-natured. Fatsos are good-natured.

ÉVI. All quiet . . .

VÉNA. . . . on the Western front – (*Stops.*) What's that from? . . .

ÉVI. The whole place is like a horror picture. I could get scared.

VÉNA. If it weren't for me.

ÉVI. There are things tickle you, bite, sting, crawl on you . . . Nature . . . Nature!

VÉNA. She's too thick. Creature upon creature.

ÉVI (*shuddering*). Ugh!

VÉNA (*tickles ÉVI's neck with a straw*). Imagine a great big catfish. There's his pink mouth and whiskers.

ÉVI (*catches his hand*). Last year's blade of grass. (*She crosses to the track.*)

VÉNA. What did you mean you're my unlawful wife?

ÉVI. Barbarian. Am I not?

VÉNA. You belong to me.

ÉVI. By what right?

VÉNA. The right of might.

ÉVI. If you conquer a territory you go and make it legal so nobody can take it away from you, don't you?

VÉNA. Barbarians don't.

ÉVI (*standing by the track*). Where can that train be?

VÉNA. Maybe it got involved on the way.

ÉVI. What if that territory found itself somebody else to run it?

VÉNA. In that case – between that somebody and me – there would arise territorial disputes. (*Closer to her.*) Cat, I would claim a minimum of two hills and one valley. I'd let that other take what was left.

ÉVI. Well, frugal you're not.

VÉNA. I would rally all my troops and would not rest till I

reconquered you in your integrity.

ÉVI. I would never be through with wars.

VÉNA. And you'd love it, cat, pussycat.

ÉVI. Don't you ever drag me into the countryside again.

VÉNA. Does it bore you to go hiking with me?

ÉVI. We fight our way through brush like badgers, ford rivers like horses and, like a couple of idiots, we get stuck at a whistle stop. No train ever ran through here. Look at the rails. They're covered with rust.

VÉNA. It's been raining.

ÉVI. Don't remind me. I feel like a shirt – wash-and-dry.

VÉNA. I'll iron you.

ÉVI. And wet matches. Won't *one* catch?

VÉNA *hands her a box of matches.* ÉVI *tries in vain to strike one.*

They crumble like cheese. Where are we? – Where are we, you and me?

VÉNA. Don't ask me. We're somewhere.

ÉVI (*sighs*). Are we?

VÉNA. Well, we're not *no*where, are we?

ÉVI. Nowhere! That's all we'd need. When I think I could be . . .

VÉNA. Cat, pussycat . . .

ÉVI. . . . out of these shoes, and the coffee brewing . . .

VÉNA. You ought to have that stove fixed. It'll asphyxiate you one day.

ÉVI. *One,* that's all.

VÉNA. It'll asphyxiate me, too. That's why I won't marry you.

ÉVI. Oh you, you would have got a new one right away, wouldn't you? You with your life insurance! – You have one, haven't you?

VÉNA. Wasn't my idea. My mother. She said, 'a piano might fall on you . . .'

ÉVI. '. . . and I will collect.' You've got a foxy mommy.

VÉNA. She cares.

ÉVI. She shouldn't have let you be a removal man then. Should have sent you to school.

VÉNA. I'd have to have the brains.

ÉVI. Would you now? You're a shrewd enough.

VÉNA. That's not brains. That's life.

ÉVI (*throwing her arms around his neck*). What does your mother think of me, anyway?

VÉNA. She likes you.

ÉVI. Oh sure.

VÉNA. She knows I won't marry you. She's morbidly jealous.

ÉVI. Of you?

VÉNA. Of my cash. I can take my love wherever I choose but the cash I must take home.

ÉVI. That's clever. Paying her all your life for bringing you into the world.

VÉNA. I'm not here for free. Some pay money for eats and drink and stuff. Me, I even pay for breathing.

ÉVI. Because of her you're stuck with menial work.

VÉNA. Gives me exercise.

ÉVI. You could play tennis.

VÉNA. Tennis!

ÉVI. White trousers, racquet under your arm –

VÉNA. Knock myself silly chasing that ball?

ÉVI. Oh well, if that's all you see in it . . . what is one to do with you? You rob yourself of so much beauty – and you don't even know it.

VÉNA. You're beautiful enough for me.

ÉVI. I'm cold.

VÉNA. You've been cold ever since I've known you.

ÉVI. Like that time in the park. That was April, though.

VÉNA. I don't remember that it was April.

ÉVI. It's written down. In my head. Let's take a walk, come on.

VÉNA. Oh no, not that.

ÉVI. It'll warm you up.

VÉNA. I'd rather unpack the blanket.

ÉVI. What a prosaic soul!

VÉNA. Must be age.

ÉVI (*crossing to shed*). Notice any such signs in me?

VÉNA (*laughs*). Well, who keeps talking marriage? (ÉVI *stops to read a poster stuck on the wall of the shed.*) That's age.

ÉVI (*stubbornly*). That's love.

VÉNA. Oh, come off it.

ÉVI. That is precisely what your prosaic soul will never comprehend. (*Reading from the poster.*) 'Dance music by comrade Posch and his Brass Band.' How posh can you get?

VÉNA. Why is it, the moment you hit thirty, all of you, you get all hot about the family hearth?

ÉVI (*continues reading*). 'In the Grand Hall of the Union Lodge.' Must have been lovely.

A silence. ÉVI *studies* VÉNA.

Such a body, and it won't dance.

VÉNA. Maybe it don't dig rhythm.

ÉVI. Did I tell you? No, I didn't. Listen, the manager came to me yesterday – seems they'll be turning that old gate house into a little wine bar, a kind of bistro – and would I run it for them.

VÉNA. Do! Take it.

ÉVI. They need an attractive female who knows how to smile at the tourists and throw in a bit of French or German here and there.

VÉNA. What's in it for you?

ÉVI *gives him a look.*

The manager, eh?

ÉVI. Aren't you silly. People *like* me – He was happy to make me the offer.

VÉNA. Take it, take it.

ÉVI. There are others who'd take it. Plenty of others. There's this Prokoš, comes on inspection. One day he opened a matchbox full of gold . . . that's to make rings, he said –

VÉNA. Must have picked his late grandmother's teeth.

ÉVI. Oh – honestly!

VÉNA. Not only are you growing old, cat. You're growing stupid, too.

ÉVI. Could be.

VÉNA. You talk considerable nonsense lately.

ÉVI. I don't mean to.

VÉNA. Well, don't – or you'll get used to it.

ÉVI (*sits on the bench, dejectedly*). It's not enough for me.

VÉNA. Now, cat . . .

ÉVI. Not enough, not enough. (*Looking at the back of her hand.*) I'm all blue.

VÉNA. It's your blood, it goes off.

ÉVI. Didn't it ever occur to you? Don't say it didn't.

VÉNA. I am not saying anything.

ÉVI. See! – Wouldn't you want a child?

VÉNA (*in surprise*). What?

ÉVI. A tiny bit of a boy. You'd always be tripping over him. And he would be the spit of you.

VÉNA. Wouldn't he just!

ÉVI. It wouldn't be so bad.

VÉNA. The family hearth.

ÉVI. You'd have to rustle up the firewood.

VÉNA (*sits beside her on the bench*). I would get crates from the greengrocer and I'd bring home piano legs and desk legs that I broke off moving widows and school teachers –

ÉVI. Would you really?

VÉNA. Speaking of the hearth . . .

ÉVI (*props her back against him and cuddles up*). Tell me something nice.

VÉNA. We moved an old lady to Kampa once. She was assigned a room and in the room there was a hearth, a huge fireplace. It reached half across the place – an historically valuable, State-protected landmark. The trouble was the old baba couldn't get her cupboard in. She kept imagining the cupboard where the fireplace stood – over and over, until she was stultified. Just kept seeing that stupid cupboard where the fireplace stood. So, finally she went and tore that splendid fireplace down. That thing of beauty.

ÉVI. What did they do to her?

VÉNA. Nothing. Who's going to sue for a pile of bricks? So, the cupboard was installed in all its glory, and there was still room for a small runner so that baba had somewhere to pace up and down in triumph over them all.

ÉVI. That wasn't a nice story.

VÉNA. From that time on, 'hearth' is a hollow term – like a great many heartwarming words. In due time, they will be joined by 'love' when love will have been totally wiped out.

ÉVI. Uh –

VÉNA. Only in ancient rocks will they discover fossilised kisses. Commissions of experts will hold conferences over a few traces of a caress . . .

ÉVI (*throws herself around his neck*). Darling – (*Stops him with a kiss.*)

VÉNA. Kitten –

ÉVI. You're making a pile of bricks out of me, too.

VÉNA. You're no housewife. (*He lies down on the bench, his head in her lap.*)

ÉVI. But I will take the bistro.

VÉNA. Changing trades like that! My grandfather was a metal worker. That's what he was born and that's what he died.

ÉVI. I don't want to die.

VÉNA (*closes his eyes*). Who's talking of dying?

ÉVI (*gazes at him*). You are my burden, my yoke. You're like a lamb when you sleep.

VÉNA. Suppose I married you. What would I do with you?

ÉVI. You would find something to do.

VÉNA. We don't need to marry for that.

ÉVI. Why don't you go to sleep?

VÉNA. How can I?

ÉVI. How can't you when you have such a nice pillow.

VÉNA *turns his face into her lap and stops his ears.*

Did I tell you my little turtle died? I kept her in my closet in a box. I thought she was hibernating, so I waited until Easter . . .

then I found out it was all up with her.

VÉNA. How, pray, did you find out?

ÉVI. Lovely little turtle. I was looking forward to her growing up. All that time I believed I had something alive to keep me company – and it was not the least bit alive.

VÉNA. It was dead.

ÉVI. It was not alive – You've got a pointy nose. (*She lifts his head by the hair.*) It's a barbarian I'd have but I would *have* him. In time, he might listen to reason. He could be tamed.

VÉNA. Me?

ÉVI. You would have to be virtuous.

VÉNA. 'Virtuous!' Never.

ÉVI. What do you want to be all your life?

VÉNA (*lies back again and thinks for a moment*). What's a not too dirty a word, meaning the opposite of virtuous?

ÉVI. Shameless.

VÉNA. Shameless – that's what I want to be. Véna Shameless.

  Silence. ÉVI *leans over him.*

ÉVI (*plays with his hand*). Still, you could have cleaned your nails.

VÉNA. Sometimes I get the feeling that if I really concentrated, I mean really, I could *be* what I want to be.

ÉVI. A demon?

VÉNA. Maybe a demon. (*He rises.*) I'll go and concentrate, all right?

ÉVI (*with a sigh*). Go ahead.

VÉNA. I'm serious.

ÉVI. Hurry up. The train may be here any minute. (*She glances at him.* VÉNA *stands a few steps away covering his eyes.*) What do I do?

VÉNA. You must keep quiet.

ÉVI. Is that the only way?

VÉNA. That's why there are no demons nowadays. That's why they walk only nights and in desert places. (*Uncovers his eyes but keeps them shut.*) I'm ready.

ÉVI (*softly*). What's it going to be?

VÉNA (*in fuller voice than before*). I have negated myself – I am nothing – I am blotted out.

ÉVI (*a whisper*). Blotto –

VÉNA. Shush! – I am yet to be created. – You may address me now, and the way you address me, that's what I'll be, that's what you'll make me. It'll all depend on what you use to call me out of the dark. Remember, it is just like when the first man saw a lump of matter in front of him and called it 'tree'

ÉVI (*frivolously*). Or 'cloud' –

VÉNA. – or 'rock'. So you'd better bloody watch out how you evoke me.

> ÉVI *looks at him intently.* VÉNA*'s eyes are closed.*

Well?

ÉVI (*after a beat*). My angel.

VÉNA (*opens his eyes in disgust*). Oh, get lost. Is that all you could think of?

ÉVI. You shouldn't have made that face.

VÉNA. I didn't make an angel face, did I?

ÉVI. A little Véna face. I had to say something sweet to you.

VÉNA. What do I do now? – Float? – 'Something sweet!' Women are crazy for puddings.

ÉVI. Try again.

VÉNA. I can't concentrate now. You were supposed to create the world!

ÉVI. I can see the mess *you* would make of the world! You could never think up anything as tender as a finch. And all your trees would look alike, I know you!

VÉNA. Powerful and gnarled.

ÉVI. No snowball bushes, no meadowsweet –

VÉNA. Platypuses and otters, sewer rats and lizards, orangutans and mastodons, rhinos and ant-eaters. And instead of rosebushes – one great thorn piercing the heavens.

ÉVI. And gliding over the desolation there'd be my angel. He'd make it that way on purpose, to be sure he would stand out.

VÉNA. That's always been my ambition!

> *A silence.* ÉVI *shakes a pill out of a tube.*

What have you got there? Give me one. (*Grabs tube.*)

ÉVI. Aspirin.

VÉNA (*ironically*). Aspirin.

ÉVI. Have one. I will, too.

VÉNA. Why should I?

ÉVI. Puts you in a good mood.

VÉNA. All the better to spin a yarn. (*Looks at* ÉVI *and swallows pill.*)

ÉVI. You'll feel better. That's all.

VÉNA. What if it knocks me out? You may have to carry me onto the train. – Well, I swallowed it – so what?

ÉVI. It doesn't work right away.

VÉNA. Don't expect me to make a declaration of love. – Or ask for your hand.

ÉVI. That'll be the day.

VÉNA. My mother used to take this stuff when she worked at the café. Made her talk all right.

ÉVI. Helped her to 'realise herself.'

VÉNA. When business was slow, she would lean against the cash register and grind out poems.

ÉVI. Did she compose them herself?

VÉNA. How can I tell a composed poem from a written one?

ÉVI. We'll see when you start your poem.

VÉNA. There'll be no poems. And if there were – it doesn't count, with dope. – Where'd you get it? On prescription?

ÉVI. The girls gave it to me for my birthday. My thirtieth.

VÉNA. Big deal –

ÉVI. They gave what they could.

VÉNA. I took you to see Harold Lloyd.

ÉVI. You said – it would be fun!

VÉNA. Well, wasn't it?

ÉVI. The way he kept hanging on those ledges . . . Gave me goosepimples –

She sighs.

A something roasted would hit the spot.

Glancing at her watch.

If the train gets here at midnight we could be at home by two. (*Sits on the bench.*) Will you stop by?

VÉNA. If I were in your shoes I'd have had enough of me for a week.

ÉVI. I am the one in my shoes. And I never have enough.

VÉNA (*sitting next to her*). Well, that's nice of you. (*He kisses her.*) Hey, it's beginning to work.

ÉVI. Sure, sure – we know what works with you.

VÉNA (*embracing her*). That was great when he chased after the wedding.

ÉVI. What?

VÉNA. Lloyd, the way he chased the wedding.

ÉVI. Had he missed it, she would have married the wrong guy.

VÉNA. It wasn't about getting married.

ÉVI. Then what was it about?

VÉNA.The acrobatics! Not the wanting to marry her or any such nonsense.

ÉVI. That's not nonsense.

VÉNA. Even old Lloyd was clear about that. That's what he was making fun of. It is nonsense.

ÉVI. It's not nonsense.

VÉNA. It is.

ÉVI. It's not.

VÉNA. It's not.

ÉVI. It is!

VÉNA (*in triumph*). There you are! All I have to do is mix you up and you don't know what you're saying.

ÉVI. What did I say?

VÉNA.That it was nonsense.

ÉVI. I didn't say that.

VÉNA. All you want is to say the opposite of what I say. Automatically, you contradict me. Woman's logic!

ÉVI. I don't give a damn about logic.

VÉNA. Of course not, you with your lyrical soul!

ÉVI. You would love to knock it out of me, wouldn't you?

VÉNA. Absolutely. (*Puts his hands round her throat, ironically.*) I could put the wind up you!

ÉVI. Go ahead. Just go ahead.

VÉNA. Enough. Futility's coming over me.

ÉVI. Oh, stop blabbering.

VÉNA. Where does it say two people who are together must blabber all the time? Who says so? (*He stretches out on the bench.*)

ÉVI. We don't have to talk.

VÉNA turns on his side.

We can be quiet.

VÉNA. Gape at the stars.

ÉVI. What?

VÉNA. The stars. Gape.

ÉVI. 'Gape, gape' – Don't talk like that.

VÉNA. One should be alone.

ÉVI. One is alone, anyway.

Silence.

VÉNA. The thing is, one won't admit it. You keep on forcing yourself to do things, and forcing everyone else. When the day's over, you slam the door, you lean on it – and 'to hell with everybody' and 'Good god, who needs it?' –

ÉVI. So, be alone and stick to it.

VÉNA. Serves me right. I can't stand being without a woman. But you find yourself a woman, and what have you got? A whole bunch of girl friends, childhood sweethearts, lovers . . .

ÉVI listens to him for a while, then wanders off, behind the shed.

Know what I'd like to do? Lock myself in, stare at the ceiling, and cure it deep brown with cigarette smoke. There were times I used to mix things up like crazy – like the time in the park. I said you had a head like a Botticelli angel and other stupidities. I've a hunch though it wasn't what I *said* . . . For remember, you told me what a wonderful hold I have – the way I take things in my hands, you said – that stuck in my mind – I even thought: the Grip Royal beats 'em all! I never went for the 'soul' stuff anyway – First thing I noticed about you was that time at the movies – the way you bit into that ice-cream – the greedy way you nibbled at it – I've always been sweet on girls with a sweet tooth.

ÉVI *appears on the roof of the shed. She peers out into the darkness.' Once in a while, she glances down at* VÉNA *who is now lying on the bench.*

For all I know, I may be pretty good at taking things in my hands. The only damn talent I've got. Well, a removal man . . . Fact is, whatever I can't get my hands on gives me trouble. A lot of trouble. You too – why, when I don't actually see you I . . . all of a sudden I get awful suspicious. Those are the times when out of the blue I dial your number – those are times I could go off my rocker – I could, you know – sometimes I keep ringing you for an hour! You're not in, and where the hell can you be, or you're in the tub and can't hear the phone for the water running, then at long last you answer and I hear you whining at the other end, and right away it gets on my nerves because all I wanted was proof I hadn't made you up! I didn't want no *conversation* with you! There are times I hang up the moment you pick up the phone, at two in the morning, that's no wrong number, baby, that's me.

Silence.

What're you thinking?

Silence. VÉNA *lifts his head, looks for* ÉVI *rises, walks to the track, then to the shed. He stops at the door.*

Cat? . . . Cat, you in there? You're cold, eh? – Why don't you say so? (*Goes into the shed.*) What's the idea? Where are you? (*Comes out.*)

ÉVI. You're getting warm.

VÉNA. Hey, stop it. I don't like it.

ÉVI, *who was lying flat on the roof, looks up.*

ÉVI. You're hot!

VÉNA. What're you doing up there – want to fall down?

ÉVI. Having a think.

VÉNA. That roof may be rotten.

ÉVI. I love heights. I love heights.

VÉNA. The whole thing'll collapse. Stop it!

ÉVI. Do I still have a sweet tooth? I wonder.

VÉNA. All you remember about books is the titles.

ÉVI. That's how I know what books are about.

VÉNA. Sometimes that's not what they're about.

ÉVI. Sometimes it is. (*She kneels on the roof and looks up at the sky.*) It's lifted up a bit. Not so close any more.

VÉNA *spits on the track.*

Situation Two

ÉVI *motionless, is kneeling on the roof.* VÉNA *stands by the track.* TWO YOUNG MEN *from Situation One enter from the back.*

FIRST YOUNG MAN (*to* SECOND). What did you have to get me in deep water for? (*Wringing the wet legs of his trousers.*) Get lost.

SECOND YOUNG MAN (*holding his eye, to* VÉNA). Hey, you, has the kid been around?

FIRST YOUNG MAN. He had a woman with him before.

VÉNA. Well, what's new, mugger boys?

FIRST YOUNG MAN (*to* SECOND). Say something.

VÉNA. How'd you make out?

FIRST YOUNG MAN. It might just stop me clobbering him.

SECOND YOUNG MAN (*to* VÉNA). It's a wonder I didn't put an eye out. A wonder I didn't leave it on a twig somewhere.

VÉNA. He gave you the slip.

FIRST YOUNG MAN. He's an expert at that.

VÉNA (*chuckling*). He figured what was in store for him.

FIRST YOUNG MAN (*examining his trousers*). New trousers. Wringing wet. Brand new.

SECOND YOUNG MAN (*to* VÉNA). He took a plunge in the brook.

FIRST YOUNG MAN. Just look at'em!

VÉNA. Outlaws of this land! There are two of you. Why didn't you ambush him?

SECOND YOUNG MAN. I could've buggered off to bed by now.

FIRST YOUNG MAN. I'll tear him in two like a snake.

SECOND YOUNG MAN. He makes me tramp through the rye, drags me through the brush, wade the brook . . .

FIRST YOUNG MAN. When I look at you I wonder what the kid ran so hard for.

SECOND YOUNG MAN (*to* VÉNA). And the young lady, how's she? (*To* FIRST YOUNG MAN.) Maybe you didn't notice, but he's got a pretty good-looking granny. I had hold of her for a moment –

FIRST YOUNG MAN. I'm an idiot. We're off.

ÉVI (*up on the roof*). At last, a bit of intelligence.

SECOND YOUNG MAN (*stops*).What did I tell you. She's in there.

FIRST YOUNG MAN (*stops*). Up there, look.

SECOND YOUNG MAN. Some silhouette!

VÉNA. So long, so long.

SECOND YOUNG MAN. And what might your business be up there?

VÉNA. Go hit the sack. Go.

SECOND YOUNG MAN. Pity there's no rosy dawn behind you. You'd have a sharper outline.

ÉVI. I like myself better in soft focus.

SECOND YOUNG MAN. Give us the profile.

VÉNA (*kicks him in the rear*). How's that for profile?

SECOND YOUNG MAN (*turns around, to* FIRST). You stand for that? Call yourself a friend!

> FIRST YOUNG MAN *hesitates, then steps toward* VÉNA *who takes one step back and watches both men.*

FIRST YOUNG MAN. You asked for it –

> *Lunges at* VÉNA.

> ÉVI *lets herself down from the roof. She is hanging by the hands.*

ÉVI. Help! – somebody help me!

SECOND YOUNG MAN (*loses interest in* VÉNA). Say the word – (*Starts towards* ÉVI *but* FIRST *pushes him aside.*)

FIRST YOUNG MAN. Wanna drop her?

SECOND YOUNG MAN (*flares up*). Quit bragging. Fancy yourself, do you?

FIRST YOUNG MAN. Shithead you!

> FIRST YOUNG MAN *pushes* SECOND *who falls but drags down* FIRST *with him.*

VÉNA (*helps* ÉVI *down, and takes her in his arms*). Kitten –

FIRST YOUNG MAN *and* SECOND *get up.*

FIRST YOUNG MAN (*to* SECOND). I'll fix you later.

SECOND YOUNG MAN. To think I've invested two fivers in him.

FIRST YOUNG MAN. Get movin'. Take off.

SECOND YOUNG MAN (*retreating*). T'morrow they'll all know how you fell in the brook – I'll see to that – (*He runs off.*)

FIRST YOUNG MAN. I'll break your head first, you bastard . . . (*He goes, running after* SECOND. *They are gone.*)

VÉNA (*still holding* ÉVI). Why did you do that?

ÉVI. I wanted you to take me down.

VÉNA. You sure?

ÉVI. Didn't dream it would last that long. (*She puts her arms round his neck.*)

VÉNA (*carrying her to the bench*). You're not the least bit heavy.

ÉVI. That roof is rotten all right.

VÉNA. What did I tell you. (*He puts her down on the bench.*) You've no sense.

ÉVI. I know. (*She hides her face in her hands.*) I know. It scares me. Sometimes, I wonder what might . . .

VÉNA (*He sits beside her*). Well – what might what?

ÉVI. (*pressing her hands over her face*). Do like this.

VÉNA. What for?

ÉVI. Do it.

> VÉNA *covers his face with his hands.*

> What do you see?

VÉNA. Nothing.

ÉVI. Close your eyes tight.

VÉNA. Kind of a pinky darkness.

ÉVI. Wait, you'll start getting pictures.

VÉNA. I'm getting shimmers now.

ÉVI. See?

VÉNA. Minnows and tiddlers.

ÉVI. I get little flowers.

VÉNA. I'm going to smell fishy.

ÉVI. Oh, it's lovely. How do we see? Our eyes are shut. With the soul, I guess.

VÉNA (*resting his head in her lap*). I rule this territory. Here is where I shall settle.

ÉVI (*with eyes still shut, she runs her fingers through his hair*). When you were born – did you have all that hair?

VÉNA. I had a bare skull and jaundice.

ÉVI. Ugh.

VÉNA. This is the way I looked. (*Makes a face.*)

ÉVI (*eyes still shut*). There's something for my fingers. All that hair. I could bury my fingers in it forever. Keeps them warm, too.

VÉNA. Tell me about me.

ÉVI. I can't see you.

VÉNA. With your fingers. Tell me with your fingers . . . as if I was written in Braille.

ÉVI. All right. – Your forehead's all knitted up.

VÉNA. Kitted up?

ÉVI. Knitted up. Some people's foreheads are so transparent, it's a wonder the thoughts don't jump out. Others are thick with meat – lumpy – the skin like shoe leather. You're neither fish nor fowl.

VÉNA. So I am cheese. Go on.

ÉVI. Your eyes are spotted like a tiger. In each eye you've got a few extra little eyes. The big one is for me, the little ones for the other girls.

VÉNA. Go on. Go on.

ÉVI. A scar on the nose. Who scratched you?

VÉNA. You. In self-defence.

ÉVI (*kisses him*). For the first and last time. May I skip?

VÉNA. What are you going to skip?

ÉVI. The mouth. It's indescribable.

VÉNA. Fine.

ÉVI. Now I'll skip to the collar bones. That's my weakness.

VÉNA. Oh? What do you see in them?

ÉVI. Strong like two hasps. So they make deep pits above. Come rain – two little ponds. For birds to drink out of.

VÉNA. They'd splash all over me.

ÉVI. Beautiful ribs, and likewise, the spine.

VÉNA. When I stretch, a skeleton tries to get out.

ÉVI. You've got him caged in. He can't get out. If you didn't have these bones, you wouldn't be so fragile. If you were to be run over, you wouldn't even crack, you would just pop like a bladder.

VÉNA. Next.

ÉVI. Shoulder blades. When you walk, they're like fledgling wings.

VÉNA. Wings. Ha!

ÉVI. You can't see them. You crane your neck – they fly away.

VÉNA. That's how I can handle all those pianos. I fly them upstairs.

ÉVI. Now, I want to take it all in one fell swoop.

VÉNA (*shakes his head*). Item by item, nice and orderly.

ÉVI. Belly. You haven't got one. Just a dimple in the middle.

VÉNA. Belly-button.

ÉVI. I didn't feel like calling it that.

VÉNA. What's wrong with belly-button? That's where they tied us up. Like they knitted us out of some yarn . . . and then they had to make a knot so we wouldn't unravel when we started to walk.

ÉVI. Next the legs.

VÉNA. You're skipping.

ÉVI. I can skip.

VÉNA. I'll skip yours, too, then.

ÉVI. Why waste words? – The legs. You could sky-walk if it weren't for gravity.

VÉNA (*sits up next to her, his chin on his knees*). Closed for inventory. Some other time.

A silence.

Let's pretend we're hiding in the woods.

ÉVI. It's fun the way we make things up like this . . .

VÉNA. Is it?

ÉVI. Yes. A lot of fun.

VÉNA. When nothing else works any more.

ÉVI. That head of yours. There's always something there that's not in mine.

VÉNA. The heads are the same but the ways are different. With you, it's thoughts.

ÉVI. That's what I mean. With you it's always different.

VÉNA. It comes to the same in the end, believe me.

ÉVI. I'm scared. (*Rises and walks a bit along the path.*) What will become of us?

VÉNA. What will become of us we already are. – We've been that for ages, kitten . . . We were ahead of ourselves, and now, things are catching up with us.

ÉVI (*stops*). What do you mean?

VÉNA. Everything's going to be the way it already is.

ÉVI. The whole world?

VÉNA. The whole world.

ÉVI. Us too?

VÉNA. Us too. Only in your grave will you see how dead you were at twenty.

ÉVI. Where did you get that idea? – Come closer, won't you?

VÉNA. It's the same distance for you.

ÉVI. But if *you* do it . . .

VÉNA (*doesn't move*). It would be my move –

ÉVI. The other day, I poked around in my brother's briefcase. Leafed through his anatomy book. Have you ever seen the way we look inside?

VÉNA. Sure.

ÉVI. Harakiri must be horrible.

VÉNA. Hara – what?

ÉVI. Madam Butterfly. She slit her belly.

VÉNA *gives her a shocked look.*

They don't show it on stage.

VÉNA. Oh. They just sing about it, is that it?

ÉVI. She did it out of unrequited love.

VÉNA. I'd be surprised if she'd done it out of anything else. (*He is standing behind her.*)

ÉVI (*feeling his closeness*). Breathe on me.

VÉNA. Three beers, and stale.

ÉVI. Please, let me feel your breath.

VÉNA *breathes on her neck.*

It's crazy. (*She presses her hand on the place.*)

VÉNA. Sure is.

ÉVI. I must have radar inside me or something.

VÉNA. You don't say.

ÉVI. Is there anything more material than breath?

VÉNA. A nightmare is. Chokes you.

ÉVI. Remember seven years ago when you sat next to me at the movies? Whenever you turned towards me I felt you on my neck.

VÉNA. Did I huff and puff?

ÉVI (*slaps him lightly across the mouth*). You breathed on me. It was beautiful. Had I been a window I'd have been all misted up. Honest.

VÉNA *laughs.*

When you laugh you cry! – What do you do when you cry?

VÉNA. I don't cry then.

A silence.

ÉVI. I could have written it in music, the way you breathed . . . in eighth and halves – the pauses . . . I sure knew the score.

VÉNA. A man breathes one way when he lugs a sofa to the fourth floor, and another when he breathes in the neck of some desirable girl.

ÉVI. Some desirable girl – Are you saying something rude again?

VÉNA. No, no.

ÉVI. I can't tell any more what's rude and what isn't.

VÉNA. You're just corrupt. You can't tell the difference any more.

ÉVI. Well, you can take the credit. I was different when you first knew me, wasn't I?

VÉNA. Sure. You had distinguished manners. You smoked Turkish cigarettes in an ivory holder and dragged an impossible handbag over your shoulder.

ÉVI. I was stupid.

VÉNA. The only thing that's not changed.

ÉVI. You've become such a bastard. I'm amazed. You still don't want to walk?

VÉNA. I don't. I don't.

ÉVI (*with a sigh*). If only something would happen. Even the moon is gone.

VÉNA. Behind the pine tree.

ÉVI. Behind a cloud.

VÉNA (*takes a look*). A pine tree, you cuckoo.

ÉVI. Suppose it's a cloud. Couldn't it be a cloud?

VÉNA. Cuck, cuck – it couldn't.

ÉVI. I see a cloud.

VÉNA. Say it again.

ÉVI (*turning her back on the tree*). Cloud! Cloud! Cloud!

VÉNA (*steps towards her and forcibly turns her head around*). Now look. Does this look like a tree or doesn't it? – Come, take a good look.

ÉVI. You'll strangle me! – Help! Let go of me. Brute! (*She struggles, kicking* VÉNA, *hitting him with her fists; suddenly she goes limp.* VÉNA *lets go. She stands, feeling her neck.*) I'm hanged.

VÉNA. In your own collar.

ÉVI. You strangled me.

VÉNA. That's what you deserve.

ÉVI. My head is two yards above the rest of me.

VÉNA. Oh, I didn't squeeze that hard.

ÉVI. All because of a stupid tree! Why is it there? I don't get it, and I don't care. I'm not the least bit interested. Not the least bit! It's stupid of it to grow, anyway.

VÉNA. You may be glad to get under it.

ÉVI. I'd rather get soaked.

VÉNA. Ho-ho, you of all people! You even use *me* for a shelter.

ÉVI. Yes! I do. When the storm howls through my life, I do!

VÉNA. Blah. Blah-blah-blah.

ÉVI (*holding her head*). You're driving me crazy.

VÉNA. If that's what you want.

ÉVI. Well, you sure don't turn me on.

VÉNA. Don't be such a cow.

ÉVI. My God. Is he rude!

VÉNA. Even my mother, when she first saw you – and she knows
about people . . .

ÉVI. Does she! Sure sees through you!

VÉNA. Blah-blah-blah.

ÉVI. Now and again, she drops in for a vermouth. 'Honey,' she
says, 'a double of the usual. When are you going to carry off my
baby? What do you expect me to do – die washing and ironing
for him?'

VÉNA. Oh shut up.

ÉVI. And after the second double it's, 'Sweetheart, for you he's all
candy floss – but for me rudeness and dirt. You can have him –
a bargain!' – How do you like that?

VÉNA. Where are you heading?

ÉVI (*steps close to him*). Behind the pine tree. You're right, as always.
I won't say another word. (*She stands close behind him, slips her
hands into his trouser pockets.*)

VÉNA. You're a tramp all the same.

ÉVI. Come on –

VÉNA (*chanting*).Tramp – tramp – tramp –

ÉVI. Come on, now!

VÉNA. My sweet honey blossom.

ÉVI. Whaat?

VÉNA (*covering up*). What a switch, eh? Some cut, wasn't it! All I do
is roll over, and the wolf turns into a lamb.

ÉVI. What're you trying to do to me?

VÉNA (*trying a joke*). The train isn't coming – I've got to do
something.

ÉVI. Does something have to happen all the time? Can't we just
be . . . as is?

VÉNA. You can't even wait 'as is' . . . Mouth keeps going.

ÉVI. The way we used to just take off for the country . . . just take
off – It was marvellous. Satisfactory. Beautiful.

VÉNA. You know, you can lead a horse to water but one day the
river's dry.

ÉVI. Oh, forget it.

VÉNA. Well, stop needling me.

ÉVI. As if *I* could needle you. Me! I know, time seems too long
when you're with me now.

VÉNA. God, how I love it – that long time growing longer . . .

ÉVI. Don't get carried away.

VÉNA. Long, long – as long as it can grow. Everything long –
Sundays, summers, legs . . .

ÉVI. Women –

VÉNA. Also.

ÉVI. Well, I'll no longer get any longer.

VÉNA. And those fabulous cuts. The way a jazzband gets going real
cool . . . up and up she goes and a bit higher still . . . nobody's
got no head no more, everything's peeled off the ground – and
then a little something dies away in the sax, and it's all over –
The way everybody goes limp – that moment they all turn
stupid, lovely dumb . . . No one knows where they're standing,
what they're standing on, what with . . . Just try and get to a
chair – you won't be able to take two steps. Out of the blue – it's
scary like the earth's gravity – How about that? Aren't they
magnificent cuts, hey?

ÉVI. What's so magnificent about that?

VÉNA. It's a well-known fact that when a landlady shouts at a sleep-
walker out on the window-ledge, the sleep-walker ends up in
the dustbin below.

ÉVI. A sleep-walker shouldn't be shouted at.

VÉNA. But the sleep-walker is a booby and the landlady doesn't
know any better. All she does is snoop around like an old mole
– roots into everything . . .

ÉVI. What's the difference?

VÉNA. Some people carry their own mole around inside them. They do! They strut along, very pleased with themselves . . . and then suddenly the mole pops his head out, 'Look, look, the Emperor's got no clothes!'

ÉVI. You're trying to put one over on me.

VÉNA. Look, my darling, what I mean is –

ÉVI. So that's what it's all about.

VÉNA (*slowly*). Next time you ask me about the family hearth – why it won't work – just take it I've said all I'm going to say. The password is 'mole'.

ÉVI (*a beat*). Aha!

A beat.

You're scared, is that it?

VÉNA. (*casual gesture.*)

ÉVI. Scared of the role, eh? You wouldn't know where to put your hands during the ceremony. What face to fit the occasion.

VÉNA. That's all I meant. Yes.

ÉVI. All right – marry me at midnight with your eyes closed.

VÉNA. It wouldn't be the real thing. (*Irritated.*) You can't do that goddamit! That's what kids do – close their eyes when a car is about to hit them or when they jump out of a window . . .

ÉVI. More of your pearls of wisdom.

VÉNA (*stubbornly*). I want to know what I'm doing.

ÉVI. Fanatic.

VÉNA. Why not?

ÉVI. But that's how things are. Some things you do for yourself. Others are – well – written out for you.

VÉNA. Who wrote this out then?

ÉVI. God. City Hall. How do I know?

VÉNA. Nobody knows. They all just pretend to know. Everybody pretends to everybody else. Take them together and they still know nothing! That's what eats me up. The know-alls.

ÉVI. You're not a know-all?

VÉNA. Me? Ha!

ÉVI. But you are. With me you are.

VÉNA. I'd have to be damn sure of you.

ÉVI. These seven years – and you're not?

VÉNA. Not even in a hundred.

ÉVI. Then there are people who are afraid that any moment, someone might shout at them: 'Hey there, wait a minute, it *is* you, isn't it? Yes – you out there!'

VÉNA. That's not nice.

ÉVI. You want to be anonymous all your life?

VÉNA. A while ago, you described me. From head to toe.

ÉVI. Everything has its own name.

VÉNA (*sighs*). Évi –

ÉVI. My name is Eve.

VÉNA (*laughing*). You have a cunning name, cat.

ÉVI. Think of the Bible and shut up.

VÉNA. That's just it. It's because of you I was chased out of Paradise.

ÉVI (*wih a sigh*). That's why you can't be alone. You'd have no one to blame.

VÉNA. Darling Évi, you're not in a shooting gallery. You can shoot here, too, but you don't win. Even if you hit the bull's eye you don't win.

ÉVI. That's why I don't bother shooting, sweetheart. I know there's nothing to win any more. Nothing to lose, either. That's the one thing that gives me courage. –

VÉNA. What is it we want? (*He kneels by the bench and rests his head on it.*) As if we didn't know.

ÉVI (*after a beat, a little anxious*). Let's stop torturing each other, shall we?

VÉNA (*holds her tight*). Cat, I cannot be without you. That's what it always comes to.

ÉVI (*holds him*). But I can't see what's ahead. We knock around together the whole wide world . . .

VÉNA. But I never take you up the tower, huh?

ÉVI. You're scared you might push me off, I guess.

VÉNA. Is there no other solution?

ÉVI. You'd rather knock around down here. No danger, no vertigo, no place to fall off of.

VÉNA (*embracing her knees as she stands close to him*). How does one get up there?

ÉVI. You'd have to be way above everything for all people to see us. – Let them! *I* wouldn't mind.

VÉNA. You wouldn't?

ÉVI (*resolutely*). No.

VÉNA (*a quiet chuckle*). Now I don't mind either.

ÉVI (*with conviction*). It's not all that difficult. You know why?

VÉNA. Maybe I do.

ÉVI (*stroking his head*). Well, tell me if it's the same way with you as it is with me. Come on, tell me.

VÉNA. You want to hear it?

ÉVI (*passionately*). Yes! At least once. I have a right.

VÉNA. But I'm afraid –

ÉVI. Don't be.

VÉNA. – that I might say something rude again.

ÉVI (*stops*). Better not tell me then. (*A beat.*) Or do, do tell me.

VÉNA. Well, the fact is – we've taken those pills.

ÉVI. So?

VÉNA. That's it. We're going up – we're high – and that's all there's to it. It's the dope, that's all.

ÉVI (*breaks away*). You mean you don't believe it just happened by itself? (*She kneels beside him.*) You think I don't know what I'm saying?

VÉNA (*shakes his head*). It was midnight with our eyes closed. – See him? The mole?

ÉVI. You filth! (*Pushing him away.*) How can you believe it was only that? My God! (*She rests her head on the bench.*)

VÉNA (*stands mournfully*). Maybe I don't really believe it.

ÉVI. He really does!

VÉNA *puts his hands in his pockets*, ÉVI *starts crying.*

VÉNA. Don't cry, cat. To hell with it all.

ÉVI. You dirty mole. You filth.

VÉNA (*shrinks even more*). I'm never sure which of the two is me, the one who enjoys or the one who destroys. (*A beat.*) Say something. Tell me.

ÉVI *rises.* VÉNA *reaches for her. She pulls away and crosses to the track.* VÉNA *remains where he is, watching her.*

Situation Three

BOY *enters from darkness upstage, his head down, staring at the ground. He does not notice* ÉVI *until he is quite close to her.*

BOY (*softly, very low*). It's me.

ÉVI (*as though she is speaking to* VÉNA). What's there to say?

BOY. It's awful important to me. Please . . .

ÉVI. (*only now noticing the* BOY, *annoyed*). Oh, why do you bother? Why don't you quit?

BOY. I can't help it. Can I help it?

ÉVI. Look, be sensible. Go home.

BOY. Gotta find it first.

    ÉVI *lets out an exasperated sigh.*

    BOY *turns to* VÉNA.

    You haven't found it, by any chance, have you?

VÉNA (*indifferently*). No.

BOY. I thought maybe I dropped it someplace around here.

ÉVI. Dropped what?

BOY. My wallet.

VÉNA (*shaking his head 'no'*). Right, cat?

BOY. God, this is terrible!

VÉNA. Listen, they're after you. Take my advice –

BOY. What if they found it?

VÉNA. Have you been running from them all this time?

BOY. I can't fight her brother, can I? We haven't known each other long enough for that. Only today she gave me her picture. It was in the wallet.

ÉVI. Well, let's look for it, shall we?

    All three look around in the area of the shed.

VÉNA. What's that guy so mad at you for, anyhow? He's just her brother, isn't he?

BOY. He already promised her to that other one . . .

VÉNA (*stops*). He what?

BOY. He could've bust a gut when he saw her dancing with me all night. He took her home, and then came back and started after me – I'll go nuts if I don't find it.

VÉNA. Tough. All your cash –

BOY. Keep the cash!

VÉNA. So, she'll give you another picture.

BOY. I can't tell her I lost it.

VÉNA. Well, fella, I'm sorry for you.

BOY. I'll be back. I'll try get matches somewhere.

VÉNA. Listen, they'll beat the hell out of you.

>BOY *waves his hand and starts off.*

You know – 'it's not just for one flower the sun shines.'

BOY (*turns, looks at them*). Sure. You can talk! (*Goes.*)

VÉNA (*watching him*). Poor old bugger.

ÉVI. I'm not so sure.

VÉNA. He hasn't been around too long.

ÉVI. Aha, age again.

VÉNA. Let's drop it, cat.

ÉVI. Drop what?

>*Silence.*

VÉNA. Some lovers! Washed out. (*Goes into the shed.*)

ÉVI. Pals, that's us. Too much so.

VÉNA (*from the shed*).That's right. Pals. Comfortable. Like a pair of old slippers.

ÉVI. It's grown stale on us.

VÉNA (*comes out of shed tying up his rucksack*). We are each other's past. We remind each other of each other.

ÉVI. And it gets on your nerves.

VÉNA. *You* get on my nerves, not *it*. The 'it' is gone. But you're still around. Can't get rid of you.

ÉVI. If only you could be serious for one minute.

VÉNA. The dope must be wearing off. – I am serious.

ÉVI. You always talk that way.

VÉNA. Maybe at last you'll get the point.

ÉVI. Just one honest word. That's all I want to hear. Don't I rate that?

VÉNA. But you do *not* want to hear it.

ÉVI. You wait! One day I'll fly off the handle and simply say goodbye –

VÉNA. That would be sweet of you, cat, but you won't do it.

ÉVI. I will.

VÉNA. You won't.

ÉVI. (*absentmindedly trying to strike matches*). I will.

VÉNA. No, you won't.

ÉVI. Yes, I will.

VÉNA. All right. Do it then. Now.

ÉVI (*as one match catches*). All right, I will not do it. Just to show you, I won't. (*She is playing with the lit match.*)

VÉNA. You will not do it. That's a fact.

ÉVI. Oh, who would I be looking for anyway? You'll do.

VÉNA (*glancing at her, he notices the lit match*). Whadya doing? It's lit!

ÉVI. It's lit.

VÉNA. The cigarettes! Where'd you put the cigarettes?

ÉVI (*realising*). I've packed them — Hurry! They're right on the top!

VÉNA (*trying to undo the tied sack*). I just tied it up! –

ÉVI. I'm burning my fingers!

VÉNA. Goddammit!

ÉVI. Too late –

VÉNA *gets the cigarettes, rushes to her, but* ÉVI *drops the burnt-out match.*

It's too late.

VÉNA. Try another one. Maybe they're dry now.

ÉVI. Only two left.

VÉNA. Try them. But careful – Let me do it. (*He takes the box, strikes the match, it breaks. He picks it up, tries again, in vain.*) Nothing. They crumble like cheese.

ÉVI. The expert –

VÉNA (*handing her the box*). Here – the last one.

ÉVI (*holding up the match*). It's got no head. (*She throws away match and box.*)

VÉNA. You could have held that match longer.

ÉVI. You could have got the cigarettes faster.

VÉNA. Hell – we'll get a light on the train.

ÉVI. If it ever comes.

VÉNA. I heard a hoot a while ago.

ÉVI. An owl.

VÉNA. A train. (*He kneels, puts an ear to the rail.*)

ÉVI. Well?

VÉNA. I seem to hear a faraway rumble.

ÉVI. You've a hum in your ear.

> VÉNA *bends down and picks up something.*
>
> What've you got there?
>
> VÉNA *hands it to her.*
>
> The kid's wallet!

VÉNA. I can see that.

ÉVI. We must call him back.

VÉNA. And how'll you do that?

ÉVI (*calling out*). Hello! Hey you, there –

VÉNA (*sneers*). 'Hey you there'! His name is Ivan. (*Calling out.*) Hey – Ivaaan!!

ÉVI. Come back!!

> *They listen. Silence.*

VÉNA. He's over the hill.

ÉVI. What can we do . . . The train will be here soon.

VÉNA (*opens the wallet, examines the contents*). Dance ticket, a little money –

ÉVI. How much?

VÉNA (*looks at her*). Interested?

ÉVI. Yes. It interests me to know how much a kid like that has left after a dance.

VÉNA (*counting the money*). A hundred-forty . . . three crowns. Cheapskate. Didn't even buy her a lemonade. Seven crowns admission, that's all he parted with.

ÉVI. How can you be so sure?

VÉNA. He's the type whose mama checks the book-keeping.

ÉVI. You mean *your* type. Must've slipped out of his pocket when you grabbed his jacket.

VÉNA. Might have. Yes.

ÉVI. How are you planning to get it back to him?

VÉNA. Well, I am not going to run after him – Besides, what makes you so sure I'm planning to get it back to him?

ÉVI. Oh – you're going to steal it, is that it?

VÉNA. Why steal it? I can just keep it.

ÉVI. A hundred forty-three crowns?

VÉNA. Never mind! It would come in handy if right now we could buy a bottle. However, I can see that in the middle of a desert, money's for the birds.

ÉVI. You can stop for a drink when we get to Prague.

VÉNA. That's no fun. I want one now.

ÉVI. 'Now' won't work.

VÉNA. That's what's the matter with things. I don't enjoy what I can't have now – (*He throws the bills up in the air.*)

   Worthless –

ÉVI. Bits of paper. They're like me. (*She puts her foot on a bill.*)

VÉNA. Don't step on them.

ÉVI. Why not?

VÉNA. Might come in handy.

ÉVI. But now it's for the birds.

VÉNA *starts picking up the bills.*

ÉVI *picks up a hundred-crown bill, offers it to* VÉNA.

Here, for a kiss.

VÉNA. A hundred? Pretty steep.

ÉVI. I want the best.

VÉNA *kisses her. She pushes him away.*

Go away. You're a liar. Your lips are liars.

VÉNA (*examining the wallet*). He doesn't even have his name in it. (*He takes out a snapshot*). Pretty as a picture.

ÉVI (*glancing at it*). That's all it is. A picture.

VÉNA. That's what's nice about it. (*Sticks snapshot in a corner of a poster on shed wall.*) Just a pin-up.

ÉVI. Suppose he finds it?

VÉNA. He'll be glad. (*He pockets the wallet.*)

ÉVI. A thief, too. A liar and a thief.

VÉNA. If he really is an idealist he'll be glad.

ÉVI. But we'll be in hot water. That's a piece of evidence.

VÉNA (*looking at the snapshot*). Some piece! Now, there's the kind of Suzy things revolve around. Where, oh where will we be when the kid finds it?

ÉVI. Maybe we won't be at all.

VÉNA. Maybe we'll be killed.

ÉVI. Kill each other.

VÉNA. One would be left.

ÉVI. That would be you. You'd kill me like a fly.

VÉNA (*taking a knife from his belt*). With this knife.

ÉVI. Maybe.

VÉNA (*putting the knife to her heart*). Straight to the heart.

ÉVI. If you press –

VÉNA. Like so –

ÉVI (*after a beat*). Ouch –

VÉNA. Hurt?

ÉVI. Pricks.

VÉNA. Still?

ÉVI. It hurts! (*She grabs his hand with both of hers.*)

VÉNA. Hey, stop it! (*He breaks away from her.*) What's got into you?

ÉVI. You would really kill me.

VÉNA (*embarrassed*). So, I'm never serious –

ÉVI. Could you really kill me? Like a fly?

VÉNA. Now, don't start again.

ÉVI. You would actually kill me.

VÉNA. I wouldn't even know it.

ÉVI. Oh yes, you would. I would make sure of that.

VÉNA. All you need is get numb for a moment, stop thinking for a moment – and it's no different than sticking it into a loaf of bread.

ÉVI. You'd know the difference all right.

VÉNA. Afterwards – maybe.

ÉVI. Better put that knife away. (*Takes the knife and puts it back in his belt.*)

VÉNA. Were you really afraid?

ÉVI. You'd get into trouble. Killers do, you know.

VÉNA. If they get caught.

ÉVI. Even if they don't. Conscience.

VÉNA. What if they haven't got any?

ÉVI. They have. Everybody's got one.

VÉNA. If I can kill a person – I can kill a conscience.

ÉVI. It's different with thoughts – you can't just . . .

VÉNA. Who told you that? – All the murdered thoughts I've seen! Whole graveyards of them! (*He takes out the wallet and puts it on the ground underneath the poster.*) There, and may the Lord watch over it. (*Crossing over to* ÉVI.) Neither thief nor murderer.

ÉVI. Look, you actually wounded me. I've got a red dimple here.

VÉNA. Why didn't you scream?

ÉVI. I said ouch.

VÉNA. That's no good. A victim must fight back. Scream, kick, bite –

ÉVI. You'd like that, wouldn't you? Sadist. I would be like a lamb just to show you what it's like to slaughter a lamb.

VÉNA. All right. The killing's off. Wouldn't work with us.

ÉVI. Is there anything that would?

VÉNA. We could sing.

ÉVI. That would be worse. Unendurable. We could get married tomorrow.

VÉNA. Speaking of things that wouldn't work.

ÉVI. It's horrible.

VÉNA. What's horrible? What now?

ÉVI. Two people being honest with each other. A lie doesn't get you far – and honesty gets you nowhere.

VÉNA. We've been lying long enough, cat.

ÉVI (*a sigh*). Pity. One should lie slower so it would last longer.

VÉNA (*he crosses to track and listens for the train*). Oh, I could've been alseep long ago instead of listening to your blah-blah. (*He sits on the rail.*)

ÉVI. It's the last blah-blah – (*She gazes at him.*)

VÉNA. It would have to be the last day. With no tomorrow.

ÉVI. Day after tomorrow we're going to the movies – I've got the tickets.

VÉNA. Day after tomorrow!

ÉVI *sits beside him.*

A silence. ÉVI *puts her head on his shoulder.*

ÉVI. Such a body, and it's afraid of a mole. Such a brow, and it can't outsmart it. Such hands, and they can't wring its neck. Such legs – and they can't run away.

Silence.

VÉNA. I could truly – truly tell you that I love you if I knew I wouldn't live till tomorrow.

ÉVI. Thank you very much. What good would that do me?

VÉNA. It would count forever. I couldn't take it back. You don't die of death. It's death that creates us. Whoever goes as a hero can't spoil it; he's got it tacked on, and that's that. The condition you die in.

ÉVI. Then you'll live a long life.

VÉNA. Me?

ÉVI. So far, you're neither murderer nor hero.

VÉNA. Why can't I go as a zero?

Silence.

ÉVI. I am no longer cold, no longer hungry, no longer thirsty – I don't even want to smoke. –

VÉNA (*his arms round her shoulders*). You're trembling. Put on my coat.

ÉVI. No, my love, your coat won't do it.

VÉNA. Is there anything that will?

ÉVI. No. Or is there? I haven't got it.

VÉNA. Who has? Have I?

ÉVI. If you had it, you would give it to me. You are not stingy. That is one thing you're not. Right?

VÉNA. I am not stingy. That is one thing I'm not.

ÉVI. But you don't have it.

VÉNA. Nobody has it.

ÉVI (*taking his arm*). Love me at least.

VÉNA. Would that help you?

ÉVI. That would help me.

VÉNA. Is that allowed – to help oneself with love? Is there nothing else?

Silence.

ÉVI. Or tell me a story. Something nice or something funny.

VÉNA. I don't know anything, Évi.

ÉVI. Remember something.

VÉNA. I can't remember anything Évi.

ÉVI. If you loved me the least tiny bit you would remember. It would just be there.

A distant train whistle.

VÉNA. (*puts his hand over hers. A beat*). D'you smell those sleepers? Must've been lying here under this rail some ten or fifteen years, and still they smell of trees. Of resin and wood, fresh grass – a whole forest. Must be the way they dry and fry in the sun all day long . . . I do love you in my way, I suppose, but there are things that I know only now – What I mean is, tomorrow they'll be gone. I go to sleep with one thing, wake up with another. It's as though overnight I had been washed away, drenched through, wrung out – If we could stretch this *now* to last for life! – It wouldn't be all that much longer, would it? It's like now I see you, now I don't, one day I look for you, the next I can't – like swinging on a pendulum: when close I start to run away. And when I'm furthest off is when I'm coming close. You ought to stop me, never let me go. I'm close? Then grab. What with I don't know. Not hands, no, you'd break something inside me – whatever spring it is that makes me work –

ÉVI. Now I don't want a thing. I'm not afraid any longer.

VÉNA. But afterwards?

ÉVI. Leave that for afterwards. Just hold me for a while. Don't say a thing.

Train whistle again. The sound quickly approaches, changes into a sharp dissonance, everything goes dark abruptly.

The End.

DOG AND WOLF ■ DANIELA FISCHEROVÁ

Translated by A. G. BRAIN

DANIELA FISCHEROVÁ was born in 1948, the daughter of the composer Jan Fischer. In 1971 she graduated from FAMU – the film section of the Academy for Performing Arts in Prague – and was employed as a scriptwriter for film, television and radio. She also wrote puppet plays and children's books. Fischerová enjoyed a wide acquaintance among Prague writers and theatre people and wrote her first stage play – *Dog and Wolf* (*Hodina mezi psem a vlkem*) – in 1978. It was given four performances in Prague in 1979 before the theatre was ordered to take the play out of the repertoire. Fischerová wrote two more stage plays which were allowed performance before 1989; *Princess T* (1984) and *Legend* (1988). *Dog and Wolf* was revived by the students of the Drama Academy in June 1989. In 1992 two of her plays – as yet unstaged – were highly commended for the Alfréd Radok award (*Phantomime* and *Sudden Misfortune*)). *Dog and Wolf* was the first play by Daniela Fischerová to be staged in Great Britain – in June 1993 by the students of the Rose Bruford School in London, directed by Petr Palouš.

Characters

FRANÇOIS VILLON, accused
BISHOP D'AUSSIGNY
RÉGNIER DE MONTIGNY, alias the Wolf
PHILIPPE SERMOY, priest
FATHER VILLON, the accused's guardian
GUY TABARY, confederate of the accused
MOUSTIER, bailiff
PICHART, bailiff
THE MOTHER of the accused
CATHERINE DE VAUSSELLES
ANGÈLE, harlot
JEANNE, harlot
MARGOT, alias Fat Margot, landlady
CHORUS

Dog and Wolf was first performed in Britain at the Lilian Baylis Theatre, Sadlers Wells, London by the final year students of the Rose Bruford College. The cast was as follows:-

JEANNE/THE MOTHER/ THE DUCHESS	Kate Ashfield
RÉGNIER DE MONTIGNY*	Chris Chamberlaine
ANGÈLE/FAT MARGOT	Saffron Fish
CATHERINE DE VAUSELLES	Pebble Francis
FATHER VILLON/THE DUKE	Paul F. Girbow
FRANÇOIS VILLON	Jason Housecroft
BISHOP D'AUSSIGNY/TABARY	Jeremy Stroughair
PHILIPPE SERMOY	Robert Vernazza
MOUSTIER & PICHART, JOURNALISTS AND ASSESSORS	Played by various members of the Company

Directed by Petr Palouš
Designed by Janey Gardiner
Music by Paul F. Girbow
Choreography by Jason Housecroft
Lighting by Lynne Gardner
Stage management by Jackie Bell, Catherine Gray & Katherine Mahony

*In this production, the part of RÉGNIER DE MONTIGNY was performed by a woman.

FIRST ACT

An empty courtroom, viz. a raised semi-circle of ten seats, with places for prosecutor, judge and defence counsel emphasised. A traverse, and on it the CHORUS. *A witness box. A bench for the accused. A cross.*

The CHORUS *on the traverse starts to improvise: a polyphonic thrumming, initially uncoordinated, becomes louder; someone whistles, someone beats out a rhythm, the melody gradually comes together into a wordless musical number that accompanies the entire entry scene.*

The play's characters reluctantly assemble in the courtroom. They are dressed in historical costume, except for ANGÈLE, *the younger of the harlots, who is dressed as an angel in a long robe, barefoot and with a wreath on her head. She looks at no one, but rehearses dance steps on the apron with the intensity of a diligent schoolgirl, making bows, smiling and tending to give an impression of unreality. The older harlot,* JEANNE, *sits lolling provocatively and in spite of the fifteenth century is constantly pulling a thread of chewing gum out of her mouth and rolling the gum around with her tongue.*

To one side, apart from the rest, stands a tall, stern, elderly man almost motionless: BISHOP D'AUSSIGNY.

CATHERINE DE VAUSSELLES *walks up and down, clenching and unclenching her hands impatiently.*

The individual characters avoid one another – an atmosphere of tension pervades the scene. From the rear of the courtroom THE FATHER *approaches, as the court usher. He is ringing a small bell and carrying a thick register. he gives a small, timid smile, looks around him and says to no one in particular and everyone in general:*

THE FATHER. Yes, yes . . . Everyone here?

No one feels like replying. THE FATHER *opens the register. His manner is always kind and conciliatory, and occasionally there is already something of the bewildered old man about him.*

With your permission . . . Paris, Advent 1462. The Court of Paris versus François Montcorbier, known as Villon. Witnesses –

At this moment a latecomer arrives: GUY TABARY, *an uncouth dandy with a broad smile. He snaps his fingers cheerfully.*

TABARY. Your humble servant! Well, what an assembly! My

compliments to all present! (*To* THE FATHER.) Tabary's the name!

All pretend not to have heard him. THE FATHER *coughs.*

THE FATHER. Oh, I see . . . Madame Montcorbier, mother of the accused . . .

MOTHER (*timidly*). Here.

Another latecomer hurries in: RÉGNIER DE MONTIGNY. *He has the appearance of a modern-day reporter and carries a flash camera and tape-recorder. He ignores everyone else. He looks self-assured and provocative. He sits down louringly on the nearest armchair and spreads out his things. All stare at him.*

THE FATHER (*hesitantly*). Monsieur . . . this is a courtroom –

Without looking up, RÉGNIER *waves a ticket.*

RÉGNIER (*curtly*). Press!

TABARY. But that's . . . No, it can't be! It is! Règne!

TABARY *livens up considerably and tries to attract* RÉGNIER's *attention. He makes a sort of conspiratorial gesture, then he actually yells, but* RÉGNIER *does not react.*

Règne! Règne!

THE FATHER. Ah, yes. Of course . . . Next. Mademoiselle Catherine de Vausselles, fiancée of the accused.

CATHERINE (*emphatically and without hesitation*). No.

THE FATHER. I beg your pardon?

CATHERINE. Mademoiselle de Vausselles, yes. The accused's fiancée, no.

PHILIPPE *stands up.*

PHILIPPE (*pointedly, in rhetorical fashion*). Your register contains not merely a crude error of fact but also a crude insult. And I would make so bold as to assert that I know how it came to be there –

CATHERINE (*cutting him dead*). It doesn't matter.

A song with a modern arrangement, sung in the style of the times suddenly interrupts the action. It starts in mid-verse (like a random track from a cassette) at full volume.

TAPE RECORDER . . . But where are the snows of yesteryear?
    White Queen Blanche, like a queen of lilies
    With a voice like any mermaiden, –
    Bertha Broadfoot, Beatrice, Alice,

And Ermengarde the lady of Maine, –
And that good Joan whom Englishmen
At Rouen doomed and burned her there, –
Mother of God, where are they then? . . .
But where are the snows of yesteryear?
Nay, never ask this week, fair lord,
Where they are gone, nor yet this year,
Except with this for an overword, –
But where are the snows of yesteryear?

All turn round. TABARY *stamps enthusiastically and whistles along.*

THE FATHER. Monsieur, please . . .

RÉGNIER. Okay.

*He turns the sound down and scribbles in his notebook. The song
continues.*

THE FATHER. Father Philippe Sermoy, preacher at the Cathedral
of Notre Dame –

PHILIPPE (*dramatically*). Here.

THE FATHER. Your, er, relationship with the accused?

PHILIPPE. Victim.

THE FATHER. I beg your pardon?

PHILIPPE. His victim. Foully murdered by the accused in May of
fifty-five.

Brief silence. CATHERINE *draws in her breath sharply.* JEANNE
smacks her lips rather vulgarly at PHILIPPE *in amusement.*
RÉGNIER *stops the tape and rewinds it. There is the loud whine of a
rapidly rewinding tape.*

THE FATHER. His Magnificence the Rector of the University of
Paris.

BISHOP. Here.

THE FATHER *abruptly changes role. As he gazes at the* BISHOP, *he
becomes older and more humble and starts to tremble. He lays aside his
register.*

THE FATHER. Your Reverence . . . Forgive an old man . . . just one
question I beg of you . . . the student Montcorbier, Mont-cor-
bier François –

BISHOP. And who are you?

THE FATHER. His guardian, Your Reverence . . . Father Villon,
Canon at St Benedict's, should Your Reverence happen to know
it –

Suddenly an inhuman shriek is heard from the TAPE RECORDER. *All jump up.*

VILLON (*from the tape recorder, screaming*). Aaaaah! No more! Aaaaah!

The MOTHER *gazes at the tape recorder in fascinated horror.* TABARY *starts to fidget nervously.*

TABARY. Why that way . . . ? I mean, after all –

The BISHOP *approaches* RÉGNIER.

BISHOP (*sharply*). That's enough.

RÉGNIER (*sparring with him*). Just one second!

The shriek continues to graduate for a few seconds, before suddenly stopping of its own accord. RÉGNIER *grins insolently.*

Now. Loss of consciousness.

THE FATHER (*clapping his hands in an effort to silence the hubbub*). Ladies and gentlemen!

RÉGNIER (*matter-of-factly, aloud to everyone*). Water torture, Fourteen Sixty.

THE FATHER. Quiet please! Please! Guy Tabary, confederate of the accused –

TABARY (*crestfallen*). Here.

The song 'Where are the snows of yesteryear' is once more heard from the tape recorder and it goes on playing quietly throughout the rest of the scene. RÉGNIER *stands up and walks about with the camera, switching on and off small spotlights, oblivious of everyone else.*

THE FATHER. Margot, known as Fat Margot, landlady –

MARGOT. Yeah.

THE FATHER. Jeanne, a harlot.

Chewing noisily, JEANNE *raises a hand and then spits out the chewing gum in a wide arc.*

Monsieur Régnier de Montigny, subsequently known as The Wolf, leader of the criminal gang to which the accused belonged –

RÉGNIER *switches on a spotlight, shining it straight onto his own face. All turn towards him.* JEANNE *whistles appreciatively.*

(*Sighing*). Yes, yes . . . This way, ladies and gentlemen, please.

All exit backstage except for ANGÈLE *who runs up to* THE FATHER.

ANGÈLE. And what about me, then?

THE FATHER. Excuse me. And you are –

ANGÈLE. I'm Angèle!

THE FATHER. You are a witness?

ANGÈLE (*childishly*). I . . . I'm his bride.

> THE FATHER *mumbles to himself as he searches in his register.*
> RÉGNIER *turns the spotlight on* ANGÈLE. ANGÈLE *covers her eyes.*
> RÉGNIER *chuckles.*

RÉGNIER. She didn't exist. There is no need to look for her.

THE FATHER. I am sorry, mademoiselle.

ANGÈLE (*insistently*). But I must be in there somewhere!

RÉGNIER. Don't bother to look. She is a phantom. A romantic
fiction of Villon's biographers. May I switch off now, old fellow?

ANGÈLE (*in childish triumph*). I'm his guardian angel!

> RÉGNIER *guffaws.* THE FATHER *gives* ANGÈLE *a gentle push
> and both disappear. The song is heard again and* RÉGNIER *whistles to
> himself. He then takes out his flashgun and aims it at the courtroom.
> Blackout. A sharp light suddenly picks out a new character in the
> darkness. A young man with manacles on his wrists is standing on the
> defendant's bench. He stares into the auditorium.* RÉGNIER *gives a
> short yelp.* VILLON *notices him and starts to smile warmly, with joy.*
> RÉGNIER *gives a secret salute.* VILLON *shakes his chains in comic
> helplessness.*

> *Reporter-style,* RÉGNIER *deftly photographs the entire scene using the
> flashgun.* VILLON *is repeatedly plunged into darkness before emerging
> once more in harsh light. The exchanges between himself and*
> RÉGNIER *do not give the impression of continuous conversation but
> of individual shots.*

RÉGNIER. How do you feel?

VILLON. Like the sole of my own shoe!

> *He clownishly freezes into a pose of total abjection. Blackout, flash,
> light.*

RÉGNIER (*furiously*). What are you doing here? Why are you in
Paris?

VILLON. I'm not able to be anywhere else! I had to come to Paris!
Règne!

> *Blackout, flash, light, new pose.*

RÉGNIER (*with sudden, genuine concern*). Will they get you, Villon?

VILLON. No . . . Yes . . . I don't know . . . Is there anything I can do? (*He suddenly leans forward as far as he can go, and whispers in despair.*) Règne! Règne! Did they really hang you?

Blackout. Brief silence. Then bells start to ring, one after another, many of them, until the entire space is filled with their clamour. The lights slowly come up to show the panel of ASSESSORS arriving on stage: Nine persons in black gowns which efface their individuality. Slowly they take their seats. The two bailiffs, MOUSTIER and PICHART come and stand behind VILLON. THE FATHER stands to one side. All stare at VILLON.

BISHOP. In the name of God!

The bells cease ringing. All immediately bow their heads and then sit down.

BISHOP (*businesslike*). I hereby open the trial of François Montcorbier, known as François Villon.

VILLON (*smilingly insolent, exaggerating the nasal consonant at the end of the name Villon*). Maître François Villon.

The BISHOP stares at him without reacting.

Your grace! Although at times my studies truly did resemble a gallop astride a foaming steed, I did, after all, reach the finishing line! With characteristic compassion the glorious University of Paris proclaimed me Master of Arts – and I therefore have the honour to style myself Maître François Villon!

Gazing at him quizzically, the BISHOP raps impatiently on the table. With a smile on his face, VILLON starts to tap out the same rhythm. The BISHOP withdraws his hand and makes an almost imperceptible sign to the bailiffs. One of them tugs the manacles and VILLON collapses under the bench. A fleeting episode. The BISHOP continues speaking unperturbed.

BISHOP. Is the prosecution in court?

PHILIPPE (*rising*). The prosecution is here!

BISHOP. Indeed!

PHILIPPE takes his place. He reads with theatrical restraint, but pointedly. His phrasing is professionally immaculate.

PHILIPPE. The crime took place this year on the Feast of St Boniface at the Petit-Place in Paris. Although it was almost day-break, light still shone in the office windows of the honourable Monsieur Ferrebouc. All of a sudden, the peaceable, God-fearing scriveners labouring there were startled by a suspicious noise. A band of ruffians, led by the accused Villon, did start to hurl stones at the scriveners. The latter, all of male state, did respond with Christian entreaties.

VILLON (*turning to one of the bailiffs*). Hey! Who squealed on his mates in Blois that time?

PICHART. Shut up!

PHILIPPE. Shortly afterwards, the Bishop's notary, the esteemed Monsieur Marcel Ferrebouc did come out also and did approach the ruffians like a peace envoy, yearning only to sue for peace – when the accused did assail him with a dagger and did stab him mercilessly.

VILLON (*instantly, in utter consternation*). What? That's a lie!

PHILIPPE. Nonetheless, however despicable that act was, it was not the first crime of the accused Villon. On the contrary, it was merely the logical consequence of a sorry list of seven major and countless minor misdemeanours.

VILLON (*stamping his feet, whistling and shouting during the speech*). Humbug! Objection! A filthy lie!

PHILIPPE. It is known to the court that the accused, when still a student, did not shrink from plundering the treasury of his own faculty. The court is cognizant of the fact that for many years the accused belonged to the Wolf-Pack, a most evil gang of felons which did lay waste the country with its raids and robberies.

VILLON (*in fury*). What are you cognizant of, corn-crake?

PHILIPPE. The court knows to its horror that the accused did not stop even at sacrilege! Robbing the most holy property, a statue of Jesus Christ our Lord.

VILLON (*turning to the bailiffs, quickly*). Who shopped us?

MOUSTIER. Quiet.

VILLON. Who got the Wolf topped?

PICHART. Shut your gob!

VILLON (*in spite of the manacles he grabs* PICHART *fiercely by the neck of his tunic*). I'll shit on your grave too, honey-bunch!

PICHART *strikes him viciously across the hand with his keys.* VILLON *winces and releases him.* PHILIPPE *lays aside his papers. He stares in front of him. When he next speaks his tone has changed. His restrained professional manner is now gone; he speaks 'on his own account' – more dramatically, more the preacher now.*

PHILIPPE. Let us cast our gaze into the depths of time, and turn our eyes to that steep path of years. There once lived here a scholar, wild as wolf's milk, a divinely gifted poet, the pride and joy of Paris. But he did not nurture his divine gift. The voice of Satan called to him from the sticky darkness of Hell and off he went. He sets off after him. The divine sparks go out one by one and from the depths, dark extravagance rises up in a pall of smoke.

VILLON (*in disgust, aloud*). Yech!

PHILIPPE. What is he coming to? How low does he want to sink? Could it be blood that you long for – Yes. This man, (*indicating* VILLON.) robber, ruffian and thief – is also a murderer!

CATHERINE. Murderer?

Suddenly one of the ASSESSORS *dashes out. As the gown is thrown off* CATHERINE *is revealed in historical costume. She starts to shake* VILLON *resentfully and even a little dementedly.*

CATHERINE. You killed him! He died! Do you hear?

VILLON (*gripping her by the wrist in total dismay*). Catherine!

CATHERINE. You ruined everything! How do you think I could ever live with you?

VILLON (*limply*). Pull yourself together, sweetheart.

CATHERINE. Just look what you're dragging behind you! Havoc. Wolves with blood on their muzzles!

VILLON. Catherine, that's a myth.

CATHERINE (*hysterically*). What myth?

VILLON. A myth. A fairy-tale. About me. (*Quietly, almost mysteriously.*) Don't believe everything they tell you about me.

CATHERINE (*suddenly throwing her arms round his neck, whispering to him with urgency*). Did you kill him, François?

VILLON (*wretchedly*). They told me he died of the filth in that hospital.

CATHERINE *starts to scream in uncontrollable spasms. The* BISHOP *gestures and* PHILIPPE *comes to* CATHERINE *and with a modicum of force pulls her off* VILLON.

CATHERINE. I curse you! I curse the very day you were born! (*To* PHILIPPE.) Take your sanctimonious paws off me, you filth! You'd like to, wouldn't you? You're jealous of François! Just eat yourself up with envy! It's all your fault anyway.

BISHOP (*drily*). Who are you?

CATHERINE *turns round. In a split second she changes beyond recognition. She is now a self-confident, cold woman with a rather coolly challenging attitude. She steps into the witness box and places her hand on the Bible.*

CATHERINE. I am Catherine de Vausselles.

BISHOP. Relation to the accused?

CATHERINE. No.

BISHOP. Answer the questions.

CATHERINE. I am. There never was, is, or will be any relationship between me and the accused. I scarcely knew him. To tell you the truth I am amazed that I have to take part as a witness in this infamous trial.

BISHOP. The court is informed that you and the accused had an intimate relationship.

CATHERINE. I expect the court is not informed about the origin of this absurd rumour. Is it possible for this to be placed on record? – All right. That myth was spread at the time by the accused himself. For what reason? Out of delusions of grandeur. Out of injured vanity he exposed me to the ridicule of the mob. Yes, in that sense there exists a relation to the accused, the relation of an injured party and I wish the indictment to be augmented accordingly.

BISHOP. Hm. What can you tell the court about the accused?

CATHERINE. Your Grace, does the word buffoon say enough to you?

BISHOP. What do you know about the incident just described?

CATHERINE. About that murder? Nothing, alas. I say: Alas.

BISHOP. Were you present?

CATHERINE (*amazed*). By no means!

BISHOP. Was the victim known to you?

CATHERINE (*conversationally*). Sermoy? Vaguely. He was a sort of fashionable preacher. He and Villon would peck at each other like two cocks on a dunghill. He always gave me the impression of being obsessed; not with the Devil – heaven forbid – but with himself.

BISHOP. The witness is asked to keep to the point.

CATHERINE. There is no point.

BISHOP. That is all. Does the defence wish to question the witness?

(*He looks around but no one reacts. He taps with his gavel in annoyance.*) Where is the defence? Who was retained to defend Villon?

ANGÈLE. Me!

Another of the ASSESSORS *jumps up. The head of a young woman, though more like a child, appears from under the cowl. It is* ANGÈLE. *She throws off the gown and runs over to* VILLON. *The* BAILIFFS *laugh, the other* ASSESSORS *murmur among themselves.*

I'll defend him! (*To* CATHERINE, *as she runs.*) I'll defend him! I'm coming François!

CATHERINE (*with disdain*). Who is that?

MOUSTIER. Where'd you think you're going, kiddo? How old are you?

ANGÈLE (*falling on her knees in front of* VILLON *and clumsily unbuttoning the gown*). I was sixteen yesterday, François!

VILLON *observes her with great embarrassment and a certain resentment.*

VILLON. Buzz off, Angèle.

ANGÈLE. You think I don't understand anything. I know, I know . . . But I dare to! (*To the* ASSESSORS, *combatively.*) I dare to! (*To* VILLON.) Help me with these frightful clothes!

VILLON. We're not by ourselves, honey. There are people here.

ANGÈLE. What do you care about them? What do you expect from them? Tell them to get stuffed, François!

VILLON. I can't. Quick, quick, do up your clothes!

ANGÈLE (*passionately*). You don't really expect favours from them, do you? Can't you see they're afraid of you?

VILLON. Buzz off!

ANGÈLE (*urgently*). They're afraid of you. Really! And I can tell when people are frightened. (*She hugs* VILLON'*s knees and whispers with utter urgency.*) François, they've sewn you up!

Suddenly another of the ASSESSORS *jumps up and thumps the table with his fist.*

RÉGNIER. That's enough! (*Authoritatively.*) Why do you put up with it? What kind of pseudo-historical masquerade is this? A sentimental pancake with a jam topping! (*Rather roughly, he finishes buttoning up* ANGÈLE *and pushes her away.*) Beat it! I'm defending Villon.

PHILIPPE (*rising*). Monsieur! Who are you?

RÉGNIER. Régnier de Montigny, monsieur! And you know full well who I am!

PHILIPPE. And what, do you think, accredits you to defend Villon?

REGNIER. As regards that, monsieur, I am not, thank God, answerable to you! (*To the* BISHOP.) I request the illustrious court –

The BISHOP *silences him with a gesture. He gives him a long, searching look. Meanwhile,* ANGÈLE *creeps back defeated to her place.* JEANNE *peeps out from her cowl.*

JEANNE (*amiably*). You came a cropper, didn't you, poor cow? (*And she immediately ducks back into the cowl.*)

BISHOP (*indecisively*). The court recognises . . . Monsieur de Montigny. A former undergraduate, is that not so?

RÉGNIER. That is so, your Honour.

BISHOP. Your studies ended a trifle . . . abruptly?

RÉGNIER. You are right once more. May I defend Villon?

BISHOP. Do you think that you, of all people –

RÉGNIER. Right for the third time, your Honour! (*With a lawyer's ease.*) Pro primo: Within the meaning of the procedural code I demand that all statements heretofore recorded be declared null and void. Pro secundo: in virtue of the corpus iuris ordinalis I assert my right to speak with my client.

The BISHOP *nods.*

PHILIPPE. Would my learned friend inform me of the reason for this delay?

RÉGNIER (*defiantly, from close to*). Of course. Five years before this latest judicial farce of Villon's I was hanged.

He walks across to VILLON. *The* BAILIFFS *remove* VILLON*'s manacles and exit. The* ASSESSORS *are blacked out and we see only* RÉGNIER *and* VILLON. VILLON *smiles happily and makes a conspiratorial gesture. Then, having shaken the stiffness out of his arms he nimbly executes a cartwheel, stretches and generally behaves like a puppy in a meadow.*

VILLON (*opening his arms in an embrace, laughing*). Règne! Is it you, Wolf?

RÉGNIER (*unmoved angrily*). What are you doing here?

VILLON. Where?

RÉGNIER (*ironically*). In Paris, Paris, my friend! In the world's maw! (*Sharply.*) Among this riff-raff!

VILLON (*sings, beating out the rhythm on the wood of the assessors' seats*). But there's no tongue like Parisienne! Though Lombards, Romans spill the beans – and Genoese – I'll risk it then! – But there's no tongue like Parisienne!

RÉGNIER. Shut up!

VILLON (*with the comic sighs of a scolded pupil, he falls on his knees before* RÉGNIER). Have you forgotten what I'm like, R-r-règne! I only flower in the Paris flowerpot, everywhere else my roots rot, R-r-règne!

RÉGNIER. You're in it up to your neck! Serves you right!

VILLON. I need Paris! I've tried to do without it. You know I have. But I just can't!

RÉGNIER. But Paris is fed up to the back teeth with you! It'll chew you up and spit you back into the woods!

VILLON. No! Not the woods! Every time I see trees now I come out in a rash.

RÉGNIER. You're crazy. To business: Were you the one that stabbed that trash of a bureaucrat?

VILLON. No. (*Suddenly fierce.*) Règne! Who peached on me that time in Blois?

RÉGNIER. To hell with Blois! – Who pinned the indictment on you?

VILLON (*grabbing him by the shirt*). It wasn't you, was it? Swear it wasn't you!

RÉGNIER (*twisting his wrists, roughly*). Get your paws off!

VILLON. If it was you, I swear to God I'll dig up your carcass and cut the legs off you! (*Desperately.*) Règne! Swear it!

RÉGNIER. Cut the cackle, I'm in a hurry! – Have you got anyone to support your statement?

VILLON (*suddenly crestfallen; sitting down*). Maybe. Dogis will swear he stabbed the old devil.

RÉGNIER. Dogis. Which one is he?

VILLON. Over there. That jellyfish in aspic. Him!

The spotlight locates TABARY *in an assessor's gown. Nonplussed, he starts to bow, a trifle shyly, while the light remains on him.*

RÉGNIER. That's something at least – I'll get down to business. beat it!

He pushes VILLON *into the darkness before returning to his lectern, removing his gown on the way, so that once again he is dressed as a modern-day intellectual. He takes some notes out of his pocket.*

VILLON (*from the darkness*). Règne! What's it like to die on the gallows?

RÉGNIER (*gazing into the darkness for a few moments, before smiling*). Delightful, old chum. The victim doesn't suffer – you ask any old priest. For half an hour your brain howls and every bone in your body croaks for mercy! (*He immediately turns round, spreads his arms rhetorically and starts to lecture.*) After that, what are you supposed to believe, my friends? We go on being bamboozled like that throughout our lives. – What sort of brainstorm was it that gave rise to that version of Villon? What sort of romantic monster do we see emerging here before our eyes? Who is it? – During my many years' acquaintance with literature about Villon I have encountered again and again two phantoms. He is either some wax angel with his eyes fixed on the future who is supposed to account to us – us of all people! – Or he is an absolute crook. Criminal, highwayman, mafioso or what you will, tearing along fast and loose according to some medieval timetable. The trouble is –

A cough of dissent. A light reveals PHILIPPE, *also dressed as a modern-day academic, sitting at his own lectern. His attitude is one of ironic reserve.*

PHILIPPE. With your permission, colleague. One can hardly call it entirely bamboozlement. As far as our knowledge extends, solely in the course of the ten or a dozen years of Villon's life that literary history has illuminated, we have irrefutable evidence of seven serious offences –

RÉGNIER (*fervently*). As far as our knowledge extends! Where does it extend to? (*With arm extended, he mimes someone groping in the dark.*) How far can we reach through the mire of time? What manages to trickle through a filter six centuries thick?

PHILIPPE. Well, if you intend to throw doubt on the facts –

RÉGNIER. I intend to throw doubt on you! No civilised system of justice accepts second-hand evidence! Circumstances known only from hearsay are of interest to no one! And I would suggest that the fifteenth century is well out of earshot, God damn it!

PHILIPPE. My dear sir, we are discussing here in academic precincts, not a taproom.

RÉGNIER. To hell with you, sir! So long as we go on treating Villon
as if he was a criminal demon we'll be barking up the wrong
bloody tree – and well you know it!

PHILIPPE. A demon? Oh, no! Your run-of-the-mill medieval
footpad. An eternal type, as timeless as a flea. Every society finds
itself confronted with irrepressibly wayward individuals of that
ilk and has the joyless task of having to deal with them. And it is
all the more exacting in that such personal deviance very
seldom occurs in persons of genius.

RÉGNIER. Personal deviance! For Jesus Christ's sake! What else
but one gigantic deviance were the times into which Villon was
born? It was a period bursting at the seams! The Paris of those
days was a screeching cat that suspects an impending cataclysm!

PHILIPPE. It was no abstract bursting at the seams that ripped
open the stomach of that priest Sermoy, but François Villon in
person!

RÉGNIER. Villon – I'll tell you who Villon was! He was a hair stood
on end in horror on the scalp of his times! He was history's
counterblast, howling through the narrow gullet of the
individual!

PHILIPPE (*drily*). My dear colleague, if you are determined at all
costs to create a class hero, I would advise you to choose
someone who is not such a total scoundrel.

RÉGNIER. Do you know what the Middle Ages were. They were no
groves of academe! They were an ethical jungle! And the law of
the jungle applied! To go fiddling about with details, such as
that regrettable little tale about that ecclesiastical windbag
Sermoy, or Chermoye or however he spelt his name, who
anyway didn't die from a stomach wound but from the filth in
the hospital, because the jungle was a pigsty, because in the
jungle no one swept the floor.

PHILIPPE (*offended*). I am lost for words. Simply lost for words.

RÉGNIER (*passionately*). I am pleased to hear it!

Both sit down snorting with annoyance.

PHILIPPE. There is a question from the floor. You answer it.

RÉGNIER (*impatiently*). What?

*The lights come up on the assessors' seats, now empty apart from
JEANNE, ANGÈLE and TABARY dressed as modern-day students.
JEANNE is asking the question. She is the trendiest of the three.*

JEANNE. What is the law of the jungle, Professor?

RÉGNIER (*put off his stroke by the inanity of the question*). What? Well surely . . .

PHILIPPE (*smugly*). If I may . . . The stronger eats the weaker. Isn't that what you meant?

RÉGNIER (*rousing himself, snorts*). Rather that than the other way round – if the weaker ate the stronger there'd be plenty of leftovers, don't you think?

JEANNE. Thanks!

TABARY. Could you define the Middle Ages for us?

RÉGNIER. Willingly. – The stronger eats the weaker and between mouthfuls forces it to say *Bon appétit!*

JEANNE (*trendily*). Fantastic.

ANGÈLE. (*assiduously and naively*). I would just like to . . . I think that Villon was so . . . fantastic and great that perhaps we oughtn't to judge him like the rest of them . . . maybe he was justified in a way –

RÉGNIER (*demonstratively collapsing in his seat*). Oof! . . . Sit down, Miss, and I'll tell you. (*Jumping to his feet.*) My reply is No, no, a thousand times no! For God's sake try and grasp the fact that the Middle Ages were cannibalistic! And the view of the world from inside a cannibal's maw is rather different from what one sees with six centuries of hindsight! – Villon justified? My dear young woman! Have you any idea of inquisitional justice? Just you bludgeon out of it a concept of justice and we'll pursue the discussion further!

PHILIPPE. Well, I think you're rather going over the top there, colleague.

Riled, RÉGNIER *leaps to his feet and puts on the gown.*

RÉGNIER. I'll put paid to this absurd trial! – Young woman, have you any idea what torture is? Water torture, for instance? Hm – When they open your sweet little mouth up here and pour salt water into you, and keep on pouring and pouring and pouring and pouring –

A stifled scream in the darkness. A sharp light is suddenly focused on Villon's MOTHER, *no longer in a gown, but dressed as a poor woman. She shields her eyes against the glare.*

PHILIPPE (*jumping up*). Now that's quite enough!

RÉGNIER. Enough? To quench thirst, yes. But it's not enough! You're lying tied to a plank bed –

PHILIPPE (*gripping* RÉGNIER *by the shoulder*). Pull yourself together!

MOTHER. François! What's up with François? Your Eminence –

RÉGNIER (*emotionally*). And then it runs out of you at the bottom – if you have the luck of the devil, that is, and your kidneys are working properly – at full pelt: thrrooom!

ANGÈLE (*blocking her ears; imploringly*). No more, please. That's enough!

PHILIPPE. Enough.

MOTHER. Where can I find the Bishop?

RÉGNIER. Villon suffered the water torture for four days. Four days! Are you still as interested in justice?

BISHOP (*loudly*). Enough!

The din stops. A pool of light on another part of the stage. VILLON *is lying insensible head down on a plank bed, alongside which stands a bucket. Both* BAILIFFS *are standing over the bed. The* BISHOP *slowly walks right over to them and takes a look at the prostrate body.*

BISHOP. Did he speak?

PICHART. No.

BISHOP. Not a word?

MOUSTIER (*guffaws*). Only rude ones.

BISHOP. Hm. – Get out! Get out!

He shoos the BAILIFFS *out. He stands alone for a moment scrutinising* VILLON. *Then, as he is leaving, the* MOTHER *falls at his feet and grasps his hand.*

MOTHER. Eminence! For the love of God! Is he truly an evildoer?

BISHOP (*withdrawing his hand; reluctantly*). What is evil? What is an evildoer?

Exit BISHOP. *The* CHORUS *starts to sing with gusto. Enter* MARGOT, *carrying a table. She lays the table and starts to shake the insensible* VILLON. *Their exchanges mingle with the singing.*

CHORUS. I know flies in the bowl
    I know the man by his apparel
    I know fair weather from foul
    I know by their shout who are the rabble
    I know nightmare and sleep
    I know the Bohemian's error
    I know the might of the Holy See
    I know I know everything but me

I know all there is to know
I know the florid and the pale of cheek
I know death that reaps us row on row
I know I know everything but me.

MARGOT (*in the middle of the song*). Get off, you pig! I need to lay the table!

She tugs at VILLON. VILLON *emits a drunken groan.* MARGOT *slaps his face and pulls his hair, her actions gradually being transformed into fairly amiable mauling.*

You're drunk as a wheelbarrow again!

She pulls VILLON *by his hair into a sitting position. He slips out of her grip, takes his head in his hands and shakes it in pain.*

VILLON. Ow! My head is full of bees.

MARGOT (*mauling* VILLON, *who relents to the contact*). What a little pig you are, aren't you?

At this moment the ebullient Parisian younger generation bursts onto the scene: RÉGNIER, TABARY, JEANNE, ANGÈLE *and* PICHART. *They bear a butcher's shop sign as a trophy, and possibly other things plundered from the shop. Discordant singing, laughter, incoherent shouts.* VILLON *pushes* MARGOT *away, sits up and starts to take notice.*

VILLON. Is that Règne?

MARGOT. Aren't you a proper little pig, though?

VILLON. Pipe down for a moment, can't you! (*Shouting.*) R-r-règne!

MARGOT (*rising in umbrage*). Off, you fleabag! Pronto! Boots off the table!

The ebullient youngsters now crowd in on VILLON. PICHART *sits to one side, snaps his fingers at* MARGOT *and gets her to bring him some wine, after which he merely sips his wine in silence and listens in carefully. The rest jabber away nineteen to the dozen and the exchanges are sometimes simultaneous.*

TABARY (*excitedly*). Frank's here! Hey, Frank, wakey wakey! Your old pal's here! Tabary!

JEANNE (*likewise*). Frankie! They're really belting each other in Paris tonight. A fantastic scrap!

MARGOT (*pushing* VILLON *roughly off the table*). Off!

TABARY (*resentfully*). Careful with him, woman! That's the Maître! That's our genius!

RÉGNIER *pushes aside the crowd surrounding* VILLON, *grabs hold of him and jerks him to his feet.*

RÉGNIER. Up you come, genius!

VILLON. Règne.

TABARY (*drumming on the shop sign with his fist*). Landlady! A jug here!

MARGOT. You can whistle for it! Who's paying?

TABARY. Yours truly! Guy Tabary! What wouldn't Guy do for his pals!

VILLON. What's happened?

TABARY (*at the same time as* JEANNE). A job, buddy, no shit – a real job!

JEANNE. The gendarmes are so mad they're pissing themselves! The students plundered a butcher's!

RÉGNIER (*jumping up on a table and spreading his arms; gaily and provocatively*). Havoc! Fantastic, glorious havoc! Another bit of Paris in smithereens! Gloria! The blessed day is coming when the whole caboodle will go up in tiny pieces, leaving only a stink behind!

VILLON *jumps up on the neighbouring table. He strums a lute. He also does no more than join in the racket and the entire subsequent disputation with* RÉGNIER *is conducted in the spirit of student provocation, not philosophical discourse. They are both having fun and their argument is accompanied by laughter.*

VILLON. I beg to differ! I have Paris under my merciful thumb. Paris is the ear of the world! Who else would listen to me?

MARGOT (*irate*). I'll kick the whole damn lot of you out of the door! The next thing there'll be the gendarmes here after you!

RÉGNIER. There's only one word that needs whispering into that shameless ear, and that's the word (*Yelling.*) NO!

TABARY (*drunkenly hugging* MARGOT *and butting into the dialogue between* RÉGNIER *and* VILLON). To hell with the gendarmes, Margot! You know what I do on the gendarmes?

JEANNE. From a great height!

TABARY. Tabary always does it from a great height folks!

VILLON. I beg to differ! I don't intend to scrape along with just a single word. and I won't stop until I have given all the words in France a good run for their money!

TABARY. I'm a student! I've got academic rights! No gendarme is allowed to lay a finger on me!

MARGOT. Stop drooling, blockhead. When they catch you they'll make mincemeat of you. and serve you right!

RÉGNIER. The world is rotting. Let it rot away! Join me, Villon! I declare an all-out onslaught on the world! It needs the two of us to point it the way!

VILLON. Am I to be permitted use of all the words? I demand freedom!

RÉGNIER. There is no such thing as freedom! Freedom is only necessity in disguise! Let our slogan be a deafening NO!

VILLON *and* RÉGNIER *laugh. The drunken* TABARY *staggers up to them.*

TABARY. Sure thing, Règne. Count me in, always. I'm a devil. Devil of a feller.

RÉGNIER (*jumping down from the table and taking a drink; amiably*). You dope. They'd only have to waggle a finger at you from heaven and you'd start singing Alleluia inside your mousehole.

TABARY (*offended*). So? What's so wrong with that? We all want to go to heaven. (*To* VILLON.) Don't you want to go to heaven?

VILLON (*laughing and strumming*). Paris is good enough for me. After all . . . there's no tongue like Parisienne!

TABARY (*assailing* VILLON). You don't want to go to heaven?

VILLON. The cat's heaven and the mouse's hell look exactly the same. It all depends who's the cat and who's the mouse.

RÉGNIER (*prodding* TABARY *and laughing*). Which are you, Tabary, eh?

TABARY. Both.

VILLON *goes on strumming.*

MARGOT (*hitting* VILLON*'s hands with the ladle*). Get down, you pig!

VILLON (*laughing*). Ouch! (*Blowing her a kiss.*) Don't interrupt, you sow! I am just thinking up a rhyme for you!

JEANNE. Do you know what? There are thirty dead already. Not bad, eh?

TABARY (*roaring*). Quiet! Quiet! A song from the Maître!

Immediate silence. JEANNE *jumps up onto the table and squats at*

> VILLON's feet. VILLON *laughs a very happy laugh. Then he starts to sing with a clear and confident voice.*

VILLON (*singing*). Item: to Fat Margot who's so fair
>   of face and painted, as I see,
>   devoted as she is, I swear
>   I love her for herself and she
>   loves me the way I've got to be.

TABARY (*enthusing*). Christ what a guy! What a fantastic idiot! What a devil!

VILLON (*singing*). I love and serve my lady with a will,
>   but that's no reason you should call me mad.
>   For her I'd hitch on sword and shield to kill.
>   She is the goods to please my every fad.
>   When customers arrive, I lightly pad
>   to bring in pots and wine. I serve them cheese
>   and fruit, and bread and water as they please
>   and say (depending on the tip I'm paid)
>   'Do call again and come here at your ease
>   to this whorehouse where we do a roaring trade'.

>   But then fine feelings end and turn to ill.
>   When she comes home without the cash, I'm had.
>   I cannot stand her, she has blood to spill.
>   I hate her, grab her belt, gown, shift and plaid
>   She thwacks my thigh and, after what we've had
>   dead drunk we sleep like logs – and let the fleas.
>   Though when we stir her fanny starts to tease.
>   She mounts; I groan beneath her weight
>   – I'm splayed!
>   Her wantonness is killing me
>   in this whorehouse where we do a roaring trade.

>   Vary the wind, come frost, I live in ease.
>   I am debauched, the same as she's
>   Layman or laity – no matter of degrees!
>   Layer on layer of onion overlaid,
>   Our filth we love and filths upon us seize;
>   Now we flee honour, honour from us flees
>   in this whorehouse where we do a roaring trade.

TABARY *sarcastically kisses* VILLON's *shoe and all laugh. From the first stanza* VILLON *is joined by the guitars of the* CHORUS *who also join in the words as the song progresses.* MARGOT *accompanies the song with furious blows of her ladle to* VILLON's *calves.*

MARGOT. Get the hell out of it, slobberchops! Go on, beat it!

Suddenly a row from outside breaks in on the singing: crashing, the clatter of hoofs, the neighing of horses and shouts. All fall warily silent. ANGÈLE runs to check out the situation and returns straight away.

ANGÈLE. François! Run! The bailiffs are coming!

The characters disperse in all directions, someone knocking over the table in the process. Confusion and growing noise from outside.

RÉGNIER. Dowse the lights!

Someone dowses the lights. Blackout. A horse whinnies.

MARGOT. My God, I just hope they don't throw the lot of you in the clink!

A sharp metallic note rings out. A dazzling light suddenly breaks the darkness, illuminating the fleeing VILLON.

VILLON. Dowse that light, you fool! Who's shining that light? Put it out!

The din of a street fight is suddenly cut, only the metallic ringing continues. VILLON shields his eyes against the glare of the light which comes closer and closer to him. He wants to flee but from the darkness someone (MOUSTIER) grabs him by the shoulder and violently sits him down.

PICHART. How many interrogations so far?

MOUSTIER. This is the ninth.

A dim light comes up on part of the stage. PICHART is just tying VILLON to a chair and shining a light into his eyes. It is an interrogation scene. MOUSTIER is holding some metallic instrument of torture. He has just banged it with a piece of metal and is listening with relish to the quivering note.

VILLON. Take that light away!

PICHART. But I want to be able to see you. Well . . . where did we come by that sweet little scar, eh?

VILLON. I already told you!

PICHART. Oh, but you didn't.

VILLON. I did.

MOUSTIER comes to stand by VILLON, agitating the fork meaningfully right by his ear.

PICHART. Leave him! He'll tell us. (*Tenderly.*) I like listening to him. He's got a voice like a lark. A proper little singer, eh? (*Suddenly roaring like a sergeant major.*) Talk, you rat!

VILLON (*broken*). Philippe Sermoy cut my lip with a dagger.

PICHART. When? Where? How? And why?

VILLON. When: The Fifth of June. Where: In front of St Boniface's Church. How? Like this.

He lets out a roar and jumps up, chair and all, to launch a karate-style attack on PICHART. *The bailiff falls down.*

(VILLON *dramatically*.) Like that! Sneakily, without warning! Like a footpad! Like a fateful blow!

MOUSTIER. Jailer! (*To* VILLON.) You bastard! Jailer!

He pushes over VILLON, *still bound to the chair. The* BISHOP *emerges from the darkness. He looks on. He then gestures them to raise* VILLON, *who spits at the* BAILIFFS. *The* BISHOP *shoos them out. He then draws up a chair and sits down opposite* VILLON, *who behaves truculently. The* BISHOP *is polite and makes no effort to butter him up.*

BISHOP. You don't mind the light?

VILLON. No.

BISHOP (*rising and pushing the light aside*). All right?

VILLON. Hm.

BISHOP (*a moment's pause and then thoughtfully*). You see, a certain order applies here. An order of things. A divine order.

VILLON. Hm.

BISHOP. It has to be preserved. When an order goes wild it turns into a whirlwind of good and evil, in which only the evil gradually thickens.

VILLON *stays silent. The* BISHOP *suddenly shakes his head as if marking a change of mood. Lightly and with a smile he says.*

You were a student weren't you?

VILLON. Hm.

BISHOP. Students. The black sheep of Paris . . . Do you like Paris, Villon?

VILLON (*warily*). Why?

BISHOP. I've heard all sorts of things about you . . . In fact, I had two or three of your ballads transcribed . . . You're a capable young man, Villon.

VILLON. Hm.

BISHOP. Would it interest you to know which ballads they were?

VILLON (*unable to resist, he smiles, and starts to respond*). Yes.

BISHOP. (*He also smiles, but unexpectedly dismisses the question with a wave of the hand; in a friendly tone*). By the way . . . Sermoy – you knew him didn't you?

VILLON. Sermoy? The ace ass of Paris!

BISHOP (*mildly*). We are speaking of a servant of God, Villon.

VILLON (*zanily*). A prize ass, naturally. The prize ass of Paris.

BISHOP. And the two of you . . . had a disagreement?

VILLON. Disagreement? A thousand disagreements. He gripped the pulpit with one hand and with the other he held onto the saints' shirt-tails when he was slandering me. (*Suddenly intense.*) He threatened to kill me!

BISHOP. Well . . . the opposite would seem to have happened . . .

VILLON. What was I supposed to do? What would you do if someone jumped on you from behind?

BISHOP. From behind? It was from behind?

VILLON (*suddenly crestfallen*). Of course . . . Ah, nothing.

BISHOP. And was there . . . a motive?

VILLON *says nothing. The* BISHOP *stands up, points the lamp high above his head and laughs.*

Full moon!

He gestures to the BAILIFFS *who wordlessly remove* VILLON*'s bonds and disappear.* VILLON *covers his face with his hands. After a moment he takes away his hands and asks softly.*

VILLON. Is she here?

But the BISHOP *is no longer there.* VILLON *stands up and looks around anxiously.*

Catherine! Catherine! Are you here?

CATHERINE *runs in out of the darkness. She is not the same as in the first scene. Now she is young, maidenly, unpretentious, in love, a trifle hectic.*

CATHERINE. I thought you'd never remember! (*Tossing him a lute.*) This is yours isn't it?

VILLON *catches the lute. Suddenly he bursts out laughing. He undergoes a change of mood: he too is young, happy, enchanted and cheerful.*

VILLON. Oh heavens open and swallow me up! – Catherine! Is it you?

CATHERINE (*with feigned disgust she takes his rags between finger and thumb*). You're a very shabby fellow for a student!

VILLON (*laughing*). Oh, I beg your pardon . . . (*He takes down his student gown from the floodlight and puts it on. He starts to strum.*) But there's no tongue like Parisienne . . .

CATHERINE. And what have you been up to this time?

VILLON (*roguishly*). Full moon! Hey, and what a moon! A monstrance!

CATHERINE (*pulling his hair*). I asked you something!

VILLON. Oh, but Mademoiselle knows everything! Has she heard some little bird, perhaps?

CATHERINE. Paris is full of it!

VILLON. There's no tongue like Parisienne.

CATHERINE (*impatiently*). Well?

VILLON. Day in day out, black flocks of rumours fly out of Paris and knock at the Gates of Heaven, howling like Melusine: Villo-o-o-n! Villo-o-o-n! Villo-o-o-n!

CATHERINE *releases his hair, and stands nervously clenching and unclenching her hands.* VILLON *notices her gesture. He stops strumming and takes her by the wrists. Guiltily she stops what she was doing.*

What's that you're doing?

CATHERINE (*trying to pull her hands away*). Nothing.

VILLON. I've frequently noticed it: showing and hiding her claws. Like a frightened cat.

He places her palms on his throat. CATHERINE *sighs. Quite differently all of a sudden, with a new, uncoquettish forthrightness.*

CATHERINE. It's impatience.

VILLON (*softly and kindly*). Over what?

CATHERINE. I don't know. Nothing. I'm as impatient as . . . as purgatory. Life just drags on, it just crawls . . . everyone just drivels on endlessly. – Aren't you ever bored, Villon?

VILLON *silently shakes his head.*

I am all the time. Eternally. I get so dreadfully bored I end up counting the toes on my feet.

VILLON. What do you actually do . . . with all your days and nights, Catherine?

CATHERINE (*bitterly*). I sleep. I sleep as if for escape: whenever I get a chance. I lie down like being burnt to ashes. I dream. I dream that I'm a student. I'm as reckless and infamous as Villon. No! Much more infamous!

VILLON smiles happily. Even CATHERINE makes a slight smile.

What else . . . I try and see how long I can hold my breath, until I almost faint. I sit at a banquet and very quietly stifle myself. And I still bite my nails. No, really. Look!

VILLON peruses her hands with interest. Then he kisses her palms.

I'm horrified at the thought that one day I will chew myself up: first my nails, then my fingers, then my hands . . . like a fox in a cage.

VILLON starts to laugh quietly. He gives CATHERINE an affectionate smile and slowly draws her to him.

What am I to do, Villon?

At this point, PHILIPPE emerges from the darkness, dressed as a priest and carrying a breviary.

PHILIPPE (*reproachfully*). Mademoiselle de Vausselles?

CATHERINE (*springing back and shielding her eyes against the floodlight*). Who's there?

PHILIPPE. What are you doing out alone at such an unsuitable hour?

CATHERINE (*defiantly*). Who says I'm alone?

VILLON (*angrily, with intent to provoke*). Oh, mouthpiece of God! God in his kindness has stuck out his holy tongue at us! Let's hear you, rhetorician!

PHILIPPE (*ignoring him*). Does your mother know where you are at this time? Allow me to walk you home Mademoiselle de Vausselles!

VILLON. Don't push your luck, pal. Scram!

PHILIPPE. Did someone give you permission to go out?

CATHERINE (*sprightly, though already a trifle nervous*). I'm moonstruck, Father Sermoy. I am defenceless against the full moon. (*Letting out a sudden squeal.*) To-o-tally defenceless!

She extends her arms in front of her and starts to play at sleepwalking.
PHILIPPE *tries to catch her.*

PHILIPPE. Mademoiselle de Vausselles!

VILLON (*pushing him away, a bit roughly*). Clear off, priest!

PHILIPPE. I wasn't addressing you, Villon!

VILLON. You're not welcome, not wanted, and surplus!

PHILIPPE. Mademoiselle de Vausselles!

VILLON *picks up a long, supple stick and casually pushes the breviary out of* PHILIPPE'*s hands with it.*

VILLON. Mind you don't drop your breviary!

PHILIPPE. Don't goad me, Villon!

VILLON (*prodding him with the stick*). Chick, chick, chick!

PHILIPPE *goes to grab the stick from him but it breaks in half.*
VILLON *immediately adopts a fencing stance 'en garde' and starts to lunge at* PHILIPPE, *using the stick as a rapier. Meanwhile the* CHORUS *has appeared on the traverse. They cat-call in tempo with the unfolding skirmish.*

PHILIPPE. Control yourself! I am a servant of the Church!

VILLON. Oh, the Church has only holy men!

PHILIPPE. You'll be sorry.

VILLON (*chanting a scurrilous ditty*).

'No, cast no slur on the priestly station
And never ever jeer at it . . . '

Shoo, shoo! Goosey, goosey into the pond. Henny penny into the corn!

PHILIPPE. Don't overestimate my patience!

CHORUS (*taking up the song*). The Church has only holy men!

VILLON. ' . . . accept it all sans reservation'
Shoo, shoo, shoo!

PHILIPPE. Stop it!

VILLON. You envious little ham-actor, you!

PHILIPPE (*in impotent fury*). I'll kill you!

Scuffle.

CHORUS. 'Only by fools are they ever maligned;

Not even in private and never out loud
Should you ever dare to speak your mind,
For they are a most revengeful crowd.'

In the course of the scuffle the ASSESSORS *start to return and they avidly observe the incident.* CATHERINE *moves round them, sleepwalking, and crosses the scene, occasionally bumping into someone.* VILLON *soon overcomes* PHILIPPE *and ends up kneeling on him on the ground, so that* PHILIPPE *is totally helpless.*

VILLON (*to* CATHERINE *in merry boyish triumph*). Catherine! What shall I do with him? He's ours!

CATHERINE (*about to burst out laughing; mischievously*). Do him in, Villon! Do him in and we'll run away from Paris together!

PHILIPPE (*prone; suffocating*). Villon, stop before it's too late!

VILLON *releases him. He laughs as* PHILIPPE *picks himself up.*

VILLON. Run away and preach! And give us your blessing! Say: The Lord be with you!

Without turning round and with head bowed, PHILIPPE *goes over to the highest chair, the 'pulpit'. He makes the blessing, saying exhaustedly:*

PHILIPPE. The Lord be with you!

All those present, with the exception of VILLON *and* CATHERINE *kneel down. A church bell rings.* THE FATHER *swings a censer.*

ALL. And also with you.

CATHERINE (*bumping into* VILLON *like a sleepwalker, then feeling his face before opening her eyes; in a fit of laughter*). I saw nothing! I saw nothing! Where is he?

Still laughing she falls to her knees like the rest, whereupon her laughter is transformed into equally uncontrollable weeping. PHILIPPE *is standing on the pulpit, his face hidden in his hands. Slowly he uncovers his face. He starts to preach and all of a sudden the fanatical, eloquent and professionally self-disciplined side of his character resurfaces even more emphatically than before.*

PHILIPPE. Weeping. Weeping. I hear weeping. There is the sound of weeping in Paris.

A lengthy pause. All at once CATHERINE *looks up and stops crying.*

The Gospel according to Matthew, chapter eighteen: 'Woe to the world because of scandals. For it must needs be that scandals come; but nevertheless woe to the man by whom the scandals cometh.' – (*Pause.*) Woe. Woe to whom? By whom, as by the Gates of Hell, that voraciously yawning gullet, that moist, protruding intestine, does weeping enter our houses?

He buries his head in his hands. The last to do so. VILLON *finally kneels down like the rest. One of the other kneelers nods to him cheerfully: it is* TABARY. *He points conspiratorially at the string of some musical instrument.* VILLON *smiles.*

Brothers and sisters! The bells of Paris are stunned into silence. The stones of Paris are running with blood. – How long are we to go on ignoring the bloody antics of the students? Is their arrogance not deadly? Students. The black sheep of Paris . . . But are they not wolves in sheep's clothing? Thus asketh the Lord. (*Pause.*) And when we do not prevent evil we open the door to Satan. When we do not punish the guilty, the gale will howl within the innocent also!

TABARY *runs his fingers down the string making it howl 'like a gale'. Someone screams in surprise; someone else chuckles. Murmuring.*

(PHILIPPE *raises his voice.*) And soon a tempest will start to thunder within us too. And foul winds roar!

TABARY *and* VILLON *provide appropriate noises as accompaniment. Finally* TABARY *roars 'like a foul wind'. The 'congregation' is scandalized.*

Who did that?

From outside comes the pounding of horses' hoofs, blows, screams. JEANNE *runs in.*

JEANNE. Help! The sergeants are beating the students.

Chaos. Some run out, others remain kneeling. Shrieks. The din outside grows louder.

PHILIPPE (*shouting them down*). Brothers and sisters! Let us remain calm! We shall sing!

There is the sound of a church hymn. Some people look into the distance. JEANNE *climbs up onto the judge's seat and stands observing the incident, catcalling.* CATHERINE *goes over to the small group in which* VILLON *is standing.*

CATHERINE (*conversationally*). What's going on this time, messieurs?

VILLON. Two sergeants have killed a student. Your obedient servant, Mademoiselle de Vausselles.

JEANNE (*shouting from above*). No! Two students killed a sergeant!

VILLON (*laughs*). Even better!

MOUSTIER. Tie all the students head down to horses' backsides and drive the lot of them out of Paris!

The small group disperses. Only VILLON *and* RÉGNIER *remain on stage.* PHILIPPE *descends from the pulpit and goes over to the pair, his face grim.*

PHILIPPE. Monsieur Villon.

VILLON (*cheekily*). Present!

PHILIPPE. A few words with you.

RÉGNIER (*sitting down on the ground and uncorking a bottle. Convivially*). May I listen in?

PHILIPPE. I would rather speak with you alone, monsieur.

VILLON (*jestingly*).Règne is my counsel. I haven't the skill to dispute with a professional. Sing – no problem! But my prose is a trifle wayward. R-r-règne!

RÉGNIER *tosses him the bottle.* VILLON *sits down on the ground and takes a drink.* PHILIPPE *stands stiffly between the two of them. But now he is neither the figure of ridicule nor the preacher. This is actually one of his rare moments of frankness.*

PHILIPPE. Villon, our enmity has the whole of Paris laughing.

VILLON. R-r-règne! (*Tossing him the bottle.*)

PHILIPPE. How far do you intend to push it, Villon?

RÉGNIER (*cheerfully*). Advice of learned counsel: don't answer!

PHILIPPE. I give you fair warning, Villon. God's patience is almost bottomless. But whoever reaches the bottom disappears beneath it.

VILLON (*slightly tipsy by now*). You talk like Scripture, Father. Thank God you don't speak in rhyme or Paris wouldn't want me any more.

PHILIPPE (*seriously*). Don't mock God's gift. Maybe I don't understand you, but one thing I do know: you are burdened with a divine talent. God will call you to account one day.

VILLON. I'll tell you the way it is with us, Father. Paris is too small for the two of us. We are two fingers of one hand stuck by mistake into the same finger of a glove. (*Holding up his index and middle fingers.*) I'm the slightly bigger one. You have let your nail grow a bit longer to make up for it, Sermoy!

PHILIPPE. Why can't you understand that I want to save you from yourself, Villon? A Tempter once appeared to me on one cold night in the seminary. He laughed at everything the way you do!

VILLON. I once dreamed about you too, Father. You were hanging from the clouds by one leg and spying at night outside bedroom windows.

PHILIPPE (*offended*). Monsieur de Montigny! Do you agree with this infantile tantrum?

RÉGNIER (*in comic amazement*). Me? I don't agree with anything! That's my purpose in life!

PHILIPPE (*staring at them both for a moment, then crestfallen*). I shall pray for you, Villon.

He goes to leave. VILLON *tosses the bottle to* RÉGNIER. *The bottle accidentally hits* PHILIPPE *on the head.* PHILIPPE *turns round. He is instantly transformed into the predatory, aggressive prosecutor. The lights come up on the full panel of* ASSESSORS. VILLON *yawns and starts to fall asleep.*

(PHILIPPE *aggressively*). Objection!

RÉGNIER (*quickly jumping up and reaching for his gown; with equal vehemence*). One moment.

PHILIPPE. I refuse to have dealings with a defence counsel who regards dissent as his philosophy! I refuse to treat with a man who has become a professional in the art of hatred! I do not acknowledge as lawful a defence counsel who rejects law as a category!

RÉGNIER (*now dressed in his gown*). What am I to agree with? Hatred towards what? And law? Whose law?

PHILIPPE. Stop declaiming!

RÉGNIER. Do you really think that Villon is full of hatred? That he is rebellious? Pah! He's just a giddy goat, who's not even sure what he's up to! But in him is that secret crevice through which howls the tempest of the times –

PHILIPPE. The tempest of the times? This drunken masquerade? Looting shops? Fights with the gendarmes?

RÉGNIER. Open your eyes! You're up to your knees in law and up to your neck in congealed blood, Sermoy!

BISHOP (*tapping with his gavel; drily*). Counsel for the defence.

RÉGNIER. Yes?

BISHOP (*serenely*). Do you intend to base the defence of your client on an indictment of the Middle Ages? Of King Charles? Of France? Of holy justice? Or of me?

RÉGNIER. No. My dispute with all the natural phenomena

mentioned is now closed and filed away. But I protest against the partiality of the prosecutor who is stuck in a rut of personal animosity and is turning this trial into a Sunday sermon!

PHILIPPE. I have scarcely started. We shall move on to the other counts of the indictment.

RÉGNIER. Yes. Up to and including murder. Before we know it, you will be murdered, Sermoy. I shall be hanged. And what about Villon? What will become of him?

VILLON is asleep. ANGÈLE sits at his side, tickling him with a straw. RÉGNIER walks round the ASSESSORS but they all look elsewhere, as if RÉGNIER had asked something improper.

I am asking you: What will you do about Villon?

BISHOP. Question overruled.

RÉGNIER. A – ha!

A moment's silence, broken by a sneeze from the sleeping VILLON.

BISHOP. Bring in Villon!

THE FATHER (*taken by surprise*). Coming . . . coming . . .

The BISHOP gestures imperiously to the ASSESSORS that he wishes to be alone. The ASSESSORS rise and leave. THE FATHER as the court usher approaches VILLON. He is now playing two roles: as the court usher he summons impersonally, as a priest-guardian he is careworn and concerned.

Student Villon! Villon, François! (*To ANGÈLE, quietly.*) Run along, my dear!

ANGÈLE starts, jumps up and runs after the others, on the way taking the assessor's gown which is hanging on the back of her seat. VILLON sits up and rubs his eyes drunkenly.

VILLON. What's up?

THE FATHER (*from close to*). Oh, my boy, my boy . . . whatever will they do to you? Whatever will become of you?

VILLON (*joyfully, affectionately*). Father! Is that you?

THE FATHER (*summoning*). Villon! Villon, François!

VILLON. Forgive me, Father, that I have not been in touch. Life has been running away with me rather . . . rearing and bucking. But I just love the way it neighs!

THE FATHER. I know, I know . . . Just so long as the Rector has patience, François.

VILLON (*startled*). The Rector? Why?

THE FATHER (*summoning*). His Reverence the Rector of the University awaits student Villon!

VILLON gets up and THE FATHER *dusts him down. No one is sitting on the seats now except the* BISHOP, *who is engrossed in some papers.* VILLON *goes down on his knees and bows his head.*

Your Magnificence! (*Exit.*)

BISHOP (*looking up, waiting a moment and then not unkindly*). Well, stand up, stand up! I'm not interested in the back of your neck! You know why you're here, of course.

VILLON (*humbly*). I would not presume, your reverence.

BISHOP (*sharply*). Just you presume!

Silence. The BISHOP *starts to tap his finger impatiently.* VILLON *fixes his eyes on the finger and the* BISHOP *withdraws it. Suddenly he leans forward and roars.*

Do you at all appreciate the fact that you are a scholar of the Holy University of Paris?

VILLON (*contritely*). Yes.

BISHOP. And can't you see that your vulgar pranks have now gone beyond all bounds?

VILLON. I'm as unripe as a pear in May, Magnificence.

BISHOP. A young scoundrel is what you are!

The BISHOP *rises and walks up and down. He speaks without sympathy.*

I know your type. You swim against the tide of the times you are born into. And that means, Villon, that time is not on your side!

VILLON (*quietly, still on his knees*). I know.

BISHOP. At eighteen you're a songbird. At twenty-five a homeless cur. And at thirty a wolf. (*He crosses the room and then comes to stand by* VILLON *where he suddenly says more or less confidentially.*) But time, young man, loses its sap with every year that passes. Time dries up. You will end up an exile in the desert, Villon. (*He returns to his seat and his papers, as well as to a purely official tone.*) Is it true that you are one of the ringleaders of a number of rowdy incidents, that you are involved in plundering taverns and shops and that you provoke fights with the sergeants of Paris?

VILLON (*meekly*). Your Magnificence must surely know that the sergeants also pick fights with us.

BISHOP (*striking the table with his fist*). Silence! Do you realise that these incidents have already claimed more than thirty lives?

VILLON. I do, and I regret it most deeply.

BISHOP. Do you realise that you have repeatedly violated the code of this university?

VILLON. Yes.

BISHOP (*searchingly and almost inquistively*). And do you realise that the code is stronger than you are?

VILLON looks up. He makes no protest, being deep in thought. The two look at each other for a long time. Then the BISHOP slaps the file shut and stands up.

Go. And make sure you don't come to my notice again. (*On his way out he passes the kneeling VILLON. He has already gone past when he recalls something and returns. He speaks quietly and with emphasis.*) Listen, Villon. I've been here thirty-five years. And I have seen plenty of you. And there's something I'll tell you. Without even properly knowing about your last step, you'll overstep the limits.

VILLON. And what if I'm careful?

BISHOP (*he reflects for a moment*). In that case . . . it just might happen that the limits will lose patience and overstep you.

The BISHOP goes out. Still kneeling, VILLON rests his head on the floor. A moment later CATHERINE creeps into the chamber in student garb, her hair tucked beneath her cap. She looks around her, without at first seeing VILLON. VILLON starts to beat the floor with his fists and lets out a wordless roar of despair – merely releasing the tension. CATHERINE shrieks and VILLON spins round.

VILLON (*furious*). Who's there?

He springs at her. CATHERINE runs away but VILLON catches her. A brief scuffle during which he deftly throws her to the floor and then squats unerotically like a small boy, on her bottom.

What are you doing here spying? Who were you expecting? Talk!

CATHERINE (*smothered*). Get off me, Villon!

VILLON (*in astonishment*). What! What the . . . ? (*Taking CATHERINE's cap between thumb and forefinger he removes it, ceremoniously. In similar fashion, he then lifts a long lock of hair.*) Mademoiselle de Vausselles!

VILLON springs up. CATHERINE rolls into a half-sitting position. VILLON squats on her knees.

CATHERINE. Just you get off me right now! You're suffocating me!

VILLON. What did you expect to find here?

CATHERINE. You're taking advantage of the moment, Villon!

VILLON. Oh alas! The moment is taking advantage of me!

CATHERINE (*thumping him with her fists*). Leave go of me!

VILLON. This moment is dragging me with it like a wave! Catherine!

CATHERINE. Be quiet! It wasn't you I came to see.

VILLON. The result is the same. Thank God!

CATHERINE. I want to see the university! I want to see the Paris that never sleeps. Every fly on this ceiling knows a hundred times more about life than I do! (*Hissing.*) And tonight I'll go to a brothel!

VILLON (*springing off her and opening his arms*). You're here! You're in the living heart of the world! Paris – is Villon! The University – is Villon! The heart of Paris – is me!

THE FATHER (*off*). Who's there? Are you still there, Villon?

VILLON *and* CATHERINE *immediately hide behind the seat.* THE FATHER *looks in.*

No one anywhere? I'm locking up!

A key turning and footsteps growing fainter. CATHERINE *stands up. She now behaves with a mixture of anxiety and some sort of magic flirtatiousness.*

CATHERINE. Goodness. Is there anyone here still?

VILLON (*falling on his knees and stretching his arms up towards the ceiling*). No one. Just you and me and flies on the ceiling.

He spreads his arms. CATHERINE *dodges him.*

CATHERINE. No. Not you, Villon. There's a hoofmark on your back.

VILLON. What?

CATHERINE (*whispering as she backs away*). The whole of Paris knows it. You made a pact with the Devil. He pours rhymes into your left ear. You have his signature on your back . . . At full moon it is molten, at new moon it bleeds –

VILLON (*in the spirit of the erotic game that has now commenced*). You've got me worried. It's ages since I last saw my back. Put my mind at rest, Catherine.

He quickly strips to the waist and turns his back to CATHERINE *who examines his back fascinatedly.*

Is it there?

CATHERINE. There's a birthmark. (*Putting her finger on it.*)

VILLON. Maybe the Devil's signature is elsewhere. Try looking lower down.

CATHERINE *lightly touches his back with her finger running it down his spine. Then she places her whole hand on his back. She stares at it in silent fascination. Motionless for a moment.*

(VILLON, *sincerely*). Oh, if only this moment might never wash me up on the shore!

CATHERINE *slowly bows her head and kisses* VILLON *on the back.* VILLON *turns round. He quickly takes her in his arms, but* CATHERINE *cries out, this time without flirtatiousness, out of sheer neurotic anguish.*

CATHERINE. No! No!

VILLON (*astounded*). What's up, Catherine?

CATHERINE. Don't you dare! Let me go!

She manages to slip out of his arms. She runs to the door and starts to hammer on it with her fists.

CATHERINE. Help! Is there anyone there?

VILLON. Stop shouting. There's not a living soul here. – For God's sake, Catherine, what's the matter?

CATHERINE (*suddenly falling silent, as if having pulled herself together; quietly*). I am frightened.

VILLON. What of?

CATHERINE. Of you, Villon.

VILLON (*genuinely aghast*). Frightened of me? Why?

He cautiously holds out his arms and hugs her. CATHERINE *stands still for a moment allowing herself to be held, but all at once she lets out another shriek and starts to batter* VILLON, *screaming.*

CATHERINE. Help! Come here!

A pack of journalists runs in from all sides: PICHART, MOUSTIER, JEANNE, TABARY *and* RÉGNIER. *They carry flash-guns, tape-recorders, notebooks. They are dressed in modern clothes. Apart from* RÉGNIER, *who keeps apart, they behave like the worst sort of gutter press journalist: sensation-seeking, inconsiderate and noisy. For a moment* VILLON *'does not notice' them.*

VILLON. There's nobody here! We're all alone! Don't be frightened!

CATHERINE *breaks away and runs to the journalists who photograph the entire scene, interrupting and jostling each other.*

CATHERINE (*as she runs; screaming*). You call yourself Paris? There are yobs like you in every pub!

MOUSTIER (*pointing the flashgun at him and shouting above the din*). Smile, Maître Villon!

VILLON (*dishevelled, bewildered, unheeding*). Catherine!

JEANNE (*trendy; prattling*). Paris Matin: I'm interested in the social context of your writing! Why do you go around half-naked? Is it a protest against convention?

VILLON. Catherine!

TABARY (*admiringly*). Villon, what do you say to those of us who regard you as one of the greatest poets of all time?

PHILIPPE. And also a cynical cut-throat! What do you say to that?

JEANNE. What was the significance of sex to the young people of your day?

VILLON (*rousing himself, but unwillingly, wearily*). What?

PICHART (*aiming his flash and clicking his fingers*). Look this way! Over here!

JEANNE. Were your happenings intended to shock the bourgeois of your day?

PHILIPPE. Do you consider yourself a criminal?

JEANNE (*indignantly*). I asked first!

PICHART. Tell us about your criminal activity! List the individual crimes you committed!

VILLON. Yes. The unintentional killing of Father Sermoy –

MOUSTIER. Punishment?

VILLON. Pardoned.

MOUSTIER. Next!

VILLON. Robbery at the theological faculty in Fifty-Eight –

PHILIPPE. Do you stand by the description 'unintentional killing'?

VILLON (*glancing at him*). Naturally.

JEANNE. Was your criminal activity socially-motivated? Were you expressing the rebellion of the oppressed classes?

VILLON (*with alarm*). What?

JEANNE. Did you yearn to demolish the world you were born into? Was destruction your aim?

VILLON. No.

PHILIPPE. The world yearns for the artist to be a great man also. Have you achieved human greatness, Villon?

VILLON (*with sudden rudeness*). Get stuffed!

TABARY. How about singing us one of your ballads, Villon?

VILLON. Bugger off!

TABARY. I have something here . . . pretty good as a matter of fact. You'll like it, Villon!

He switches on his tape-recorder. 'Oh, where are the snows of yesteryear' can be heard as in the opening scene – as a modern hit. VILLON hides his face in his hands. The others fall quiet for a moment and listen. The song continues to be heard after the next exchanges. CATHERINE steps lightly out of the group.

CATHERINE (*reporter-style*). Who was the notorious Catherine of your ballads? Did she exist?

VILLON (*glancing at her, and then harshly*). Naturally. Catherine de Vausselles was the most astute whore of the Paris prefecture. She had the comportment of an ox's tail and a long black bristle grew out of her nose.

CATHERINE (*after a moment*). Thanks.

TABARY. Pipe down for heaven's sake, all of you! Listen to it!

All fall silent for a moment. The song. All at once, RÉGNIER walks over, after having said nothing so far.

RÉGNIER (*ironically confidential*). And what did they actually do to you, Villon?

All react as if they have heard something extremely indelicate. VILLON glances up in confusion.

RÉGNIER. What kind of dance did they actually lead you?

PICHART (*the first to recover*). Light! Give me a light on that chin! Move over! That's it.

JEANNE, TABARY and the two BAILIFFS kick up quite a confused bustle around VILLON, shifting floodlights, flashing with their

cameras, making a din and pushing each other out of the way.
VILLON *shields his eyes from the glare of the floodlights.*

VILLON. Take that light away!

PHILIPPE (*thrusting a microphone towards him*). You have stated that
   Sermoy stabbed you in the back. Do you still stand by that?

VILLON. Damn it, my eyes are like two fried eggs! They're fried to
   a frizzle!

PHILIPPE. You still have a chance!

VILLON. What did they do to me, Règne?

   *The song stops in mid-verse. Complete blackout. In the darkness the
   journalists disappear and then a single light comes on, directly opposite
   VILLON. The two BAILIFFS, now dressed as such, are binding
   VILLON to a chair. The BISHOP emerges from the darkness. This
   time he is grim, without a trace of friendship.*

BISHOP. You still have a chance, Villon.

   MOUSTIER *twists* VILLON*'s arms. From this moment everything
   proceeds at the pace of a high-speed interrogation intended to confuse.
   Questions fall thick and fast without leaving any time for a reply. Cries.
   The* BISHOP *sits watching impassively.*

MOUSTIER. Why did you kill Sermoy?

VILLON. That crook himself –

PICHART. Who robbed the Collège de Navarre with you?

VILLON. It's covered by statute of limitation.

MOUSTIER. Answer the questions!

PICHART. Name your accomplices!

VILLON. Who?

MOUSTIER. Who's the leader of your gang? Who is the Wolf?

PICHART. Names, names, names!

VILLON. I don't recall. I was drunk.

PICHART. We've got witnesses that you're the one who stabbed
   Ferrebouc!

VILLON. But I never saw the man in my life.

MOUSTIER. You never saw the Wolf?

VILLON. I never saw Ferrebouc!

PICHART. How and why did you attack his holiness the Bishop?

MOUSTIER. What weapon did you use to attack Ferrebouc?

VILLON. I didn't attack anyone! I was asleep at the time!

PICHART. Are you trying to tell us that Bishop d'Aussigny attacked you?

VILLON (*screaming*). No! Sermoy attacked me!

Suddenly the BISHOP *interrupts the interrogation with an imperious gesture. The* BAILIFFS *disappear. The* BISHOP *himself pushes the light one side and loosens* VILLON*'s bonds.* VILLON *collapses and rests his head on his knees.*

BISHOP (*coldly*). Pointless nonsense. Lights, shouts, confusion . . . After all, we can talk things over calmly, can't we. All right. Who was that woman who witnessed the murder?

VILLON (*worn out*). There was no woman there.

BISHOP. Name?

VILLON. No.

The BISHOP *snaps his fingers. A light reveals a woman in a veil. She stands stiffly upright and anonymous like a puppet.*

BISHOP. Well? Go to her.

VILLON. What am I supposed to do?

The BISHOP *shrugs his shoulders. There is a lute lying on the floor;* VILLON *picks it up disconcertedly and starts to strum it softly. The woman does not react.*

(*singing quietly*). Oh, where are the snows of yesteryear . . .

BISHOP. Sermoy came alone?

VILLON. Yes.

BISHOP. Continue.

VILLON *sings.* PHILIPPE *emerges from the darkness, a dagger in his hand. He waits a few steps away from* VILLON.

BISHOP. He attacked you from behind?

VILLON (*strumming*). That's right.

PHILIPPE *steps over to* VILLON *and stabs him in the back.* VILLON *lets out a groan and falls to his knees.* PHILIPPE *moves away unconcerned.*

BISHOP. Does he have a scar on his back?

CATHERINE (*pushing apart his rags and in a high, unnatural voice*). He has a birthmark.

VILLON (*turning round; savagely*). You bitch!

Incensed, PHILIPPE *suddenly stops playing the game and thrusts himself into the live action.*

PHILIPPE. How dare you use that sort of language before the church doors? Apologise at once.

CATHERINE *breaks into uncontrollable neurotic laughter.*

VILLON (*with growing agitation*). Catherine! (*To* PHILIPPE *who is gripping him in an attempt to prevent him rushing to* CATHERINE.) Out of the way, you bastard!

CATHERINE (*blurting out between bouts of laughter*). Apologise then . . . go on, apologise to me . . . go on –

BISHOP (*in a loud voice across the whole stage*). Who witnessed the murder?!

VILLON. Let go, you slobbering slug! You sapless eunuch! You holy squeaker!

PHILIPPE. In God's name don't provoke me!

VILLON. Fight back then!

CATHERINE (*hiding her face in her hands and sobbing with laughter*). I saw nothing! I saw nothing! Nothing at all!

PHILIPPE *unsheathes his dagger. They scuffle,* PHILIPPE *stabs* VILLON *in the mouth.* CATHERINE *stops laughing, takes her hands away from her face, pushes aside the veil and observes the scene in frozen fear.*

VILLON (*crazed*). You little toe-rag!

He wrests PHILIPPE *'s dagger from him and stabs.* PHILIPPE *screams and falls.* VILLON *picks up a stone and goes to throw it in* PHILIPPE *'s face. Before he can throw it,* CATHERINE *rushes up to him and falls to her knees in front of him, grasping him about the legs.*

CATHERINE (*appalled; quietly*). I saw it, Villon, I saw it.

The BAILIFFS *carry* PHILIPPE *off. The lights come up slowly on the courtroom. The* ASSESSORS *are in place, dressed in their gowns. All gaze sternly at* VILLON. VILLON *stands looking as if he has just woken up; he is totally unaware of* CATHERINE *'s presence.*

(*still kneeling, she whispers*). Run! Quickly!

VILLON (*dispiritedly, unnaturally, heedless of* CATHERINE). He was asking for it, the creep. At least it'll keep him out of the pulpit for a week of two!

The death-knell sounds.

(VILLON, *in panic*) What's up?

Enter THE FATHER – *as court usher – ringing a bell like a death-knell.*

THE FATHER. The hearing is adjourned! Clear the court!

VILLON. Father, what will become of me?

CATHERINE. What will become of me? François! Don't leave me here alone!

THE FATHER (*at* VILLON's *side; quietly and sternly; prodding him*). The game's up, my boy! You must leave Paris!

The ASSESSORS *disperse.*

Everyone out of the courtroom!

VILLON. But I can't leave Paris! Father, why have you forsaken me?

THE FATHER (*ringing his bell*). Interval of five years!

SECOND ACT

Before the second act opens the CHORUS *starts to sing.*

CHORUS: The days of my youth I must regret
      I had my fling and more than most,
      then came onset of age. And yet
      behind my back they seemed to coast
      away and not on foot or on post –
      on horseback? No. Then how?
      All of a sudden gone like a ghost
      and not a thing did me endow

      All of them gone and I remain,
      poor in my wits and wisdom, sad,
      failing, blacker than blue; no gain,
      no rents, no property I've had.
      My least kin now (it's true, I add)
      our tie of blood they sorely mock it,
      spurn natural duty, it's too bad,
      and just because I'm out of pocket.

In the course of the song, the ASSESSORS *(in gowns) gather in the courtroom.* THE FATHER – *as court usher – rings a bell.* RÉGNIER *is the last to enter, walking quickly and giving a friendly nod in the direction of the* FATHER.

RÉGNIER. Well?

THE FATHER (*he stops ringing the bell. Surprised but harried*).
    Monsieur de Montigny!

RÉGNIER. How's François?

THE FATHER. Oh, my goodness. (*Quietly.*) I've had neither sight
    nor sound of him for nigh on five years.

RÉGNIER *nods and smiles, wanting to continue on his way. But*
THE FATHER *stops him imploringly.*

Forgive me, monsieur . . . You have news of him, haven't you? Is
he alive, at least?

RÉGNIER *grins in a friendly manner and slaps him on the back before
continuing to his place.* THE FATHER *pulls himself together and*

starts ringing the bell with gusto. The BISHOP *enters. The*
ASSESSORS *rise.*

BISHOP. In the name of God. The Case of François Villon. (*He sits,
opens the register and waits. Suddenly he looks up in surprise.*) Where
is the accused?

They all look at one another.

TABARY (*with obsequious anxiety*). Notary Ferrebouc awaits in vain a
result –

BISHOP (*interrupting him and striking his gavel*). The Court asks
once more! Where is the accused?

PHILIPPE (*rising; drily and with restraint*). I wish to state that I have
legitimate grounds to suspect that the accused has fled from
Paris to evade justice. Item grounds to suspect that this
happened with the direct assistance of the defence counsel.
Item grounds to suspect that the defence counsel knows the
whereabouts of his client. Item grounds to suspect that he is in
secret contact with him. On the basis of my statement I request
that he be recalled from this case.

He sits. Commotion in the hall. RÉGNIER *lolls back in his seat,
smiling.*

BISHOP. Silence in Court! – Counsel for the defence!

RÉGNIER. Here.

BISHOP. Could you make some statement?

RÉGNIER (*looking over his shoulder out of the window – cheekily*). It's
raining outside. Item it's getting dark.

BISHOP. Excuse me?!

RÉGNIER. Twilight. The hour between dog and wolf. – Or am I
perhaps to tell you about Villon? There's nothing to tell.

BISHOP. Have you cognizance of where he is hiding?

RÉGNIER. I discharged him from my service in the year of our
Lord 1459.

BISHOP (*roaring*). Have you such cognizance?

RÉGNIER. No.

TABARY (*after a moment, again obsequiously hesitant*). If we keep
Monsieur Ferrebouc waiting, he will complain to the Crown.

The BISHOP *impatiently taps the desk with his knuckle.* THE
FATHER *approaches him clearly upset.*

THE FATHER. I humbly ask the court for a moment's forbearance.
I shall return with the accused.

The BISHOP *slaps the register shut and starts to leave.*

BISHOP (*turning on his way out; drily*). Inform the court in due time
of all the facts.

RÉGNIER (*rising; provocatively*). And let me know too.

He goes out. CATHERINE *stands up, and leaves in the opposite
direction without looking at anyone.*

TABARY (*nonplussed*). What's going on? Is this a recess or what?

No one replies to him. TABARY *shrugs and leaves also. The rest yawn,
remain silent and look out of the window.* PHILIPPE *writes something.*
MOUSTIER *and* PICHART *take out lutes and start to strum – each
of them something different. General tension. In the end,* ANGÈLE *–
naively and affectedly – exclaims loudly.*

ANGÈLE. It's stifling here. Does it always take so long for a trial to
start? (*She takes off her assessor's gown revealing beneath it the costume
of a lady at court. She throws the gown on the floor like a blanket and
stretches.*) Why don't you take your robe off too, Madame la
Comtesse! The sun is so hot! Gentlemen! Take off those robes!
The ladies won't mind!

One after another they remove the gowns. The BAILIFFS *and*
PHILIPPE *are dressed as young noblemen.* PHILIPPE *also takes out a
lute and the disparate prelude becomes louder. The* MOTHER (*now the
Duchess of Blois*) *timidly walks up and down the traverse deep in
thought.* JEANNE (*now a lady at court*) *sheds her gown also. She
stretches luxuriously and makes for* ANGÈLE *who has sat down on her
gown in the meantime.*

JEANNE. It's such a dump, this place! (*Yawns and sits down next to
ANGÈLE.*) Every decent château has a tournament. This has to
be the only place where the Lord of the Manor is mad on
poetry. A poetry contest! Tsk!

ANGÈLE (*enchanted*). Who do you think will win?

JEANNE (*indicating* PHILIPPE). That one there. That adenoidal
nerd. (*She takes off her shoe and wiggles her toes in irritation.*)
Merde, I'll chuck these shoes out! – He always wins. It's enough
to say Boo! to him and off he goes. Boo shoe true blue few
spew. Like a dose of the shits. (*Banging the shoes on the ground.*)
The toes on these are dreadful!

ANGÈLE (*indicating*). And those are all poets?

JEANNE. Yeah. So what's the hold up. Where's the Duke?

The MOTHER/DUCHESS *is on the traverse apparently looking for someone. She passes her hand over her slightly swelling belly.* ANGÈLE *notices her and digs* JEANNE *in the ribs.*

ANGÈLE. Hey! The Duchess!

JEANNE (*brightening*). Wow! Would you ever! D'you see what I see?

ANGÈLE. What?

JEANNE. Well I'll be! She must be in the club!

ANGÈLE (*touched*). That's wonderful.

JEANNE (*a scandal-monger in full flight*). Well, what a turn-up for the books! Who's the daddy?

ANGÈLE (*genuinely*). The Duke, of course!

JEANNE. Tsk! Him, he only goes for poets by now!

THE FATHER/DUKE *has appeared on the traverse. He kisses the* MOTHER *on the hand and then on the palm.* ANGÈLE *simpers,* JEANNE *sniggers.*

Though on second thoughts, maybe she goes for poets too.

THE MOTHER. Let us commence, my dear. The gentlemen are waiting.

THE FATHER. Yes, yes. Just let me get my cape.

THE MOTHER. So what theme have you chosen this year?

THE FATHER (*pressing her finger to his lips and smiling*). Sh!

Fanfares. The ladies jump up and dash to their places. JEANNE *has difficulty putting on her shoe.*

JEANNE. Oh for fuck's sake!

The poets rise, their lutes held to their heart. A few of them go down on one knee. The ladies bob curtsies as they run. The MOTHER/DUCHESS *enters, the* FATHER/DUKE *arrives a little late. All at once,* VILLON *appears on the traverse. He is worse for wear: coarsened, scarred, older. He no longer gives the impression of a charming young rake; in fact, at times he is slightly vulgar. He hisses quietly to the* FATHER/DUKE *and waves him over.*

THE FATHER (*surprised, but polite*). Monsieur! Is it me you're calling?

VILLON. Just for a second!

THE FATHER. What may I do for you?

VILLON. How do I get to the château?

THE FATHER (*taken aback but still polite*). May I ask, monsieur, who you are?

VILLON (*makes a face*). A poet – Does your patron tend to set the dogs on gate-crashers?

THE FATHER (*hesitantly*). If you are a poet . . . if you consider yourself a poet . . . the door of this house has always been open to poetry –

VILLON *has heard enough and leaps over the bench. Meanwhile* PHILIPPE *is already singing on one knee before the* MOTHER/DUCHESS.

PHILIPPE. Fair lady, before your glowing beauty – Th' assembled poets do bend the knee – So humbly now we beg of you – To ope our feast of poesy –

VILLON (*during his song in a whisper to the* FATHER/DUKE). So where's this patron of yours to be found, hm?

THE FATHER (*smiling, unoffended*). Sh!

Leaving VILLON *where he is, he goes up to his raised seat. General bowing ensues.*

Gentlemen. I won't bore you with a lengthy speech. I humbly offer thanks to Poetry which has brought you here for so many blessed years now. The theme of this year's contest is: I die of thirst beside the mountain spring. I shall await your works after sunset. I wish you a happy and free spirit, gentlemen.

Murmuring. The poets take out sheets of paper and start to scrawl. Disparate strumming.

JEANNE (*prodding* ANGÈLE *and pointing at* VILLON). Jesus! Get a load of that ragamuffin over there?

ANGÈLE (*speechless with enchantment*). Poor fellow! He's scared!

JEANNE (*tapping her forehead*). Tsk! Why?

ANGÈLE. I don't know. It's just that I can tell when people are afraid.

VILLON *turns in the direction of the voice. He glances at* ANGÈLE. *But all at once he turns away, steps into the centre of the stage and shouts boldly.*

VILLON. Which of you gentlemen will lend me a lute?

THE FATHER (*quietening the commotion, mildly*). Won't you be singing from a manuscript, Monsieur . . . Monsieur?

VILLON. Straight off, without a manuscript! That lute, gentlemen!

No one feels like lending one. At last a member of the
CHORUS *whistles and tosses* VILLON *a lute.* VILLON *laughs and*
strums it uncouthly. VILLON *waits and then launches into a song.*

After a while the CHORUS *joins in, and possibly the tape recording*
also. The song swells into a polyphonic chorale. This musical item
should sound as magnificent as possible.

I die of thirst beside the mountain spring
I'm hot as fire and tremble like a leaf
At home as in foreign parts languishing
Beside the coals I shiver without relief
Naked as a worm, gaudy beyond belief
I laugh in tears and wait bereft of hope
Only despairing do I cease to mope
Pleasure have I none, but am ever gay
Though lacking strength I'm mighty as a pope
Warmly welcomed, always turned away

Only the uncertain is sure to me, no other thing
Only things that are sure I find beyond belief
The only things I doubt are those beyond querying
Knowledge is accident that is my belief
I'm always the winner yet all things must enfief
'Good night' I say, when day it has just broke
Falling is my fear when laid on bed of oak
I've plenty of everything and not a denier
No man's heir am I and inheritance I hope
Warmly welcomed, always turned away

Blasé am I and ever labouring
Wealth to win which brings me no relief
Those kind to me I find most sickening
He who tells me true strains my belief
My friend is he who lies in my teeth
and declares a swan as black as any crow;
He helps me most who makes me suffer woe;
Lies and truth are one to me today
I nothing can recall, though all I know,
Warmly welcomed, always turned away

Merciful Prince I wish for you to know
That ignorant I am, much knowledge can I show
I'm a rebel, and no laws disobey
What is it that I want? To get back what I owe
Warmly welcomed, always turned away.

A moment's total silence. ANGÈLE *tosses a rose to* VILLON, *who sticks it behind his ear and grins. The* FATHER/DUKE *rises.*

THE FATHER (*moved*). My beloved Poetry visited our house today.

ANGÈLE. Well – isn't he fantastic?

All of a sudden the MOTHER/DUCHESS *starts to sway slightly and fall over.* THE FATHER/DUKE *just manages to catch her in time.*

THE FATHER. Please excuse us. Her Grace is exhausted with the heat. I shall expect you in the Hall after sunset. You are my guests, Gentlemen. (*Bowing ceremoniously to* VILLON.) You have lit up my old heart, monsieur. I shall expect you.

VILLON *tosses the lute back to the* CHORUS. *He closes his eyes happily. The* CHORUS *softly strums. The ladies lead the* MOTHER/DUCHESS *away.* THE FATHER/DUKE *starts to leave.*

MOUSTIER (*suspiciously, like a secret cop*). Who is that?

PICHART (*in similar fashion*). Didn't we see him somewhere?

MOUSTIER. He's a bit scarred somehow.

PHILIPPE. Seeing that the idea was supplied, that the ballad form is something we inherited, and that rhymes follow a very definite pattern . . . well, there's nothing new under the sun.

THE FATHER (*having overheard him, turning with a smile: conciliatorily*). As far as the sun's concerned, maybe not. But as far as I'm concerned, there is. Good day!

All disperse. VILLON *remains alone. He stretches blissfully and sprawls on the assessor's gown left there by* ANGÈLE. *He whistles along with the* CHORUS *'s quiet strumming. Suddenly a drawn-out howl is heard. The song immediately falls silent.* VILLON *sits up. Alert. The howl is repeated.* VILLON *howls also. He looks ill at ease. Dusk is falling. From it emerge* TABARY *and* RÉGNIER, *both in the garb of medieval footpads. They raise their arms in a familiar salute.* TABARY *eagerly rushes over to* VILLON.

TABARY. Frank! You crazy lunatic!

RÉGNIER (*harsh and hostile*). On your feet!

VILLON (*immediately getting up; uncertainly*). Wolf! Where did you spring from, Règne?

RÉGNIER (*coldly*). What are you doing here?

TABARY. Yeah. Frank in the lap of luxury! Frank at court!

RÉGNIER. I asked you a question!

VILLON (*defiantly*). I can still go wherever I want, can't I?

RÉGNIER (*leaping at him and pushing him over. He now explodes*). You can't do anything! You are totally answerable to me!

VILLON (*getting up; with equal vehemence*). R-r-règne! I can't! I just can't spend my life hidden away like a louse!

RÉGNIER (*drawing a dagger and placing it close to* VILLON's *scar*). You've got your arrest warrant written on your mug. And if it's not clear to you, I'll make you a copy, my friend.

VILLON. R-r-règne! Leave go! I'm setting off for Paris with the first frost!

RÉGNIER (*gesturing with the dagger*). Feet first! But no other way!

Medieval dance music is suddenly heard. Soft lighting comes up on couples dancing on the traverse. ANGÈLE *dashes up onto the traverse and gazes down longingly. Only* TABARY *notices her.*

TABARY. Hey, a quail! a quail à la crème!

ANGÈLE *tries to draw* VILLON's *attention.* TABARY *blows her kisses and makes some mildly vulgar gestures, paying no further attention to the fiery dispute between the other two.*

VILLON. Règne! I have to get to Paris! I just have to! And I'll get there!

RÉGNIER (*shaking his head, his manner now markedly friendlier*). Dusk. The hour between dog and wolf. The dogs trail home while the wolves set out. The wolf hunts while the dog pisses on the locked gate from inside. (*He shakes* VILLON *with urgency.*) Don't die like a dog!

VILLON (*beating his head with his fists*). I go crazy anywhere else. I'm drained. Hollow as a barrel.

RÉGNIER. Catherine goes in for youngsters now. She's not particularly choosy. Her teeth and claws are famed in Paris.

VILLON (*desperately*). What do I care about her? – Règne! I'm rotting from the feet upwards here.

ANGÈLE *dances towards them, swirling around on her own, but only* TABARY *sees her. He waves at her with the tip of his tongue but* ANGÈLE *does not notice him, having her eyes fixed on* VILLON, *who for his part does not notice her.* RÉGNIER *stands up. There is no longer any trace of friendly urgency. It is the Wolf once more.*

RÉGNIER. Listen here. Your outstanding service at court ends tonight. (*He pulls out a skeleton key and dangles it provocatively.*) The chapel at Blois has a nice little Jesus it could well do without.

VILLON (*staring at the skeleton key and then shaking his head*).

Count me out.

RÉGNIER (*striking him viciously across the face with the key*). That wasn't a topic for poetic obeisance. That was an order! Scram!

VILLON. Wolf! R-r-règne! I can't take the risk! If I'm not home by this winter, these barren forests will smother me!

ANGÈLE has danced off in disappointment. TABARY returns to the two of them.

TABARY (*yawning*). Why the hassle? It's kid's play! Easy pickings!!

In the half-light the MOTHER/DUCHESS has gone over to the cross. She kneels and prays. VILLON stares at her.

All you have to do is open up and get things ready . . . and good ol' Guy Tabary will run right in there all on his own! Softly, softly, like a snake in the moss, he'll take the little ol' Jesus –

RÉGNIER. Shut up! (*To* VILLON.) Around midnight that chapel will be open and you'll be gone!

VILLON (*in frenzied rebellion*). R-r-règne! You really think a fucking lot of yourself, don't you? Well, prepare your ears for a resounding No!

RÉGNIER (*bristling*). What?

Both fall silent, sizing each other up.

TABARY (*uncomprehendingly*). It's easy pickings! No kidding!

Still in half-light, the DUCHESS/MOTHER has stood up and is shielding her eyes.

THE MOTHER (*uneasily*). Is anyone there? Who's that talking?

TABARY immediately throws himself onto the ground. RÉGNIER suddenly grips VILLON by the neck of his shirt and for a moment stares at him from close to. Then he hands him the skeleton-key.

RÉGNIER. It's an order. And then . . . I release you. Beat it back to Paris.

VILLON. Règne –

THE MOTHER. Monsieur, is that you?

RÉGNIER vanishes. VILLON goes to meet the mother as she comes down. He is still holding the skeleton-key. He goes down on one knee before her. The MOTHER scans him short-sightedly.

VILLON. Madame.

THE MOTHER (*shyly, with tenderness*). Monsieur . . . Monsieur, how old are you?

VILLON. Twenty-eight, madame.

THE MOTHER. Twenty-eight . . .

She falters, unsure of what to say next. VILLON slowly slides the skeleton-key inside his shirt, smiling at her. THE FATHER enters carrying a scarf.

THE FATHER. Marie! Put on this scarf, you'll catch cold . . . Ah, Monsieur . . . Monsieur . . .

VILLON. Let's say Montcorbier. Yes, why not?

THE FATHER. Why did you not come to the banquet, Monsieur Montcorbier.

VILLON. I was howling with the wolves, your Grace.

THE FATHER. I beg your pardon?

VILLON. I was howling at the moon.

THE FATHER. Hm . . . Please be seated! (*Gesturing to all to sit down. Suddenly he fixes VILLON with his lively gaze.*) Will you stay in my service, Monsieur Montcorbier?

VILLON (*rather churlishly*). How should I know?

THE FATHER. Who else should know?

VILLON. The world's a mill.

THE FATHER. I would make you welcome.

VILLON. Give the devil quarter, he'll steal your daughter.

THE FATHER. What's that?

VILLON (*with an unfriendly smile*). Nothing. I am, your Grace, the sort who looks a gift horse in the mouth.

THE FATHER. Do you want time to think it over?

VILLON. I have only very little time. I'm as sparing with it as a peasant with a penny. I've a cup of it for sleeping, a cup for roaming, and a cup for something even worse . . . There's no cup for thinking things over.

THE FATHER (*very amiably*). Forgive me for asking, monsieur. Are you safe here?

VILLON (*laughing in surprise and then declaring in an unfriendly tone*). Your Grace! Nothing you see on me is mine. The tunic comes from a dead tramp in your woods. The boots from a live one. (*Leaning towards him and saying provocatively, straight to his face.*) And there's a stolen louse in my hair!

A sudden peal of laughter from the places where the dancing continues.
A howl is heard from the darkness. THE FATHER *looks long at*
VILLON. *His subsequent utterances are extremely polite and refined.*

THE FATHER. Forgive an old man for speaking his mind. – I have
been a long time on earth and quite a few poets have shown up
at this court at one time or another. God, monsieur, pointed
His finger at your mother's womb.

VILLON. Hm.

THE FATHER. Believe me. – God never pointed at me. All He did
was summon me (*Beckoning with a finger.*) and say: I give you
administration of them. I shall lend you . . . well how much do
you think you'll need for it? A thousand pounds? Ten thousand
pounds? I'll hire you a castle for them.

VILLON *is not looking at him, but instead making faces mirthlessly in*
the direction of the audience.

I used to write poems once too . . . They were faultless. So far as
I can remember, that is. It's a long time since I read any of
them. They were well-rounded and smooth . . . like an egg. But
hard-boiled, unfortunately. I would sit brooding over a ballad
for weeks and then discover I had hatched a hard-boiled egg. –
I am tongue-tied. For ten whole years I begged God on my
knees to loosen my tongue just a little, but he tied it tighter
instead.

THE MOTHER (*placing her hand on his; imploringly*). Husband –

VILLON˙ (*insolently*). So what?

THE FATHER. So . . . I'm offering you security, young man. If you
want it, that is.

VILLON. Hm. Why and what for? In return for what?

THE FATHER (*shaking his head*). For nothing. Do what you like
here. The Good Lord has lent me a pound a day for you. There
are beautiful woods here.

VILLON (*whistling to himself for a moment and rocking on his chair*). I
must say you're not very prudent. Discretion is the better part
of valour.

THE FATHER (*smiling*). Where I come from they used to say: The
wish is father to the thought.

VILLON. Days of untrammelled joy! And what do you think they'll
produce together? Phah! A hard-boiled egg, most likely!

Howling from the darkness. THE MOTHER *shows uneasiness.*

THE MOTHER. Wolves . . .

THE FATHER. The only thing that makes any sense in this world is song. If you are able to sing – and you are, my boy . . . then fear nothing and sing, sing . . . and don't ask for anything else. Generation after generation will take the words from your lips like the wind –

THE MOTHER *places a hand on his shoulder.* THE FATHER*'s excitement dissipates.*

Yes, yes. Come along, it's very cold out. The hour between dog and wolf. (*Rising.*) Well . . . Good night, then.

VILLON *bows ceremoniously.* THE FATHER, *suddenly hunched in a peculiar way, leaves as one defeated.* THE MOTHER *stops on her way out and lays her hand hesitantly on* VILLON*'s hair.* VILLON *bows his head.* THE MOTHER *goes out.* VILLON *drops to the ground and starts to crawl across the entire stage towards the cross. On the traverse above,* THE FATHER *is accosted by* PHILIPPE *as a courtier.*

PHILIPPE. Your Grace!

THE FATHER. Yes?

PHILIPPE *leans towards him and whispers something.* VILLON *goes on crawling.* THE FATHER *gives* PHILIPPE *a hearing and then, very clearly, in distinct disagreement, replies loudly.*

I think, monsieur, that you are bringing your eggs to the wrong market!

THE FATHER *goes out.* PHILIPPE *stands for a moment and then turns towards the Judge's seat. The lights come up to reveal the* BISHOP *deeply engrossed in the Bible. As a bishop he behaves more harshly, more medievally. A* BAILIFF *shouts out.*

MOUSTIER. Le Viconte de Montcourt humbly craves audience of his Holiness Bishop d'Aussigny!

BISHOP (*laying aside the Bible*). Speak, my son.

PHILIPPE (*falling to his knees; devoutly*). Your Holiness, the Bible says: Am I my brother's keeper? And can I, the humblest of the humble, be the keeper of morals at court?

BISHOP (*impatiently*). Say what you have to say!

VILLON *has crawled his way to the cross. Quietly, he tries to rip the figure from the cross.*

PHILIPPE (*humbly*). As your Holiness undoubtedly knows, the Château de Blois is open to visitors. The holy trust of our honoured lord Duke Charles . . .

BISHOP (*bringing the Bible down sharply on the table*). Time, my son, is a divine gift. Come to the point – or get out!

PHILIPPE *stands up and snaps his fingers. A* BAILIFF *hands him his gown. In a flash* PHILIPPE *is transformed into the* PROSECUTOR. *All humility disappears. The lights come up to reveal the assessors' seats now filled with begowned* ASSESSORS.

PHILIPPE (*aggressively*). To the point! I accuse! I accuse François Villon of abusing his spiritual gift. I accuse him of descending beneath his own level! I accuse him of throttling his words through his actions! I accuse!

Having stood up and taken his staff, the BISHOP *makes his way to the place where* VILLON *is struggling with the cross.*

PHILIPPE. I accuse and give warning: I give warning against a voice shaking in fear at the law! I give warning against poems whose pages are stuck together with blood!

He takes a look in the direction of VILLON *behind whom the* BISHOP *is already standing. He exclaims in a different tone – it is almost human anguish all of a sudden.*

I'm warning you, François!

The BISHOP *walks up to* VILLON. *He is alone. The* BISHOP *speaks calmly, coldly and with extreme self-assurance. He has no doubts at all of his authority.*

BISHOP. What is it you seek here?

VILLON turns in a flash. He holds the heavy cross in front of him like a shield.

VILLON. Clear off!

BISHOP. Who are you?

VILLON. Careful! I've got a knife!

BISHOP (*shaking his head*). No. I am a Bishop. You'll not lay hands on a Bishop, nor draw knife.

VILLON. Let me pass. I'll go quietly. Stand aside.

BISHOP. Do you have a nickname, Villon?

VILLON. If you don't get out of my way, I'll kill you!

BISHOP (*with a cold and calm smile*) I am the Holy Church. You'll not lay a finger on me.

He points his staff at VILLON, *taking a step towards him.* VILLON *roars and hurls the heavy cross at him. The* BISHOP *only just gets out of the way.* VILLON *wrests the staff from his grasp and uses the pointed end to pin him to the wall by the throat. The* BISHOP *gurgles.* ANGÈLE *screams from her seat among the assessors.* JEANNE *swings up onto the judges' bench. Her cowl slips down, and with unkempt hair she catcalls in her excitement.*

VILLON. You won't get me. No one will get me!

BISHOP (*hoarsely*). Guard!

The lights come up abruptly and there is a sudden hullabaloo. Both BAILIFFS leap on VILLON. JEANNE whistles, and the BAILIFFS' shouts interrupt each other. They set up a plank-bed and after a short scuffle tie VILLON to it.

MOUSTIER. You arsehole!

PICHART. We've got you, you louse!

MOUSTIER. Now you've had your chips, you punk!

The BISHOP makes a rattling cough, feeling his throat. MOUSTIER lights a torch.

Does your Holiness order the torture to commence?

BISHOP (*groggily, his voice distorted*). The Holy Church judges but does not punish. The secular power punishes. (*Suddenly turning towards the ASSESSORS and in a powerful voice, for the first time maddened with rage, he screams.*) Clear the court! What are you waiting for! Clear the court!

All rush out. Only VILLON and the two BAILIFFS remain. MOUSTIER is just bringing the burning torch up to VILLON's face.

MOUSTIER. Smells nice, eh? Go on, have a good sniff! – So let's have some names. Names! Sing, my little skylark!

PICHART. Who are the other rats?

VILLON screams.

MOUSTIER. Who's the boss man?

PICHART. Who's The Wolf? Who's the leader? I'm waiting!

MOUSTIER (*rhythmically thrusting the torch up into VILLON's ribcage*): Boss-man! Boss-man! Boss-man! Who has the whip-hand, my little friend?

VILLON. Fuck you, you son of a bitch! (*Screaming in pain.*) No more! Aaah! –

MOUSTIER. Scream away, honey-bun, scream away! At least it'll give you an appetite.

PICHART. Come on! Who's The Wolf

VILLON screeches. Suddenly his shouts are joined by someone else's. THE MOTHER/DUCHESS totters in, clearly in her ninth month by now. She leans against the wall, holding her belly. She lets out a moan.

THE MOTHER. It hurts. It hurts.

MOUSTIER. Does it hurt? Does it hurt?

VILLON. I curse you! Jump in the dungheap! I hope the worms eat you! I –

In the middle of a scream, VILLON's *head lolls to one side.*

THE MOTHER (*starting to scream*). Help! Help me, for heaven's sake! Where are you, someone?

PICHART (*slapping* VILLON *round the face*). Is he done for?

MOUSTIER (*pressing his ear up against* VILLON's *chest*). No. He's a tough bird, this one.

PICHART (*sitting down and rubbing his tired joints*). The swine. He deserves three times as much. That gang of theirs plundered half the county. They've been wreaking absolute havoc.

THE MOTHER. For God's sake! Can no one hear me?

The BAILIFFS *are taking a rest: one of them has fallen asleep, while the other has sat down to have something to eat.* ANGÈLE *rushes in in angel garb (i.e. barefoot in a night-dress). She is half-awake, alarmed and in a flap.*

ANGÈLE. Forgive me, my lady, I was asleep. – Mother of God! It can't be here yet. Surely? I'll call the doctor!

The BISHOP *enters in a white gown, followed by* RÉGNIER, CATHERINE *and* TABARY *in similar attire. It looks like a senior consultant doing his rounds with his retinue.*

BISHOP (*authoritatively*). Sure! Where are you?

ANGÈLE (*scurrying over to him in agitation*). Here I am?

BISHOP (*feeling the unconscious* VILLON's *pulse. To* ANGÈLE). Remove the bandage! (*To* MOUSTIER.) Coma?

MOUSTIER (*with his mouth full*). Hm.

BISHOP. Did he speak?

MOUSTIER. He swore.

In haste ANGÈLE *clumsily removes* VILLON's *bandage.* RÉGNIER *and* PHILIPPE *look on in interest;* CATHERINE *looks elsewhere unconcerned. The* BISHOP *starts to lecture impersonally.*

BISHOP. Male, twenty-eight years old. Compulsive conflict-prone personality, persistent vagrant, recidivist. Past history vague, father unknown, childhood spent in destitution. Superior intellect, exceptional tendency to self-expression. Currently

receding coma with magical overtones. Clinical picture:
psychopathy with criminal tendencies. – Questions?

VILLON (*groaning and opening his eyes*). An angel! There's an angel
here! Is it you, Angèle?

ANGÈLE (*startled*). Shush!

PHILIPPE. How would I put it . . . Social consciousness – there's
none apparent?

BISHOP. An odd question. – What exactly is meant by it?

PHILIPPE. Well . . . resonance to collective existence, so to say.

BISHOP. Quite exceptional resonance. Activity unacceptable,
unfortunately.

PHILIPPE. Any hope of a return to society?

BISHOP. Of course.

RÉGNIER. Will society accept that return?

BISHOP (*he stares at RÉGNIER for a moment before replying tersely and
emphatically*). No.

PHILIPPE (*sincerely shocked*). But . . . That's no sort of question for a
doctor to ask!

BISHOP. No, it isn't. – The injection, nurse!

The BISHOP *exits. The doctors go and sit around casually on the
seats.* ANGÈLE *finally manages to remove* VILLON*'s bandage and he
halls into her arms with a groan.* ANGÈLE *lets out a shriek.*

RÉGNIER (*ironically*). Wow, man! That's a powerful statement!

PHILIPPE (*still sincerely shocked, not declaiming now*). That question
of yours, after all . . . People don't live in isolation, do they?

RÉGNIER (*off-handedly, with indifference*). So?

PHILIPPE. Well after all . . . we have to make concessions to the
times and society we live in!

RÉGNIER (*snorting*). Okay, so we return him to society. It'll take
three bites out of him (*With a wry face.*) and then it'll spit him
out again, along with the plastic bag we'll send him back in. –
More's the pity! The pity is we've lost the institution of the
greenwood, which is where I'd rather send a lad like him.

CATHERINE (*turning towards them for the first time; with icy contempt*).
Greenwood? Come off it!

VILLON (*to ANGÈLE, in a daze*). Where am I?

ANGÈLE (*whispering mysteriously, angel-fashion*). In heaven. At the divine judgement seat, François!

CATHERINE. And he'll creep back out of that greenwood on all fours! A show-psychopath like him! He needs his audience.

PHILIPPE. Show-psychopath! That's a great expression! Did you find it in the books?

CATHERINE (*mockingly*). No, in my head. In the vernacular: a buffoon.

VILLON (*pointing at them*). Are they judges? And where's God?

ANGÈLE (*whispering*). He's not here. Shh!

PHILIPPE (*to* CATHERINE). Do you know him, that guy?

CATHERINE. Me? No. It's the first time I've seen him.

RÉGNIER. But he interests you though, doesn't he?

CATHERINE (*She turns to him. They size each other up; they don't like each other. Then, very deliberately*). You'd be amazed how little anything interests me these days.

She takes out a cigarette. PHILIPPE *goes to light it for her, but she lights it herself. She turns away again, rocking on her chair.* RÉGNIER *whistles 'Where are the snows of yesteryear?'*

VILLON (*pointing at* THE MOTHER). Is that the Virgin Mary, the one with the belly?

ANGÈLE. Hush, François, hush . . .

VILLON. Well when am I to be judged, then? Will they let me in? Who'll lend me a lute? Oh, come on! Gentlemen!

THE FATHER *appears on the traverse. He is dressed as the court usher, with some files or other under his arm. He tries to pass as inconspicuously as possible, but* VILLON *notices him. He immediately sits up.*

But that's Father. Father Villon! That's my guardian, girl! Hey! (*To* ANGÈLE.) Well don't stand there goggling, grab him! – Father Villon!

THE FATHER (*going over to him in embarrassment*). François –

VILLON (*catching him by the sleeve and prattling ever more feverishly, by now rather malapropos, at times aggressively*). What are you doing here? (*Conspiratorially, laughing.*) do you know we're in heaven? The trouble is God (*He snorts.*) is done for! (*He makes a wry face.*) Ah, old'un! Surprised, eh . . . ? I've come to a pretty pass, haven't I? (*With a recitational undertone.*) I wheeze like a grandpa, my God – and I'm still a young capon! – All right, let's

drop it. This here is my guardian angel, see. She's not been
much use so far, has she? (*He laughs.*) I'm falling over,
Daddy . . . Do you know they're actually torturing me? (*He
screams out.*) They're torturing me! Where are you, God?
(*Immediate transition back to prattling.*) And what are you doing
here, Father? Not that you're not worthy of heaven, but I don't
expect you've conked out yet –

THE FATHER (*interrupting him, mildly, apologetically*). François, I am
God.

ANGÈLE *falls to her knees in astonishment.* VILLON *instantly sobers
up and stares.*

VILLON (*inquisitively, without reproach*). And why do you allow it?

THE FATHER (*laughing*). François, I'm not in charge of anything.

VILLON. How come?

THE FATHER. I'm not alone here. The least of the angels
(*indicating* ANGÈLE.) has a better portfolio than mine.

VILLON. Why?

THE FATHER. In order to do something, one has to have the right
to make mistakes. I can't be both all-powerful and all-knowing,
François.

VILLON. But you created it!

THE FATHER (*cheerful and consoling*)*.* There's a tiny passage in the
hour-glass as narrow as this. The whole of time past runs into it
like sand . . . and the moment it emerges it is part of the future.
And you're stuck in that crevice, squeezed like a dried
prune . . . and now go ahead and create! (*Winking at* VILLON
almost jokingly.) It's a tight spot to be in, François!

He gives VILLON *a friendly slap on the shoulder and shuffles off
elsewhere.* VILLON *shouts out.*

VILLON. But I'm in torment! My muscles are cracking! They're
pouring the twelfth jug of brine into me! My kidneys are
bursting!

THE MOTHER *groans.* ANGÈLE *and* JEANNE *rush over to her
together with* MARGOT *as the midwife.*

MARGOT. Water! Quickly! Lots of water! (*slapping* THE
MOTHER*'s face.*) Bear up, Sweetheart!

The court ladies quietly bustle around the moaning MOTHER. *Her
moans are joined by someone else's: the* BAILIFFS *are dragging in the
dishevelled* TABARY, *pulling him along the ground and kicking him
as they go.*

MOUSTIER. So they nabbed you, eh, my little canary! Crawl, crawl! Let's hear you twitter!

TABARY. Help! Oooow!

MARGOT (*to the* MOTHER). Sssh! Sssh ! Sssh . . . !

PICHART. Names! Come on, I'm waiting!

MOUSTIER. Let's open our little beak, eh, and trill it out! (*Coaxingly.*) Or uncle will have to clip your tongue and it'll be too late . . . (*Kicking him, he roars.*) Talk, scumbag!

THE MOTHER. It's more than anyone could bear!

MARGOT. Oh yes they can, lovie. Just you suffer.

PICHART. I'm going to count to three. One –

TABARY. Not the knife! Not the knife! I'll tell you!

PICHART. Two . . .

TABARY. Régnier de Montigny –

MOUSTIER. Well, well, see what you can do when you try! Now just one more little mouthful! Come on – who's the other rat?

TABARY. I don't know! I swear I don't know!

PICHART *twists the toe of his shoe into* TABARY's *stomach.* TABARY *and* THE MOTHER *cry out.*

MARGOT. Don't give in now! Bear it!

TABARY. Villon! François Villon!

The BAILIFFS *instantly release* TABARY *and kick him away, half-dead. He screams.*

MOUSTIER. Villon! François Villon!

RÉGNIER *stands up and removes the white gown. Beneath it he is wearing a ragged tunic. Slowly he climbs up onto the traverse.*

PHILIPPE (*calling after him*). Where are you off to?

RÉGNIER (*turning and grinning*). My big moment is here. On the gallows.

Meanwhile the BAILIFFS *are dragging the bound* VILLON *back to the plank bed.*

VILLON. No, not the water! No!

THE MOTHER (*holding her belly and rushing to the middle of the stage*). Save the child, at least!

JEANNE (*yelling at the top of her voice*). Her Grace is in labour!

Everyone out!

She draws the curtain to shield the event from unauthorised gaze. The CHORUS *crowds in front of the curtain, singing.*

CHORUS. What's that?
                    It's only me.

                              But who?

                                        Your heart.
I'm hanging by just a single thread. It saps my
strength and nerve, you're so apart,
withdrawn – a corner-skulking mongrel, head
on paws. And why is this? Because you've led
a merry dance, my friend.

                              So what?

                                        It's me that takes the
knocks you know.

                    Oh, let me be.

                              But why?

                                        I'll give it some

thought.

          How soon?

                    When childhood's over, see?

                                        No further
murmur then.

                    That suits me fine.

                              What's on your mind?

                                                  To

play a nobler part.

                    You're thirty now – an age when
mules are dead.
You call it childhood still?

                    No more, dear heart.

                              Madness
it must be taking hold instead.

                    Of what? My collar, then?

Your empty head knows nothing.

                    That's not quite true at

all. I see
flies in the milk as plain as they can be:
one's black, one's white.

         Is that so, that the sign?

                                  You

want more argument?

         You're lost.

               Not me!

                       No further murmur

then.

    That suits me fine.

Mine the heartache, yours the sorrow and smart.
If you had been some simple knucklehead
Then I could sometimes take your silly part,
but fair or foul's all one, I would have said,
for all you care. You have a skull of bed-
rock or you choose the life of misery
rather than honour. Now answer that for me.

Once I am dead it's no concern of mine.

                   Some comfort

that!

    What noble oratory!

            No further murmur then.

                         That suits

me fine.

Where's the trouble?

            Bad luck from the start.
When Saturn packed my bags for me he fed
the troubles in.

            You're mad. You take the part
of serving man when you are lord instead,
Solomon writing in his scroll has said
'A wise man has,' it goes, 'authority
over the planets' influence.'

              Not so with me.
I'm as they made me. That's no creed of mine.

                    What's

that you say?

That's my philosophy.

No further murmur
then.

That suits me fine.

Very life you want?

God strengthen
me.

It takes . . .

Well what?

Repentance it must be,
Limitless reading.

Of What?

Philosophy,

Leaving all fools.

I'll see how I incline.

Okay, remember
now.

My memory never fails.

Don't wait till worse, you
see?
No further murmur then.

That suits me fine.

THE FATHER (*as the court usher*) *steps out in front of the curtain and silence falls.* THE FATHER *strikes the ground ceremoniously with his staff and reads out with pomp from a scroll.*

THE FATHER. In the King's name! His Grace Duke Charles d'Orleans and his wife, Her Grace the Duchess Marie de Clèves declare an amnesty for all prisoners irrespective of the gravity of their offence. They do this in honour of their first-born daughter – the Most Noble Princess Marie!

The CHORUS *disperses hurriedly. The curtain opens.* VILLON *is seated on the plank bed, apparently insensible. The* BAILIFFS *prod him.*

MOUSTIER (*genially*). Well, off you go then! You've the luck of the devil, you bastard!

VILLON *stands up in a daze.* THE FATHER *goes to him, his arms extended. The* BAILIFFS *stretch, yawn and depart impassively.* VILLON *starts to wobble slightly and* THE FATHER *only just catches him.*

THE FATHER (*now as his guardian: a dithery old man*). Oh, François, François . . . That was lucky. Lean on me, my boy. The Queen of Heaven herself watches over you! But now you will have to toe the line, my son!

The ASSESSORS *enter and take their places.* THE FATHER *leads* VILLON *who does not yet appear entirely compos mentis.* THE FATHER *witters senilely.*

Things are very strict in Paris now, my boy. Oh my. It's much tougher, you know. Paris is harsh and has no patience. I don't know why, but things have never been as strict as they are now. Paris is frightened, you see . . . But Paris has a long memory. Oh my. No one can keep anything secret here, oh no!

VILLON (*dazed*). What's that gallows doing there?

THE FATHER. You mustn't provoke them, my son. Above all, don't leap around. These days it's best to stay in the background . . . There's a lot of hanging, my boy.

VILLON (*not listening*). Who's that hanging there?

THE FATHER. Come, come . . . but I fancy you knew him too. What was his . . . Monti? Montigny?

VILLON (*stopping*). That's Règne?

THE FATHER. Yes, yes . . . Montigny . . . that's right . . .

VILLON *starts to sway ever more violently until he finally collapses in front of the row of* ASSESSORS – *at the feet of the begowned* CATHERINE. THE FATHER *steps up to* THE BISHOP *and declares in the tones of the court usher.*

Your honour, the accused Villon is here.

BISHOP (*waving him into the witness box*). You are Father Villon, canon at St Benedict's and guardian of the accused François Villon?

THE FATHER (*with his hand on the Bible*). I am.

BISHOP. On his return to Paris, was it you who took charge of him?

THE FATHER (*startled; now he is an ordinary old man in front of a judge*). I . . . your honour, François has changed, he's changed a great deal . . . he's learnt his lesson.

BISHOP. Answer the questions! What does the accused do for a living?

THE FATHER. He's properly employed, your honour. He works as my clerk – I myself pay his wage.

BISHOP. Are you aware that your ward is still in debt to the royal exchequer on account of the robbery at the Collège de Navarre, to the tune of . . . er . . . (*searching through his papers.*)

THE FATHER (*taking advantage of the pause; starts to prattle once more*). Poverty taught him a lesson, your honour . . . After all, he returned home with his tail between his legs. Besides, his salad days are over and he's not a young lad any more . . . But he's making amends. He keeps himself to himself and we lead a nice quiet life . . . And the time was when he was to be seen everywhere. François, I tell him (*Breaking into quavering senile laughter.*) the Good Lord knocked the feet from under you, and no mistake!

PHILIPPE (*interrupting him*). And what is it he's looking for in Paris?

THE FATHER (*puzzled*). What should be be looking for? It's his home, isn't it?

VILLON *pulls himself together and glances at* CATHERINE. *This marks the start of a double dialogue:* VILLON *and* CATHERINE, THE FATHER *and* THE BISHOP/JUDGE.

VILLON. Catherine! Is that you?

CATHERINE *turns away.*

BISHOP. Are you solvent? Are you prepared to settle Villon's debt?

THE FATHER. What sum is involved?

VILLON. Catherine! I'm back in Paris!

CATHERINE (*in irritation*). Hush!

PHILIPPE. One moment!

He leans towards the bishop and whispers something to him. From this moment they no longer pay attention but sit huddled together deep in discussion.

THE FATHER. I shall watch over him! I care for him as for my own salvation . . . Only don't lose patience with him, gentlemen!

VILLON. Back in Paris for ever and ever. Amen – Catherine!

CATHERINE. Don't disturb me.

VILLON. Are you still alive, Catherine? They told me you were still alive. How are you?

CATHERINE. Hold your tongue!

THE FATHER. Patience is a heavenly virtue, St Thomas tells us . . . the weapon of the angels . . .

VILLON. Look at me!

CATHERINE (*looking at him for the first time, and actually bending towards him; with hostility*). What do you want here?

VILLON. I'm unable to be anywhere else.

CATHERINE. *You're* unable to be anywhere, Villon!

THE FATHER. And trust, trust is a divine virtue! (*With emotion.*) Trust him!

VILLON. Everywhere else I putrefy. I spent five years in the back of beyond, Catherine. I turned my back on Paris . . . No! Paris turned her back on me. It's where she has her birthmark.

CATHERINE (*beating her chair with her fist*). Will you be quiet!

THE FATHER. He's learnt his lesson. He will not come to your notice . . .

VILLON. I'm no wolf. I'm the dog that wends its way home when dusk starts to fall . . . What's happened to you, Catherine? You used to look like a lost skylark. Now you look like a bat at midnight. Do you still bite your nails? Show me your hand!

CATHERINE (*coldly*). I've almost eaten myself all up! And now all of Paris dines off what's left of me.

VILLON. Catherine. I'm here. And there's nothing and no one will make me leave now.

CATHERINE (*leaning right over to him; maliciously and out loud*). If you think that Paris will put up with you, then you're very much mistaken. In Paris you're as unwelcome as a louse!

VILLON *stands up. He moves to centre stage. Then he spreads his arms clown-like and gives out a wild, inarticulate roar.*

BISHOP (*striking his gavel*). Silence in court! Quiet!

VILLON *sits down alone on the edge of the stage and curls up, resting his face on his knees.* PHILIPPE *continues to whisper something to the* BISHOP. *The* BAILIFFS *exchange enquiring glances and stand up.*

PICHART (*to the* BISHOP). Now?

BISHOP. Patience.

RÉGNIER *lounges back and whistles. A moment later,* THE BISHOP *points silently at a number of* ASSESSORS: TABARY, JEANNE, MARGOT *and the two* BAILIFFS. *They all remove their gowns.* MARGOT *and* JEANNE *are dressed as in the first act (*JEANNE *is* *pregnant), the other three are dressed as medieval townspeople.*

ANGÈLE (*in agitation*). Where are they going?

PHILIPPE *looks enquiringly at* THE BISHOP.

BISHOP (*with an almost imperceptible shake of the head*). Not here. (*Aloud to everyone present.*) Clear the court! Everyone out!

ANGÈLE. What's up? What's going on? (*to* PHILIPPE *who is pushing her out of court after the other departing characters.*) Leave me alone!

BISHOP (*to the* FATHER, *who remains standing meekly in the witness box.*). In the light of new and unforeseen circumstances the court adjourns the announcement of its verdict.

THE FATHER (*alarmed*). What? What circumstances? (*Looking around, shielding his eyes.*) Where is that ward of mine? François!

PHILIPPE *manages to eject the* FATHER *as well. Meanwhile* MARGOT *and* JEANNE *set out a tavern scene. The* ASSESSORS *are gone, only the crouching* VILLON *remains.* MOUSTIER *slaps him cheerfully on the back.*

MOUSTIER. Why so down in the mouth, pal?

VILLON (*his train of thought disturbed*). What?

MOUSTIER. All your birds flown away? Flies in your honey?

VILLON. Beat it, I'm not in the mood.

PICHART (*with drunken affability, though not entirely convincing; indeed both of them bear the unmistakable stamp of police informer*). Cut the cackle, you guys. We're going to Margot's.

JEANNE (*running up to* VILLON *and throwing herself on him*). Would you ever . . . ? Well I'll be . . . Is this really Frank? Well damn me!

VILLON (*rather impassive, but amiable; to* JEANNE). Yeah, yeah. I'm back again.

JEANNE. Margot! Would you believe it! Frank, you old bastard! Come on!

MOUSTIER (*with fake joviality*). Oh hugs an' kissin'. – I know what I'm missin'! Landlady – a jug!

MOUSTIER *pushes* VILLON *over to the tavern table. He snaps his fingers for a jug.*

MARGOT. Well look who the dog's brought in. Don't suck him, Jeannie, he'll give you fleas!

PICHART (*to* VILLON). The name's Pichart.

MOUSTIER. And just call me Houtin. Big Boy Houtin.

> VILLON *sits down, more or less passively. Suddenly he notices* TABARY.

VILLON (*suspiciously*). You there. What's your name?

TABARY (*shiftily*). Dogis. At your service. My name is Dogis, I'm a clerk.

VILLON. Aren't we acquainted?

TABARY. I'm sure I've not yet had the honour.

> VILLON *stares.* TABARY *looks away. The* BAILIFFS *dig each other in the ribs.*

MOUSTIER. So how's about a song? They say you're a great singer! Landlady – a lute!

> MARGOT *hands* VILLON *a lute.*

VILLON (*quietly*). How's life treating you?

MARGOT (*harshly*). Why? I'm alive – so what?

MOUSTIER. Come on songbird, let's be hearing you!

JEANNE. Frankie, just don't you go singing anything against the king, this time, though! No provocation, Okay?

VILLON (*absently*). What's that?

JEANNE. What do you think? I need peace and quiet for the baby don't I?

MARGOT. Oh, come on. Don't you go making such a you know what out of your belly!

JEANNE (*as excitable and loudmouthed as ever*). What! Less of the 'you know what'! I wouldn't mind if there was some point in it at least! It's about as useful as tickling a fly's arse! Well, ain't I right? Ain't that the way of it?

MOUSTIER (*laughing and slapping her on the behind*). How right you are, honey.

> VILLON *starts to play, strumming and whistling without looking at anyone. Then he starts to sing listlessly. Puzzled by his lassitude, the* CHORUS *timidly tries to accompany him.*

VILLON (*singing*). To hermits, Carthusian or Celestine,
> To whores who let their tits be seen
> to draw a larger clientele;
> to brawlers, conmen on the scene,
> to showmen with their apes at heel

to fools and those in farce who steal
away, whistling, six to the van;
to dolls on strings – in hand or real –
pardon I cry from every man

With sudden, irrational aggression.

Except those sons of bitches so mean
they made dry crusts my daily meal
and made me shit hard in between –

No one pays undivided attention. PICHART *mauls* MARGOT,
MOUSTIER *drinks and yawns,* TABARY *stares at the table the whole
time.* VILLON *suddenly appears to wilt and breaks off in mid-verse. By
contrast* MOUSTIER *revives.*

MOUSTIER. Ah, well. We'll be on our way again then. Up you
jump, songbird!

PICHART *and* MOUSTIER *jump up and start to leave the tavern,
yawning.*

PICHART. Hey, they've still got the lights on across the street!

MOUSTIER. Who is it?

PICHART. Old Ferrebouc's scriveners.

MOUSTIER. The ones with the cowls? The praying mantises? (*He
puts his hands together as in prayer and starts to shuffle around with
bent back mumbling in imitation of a monk.*) Bla bla bla bla bla bla
bla . . . Bla bla bla bla bla bla bla . . . Bla bla bla . . .

VILLON *looks elsewhere blankly, oblivious of what is going on.*
ANGÈLE *rushes down from the traverse dressed as a harlot.*

ANGÈLE. François! You're back, François!

VILLON (*not over-enthusiastic; still rather preoccupied*). Ah, Angèle . . .
Well, did you keep an eye on Paris for me then, my little
Angèle?

ANGÈLE. Paris is a dreadful place these days, really dreadful . . . do
watch your step, François!

VILLON. I dreamt about you once . . . you appeared as a guardian
angel. (*He laughs.*) I ought to have married you and stayed at
home. Run along now, there's a good girl!

ANGÈLE *leaves reluctantly, looking back over her shoulder at*
VILLON. VILLON *sits down on the edge of the stage and hunches
up, apparently asleep.*

PICHART (*yawning*). Ah, real fresh air. You can't beat Paris at
midnight!

MOUSTIER. Bla bla bla bla . . . Bla bla bla bla . . .

PICHART (*picks up a stone and weighs it lovingly in his hand*). Well, how d'you reckon my chances? When I was a kid I could hit a sparrow in the eye!

He takes lengthy aim and then throws. There is a loud sound of breaking glass. It is a sign for the entire stage to be plunged into darkness whereat uproar ensues, to the sound of breaking glass, shouts and blows, but all we can see is the sleeping VILLON. The CHORUS crowds, whistling and shouting, onto the very front of the stage where the only light remains. They sing the refrain of the previous number but whereas the earlier performance lacked vehemence and was more nostalgic than anything else, it is now a strident protest song.

CHORUS. Except those whoreson dogs so mean
    they made dry crusts my daily meal
    and made me shit hard in between –

    Let someone bang their ribs a deal
    With good stout weighty mallets: fan
    their heads with lead weights till they reel;
    pardon I cry from every man!

A shout is heard from the darkness.

PICHART. Watch out he's got a dagger!

RÉGNIER. Stop!

The CHORUS instantly falls silent. The lights come up. We can now see TABARY standing centre stage holding a dagger. Slowly and with surprise he lets it fall to the ground. The rest of the ASSESSORS are seated in their places. RÉGNIER shouts out.

I protest! He's been set up! Wake up, Villon!

PICHART (*shaking the sleeping VILLON*). Come on then, wake up!

MOUSTIER (*gleefully*). Okay, jerk. The fun's over!

RÉGNIER. Bastards! They've set you up, Villon!

VILLON (*to MOUSTIER, half-asleep*). Go to hell, I'm sleeping!

MOUSTIER. Tell it to the marines! Hey feller, you can't go round stabbing people like that! And Notary Ferrebouc of all people! And in a drunken state! And what's more: in the belly!

PICHART *whispers something to him.*

The leg, you say? Okay, in the leg.

VILLON. Get out of here, you creep!

PICHART *lays hold of him and pulls him to his feet. The* BAILIFFS *handcuff him and drag him protesting into court.*

RÉGNIER (*to the* BISHOP *in the meanwhile*). I demand that eyewitnesses be brought forward immediately! I demand immediate presentation of evidence!

MOUSTIER (*triumphantly, to the* BISHOP). Here!

RÉGNIER. I protest in the name of my client –

BISHOP (*roaring*). Silence! (*Calm once more.*) Prosecutor.

PHILIPPE (*rising and reading cursorily*). Yesterday, the Feast of St Boniface, a gang of hooligans attacked some God-fearing and hard-working scriveners. The Bishop's notary, Monsieur Ferrebouc, came out in front of his house in order to discover the cause of the disturbance. The accused Villon, the leader of the gang of hoodlums, pulled a dagger on him and stabbed him in cold blood.

RÉGNIER. Scoundrels! Bastards!

BISHOP. Silence, counsellor. You will be questioned later.

RÉGNIER. Questioned? I'm asking the questions! Who is responsible for this disgraceful farce?

PHILIPPE (*reading*). And since this is not the court's first acquaintance with the accused –

RÉGNIER. Answer me! Who identified Villon?

PHILIPPE *leans over to the* BISHOP *and asks him something in a whisper.*

PHILIPPE. The prosecution will call witnesses presently.

RÉGNIER. Witnesses? What witnesses? Where did it find them? Who are they?

BISHOP (*who has now had enough; jumping up*). Silence or I shall adjourn the hearing! The prosecution has the stand.

PHILIPPE. I call the honourable Monsieur Houtin de Moustier!

MOUSTIER *steps forward into the witness area and mumbles the oath with his hand on the Bible. Meanwhile* RÉGNIER *catcalls.*

RÉGNIER. Villon! What are you waiting for? Defend yourself!

VILLON (*resignedly*). They've got me, Règne.

PHILIPPE (*to* MOUSTIER). Were you an eyewitness to the accident?

MOUSTIER. I was.

PHILIPPE. Would you recognise the assailant?

MOUSTIER. Of course. (*Pointing at* VILLON.) That's him.

RÉGNIER. You're not giving up, surely? For heaven's sake! Let's hear you roar!

VILLON. It's a long time since you were here, Règne. You don't know what they're like.

RÉGNIER (*incensed*). Shut up! (*Instantly to* MOUSTIER.) Defence counsel. Where did the light come from?

MOUSTIER. What? What do you mean?

RÉGNIER. It's a simple question. Where did – the light – come from?

PICHART *pushes his way into the witness box, rests his hand on the Bible and start to mumble. He functions openly as a 'jamming station'.*

PICHART. I, Roger Pichart, declare that . . . etc.

MOUSTIER. Er . . . from the moon, didn't it?

RÉGNIER. That's a lie. Yesterday was a new moon.

PHILIPPE. The light in the scriveners' hall shone quite brightly . . .

RÉGNIER. A lie! The first stone broke the lamp. The oil stain (*Pointing at the floor.*) is still visible on the flagstones.

PICHART (*mumbling to drown him*). . . . and in the name of God do so declare and sign!

VILLON (*whistles and shouts from one side of the stage to the other.*) It's pointless, Règne!

RÉGNIER (*snappishly*). Pointless, maybe, but necessary! – I call witness Dogis!

A hubbub ensues among the ASSESSORS. TABARY *eventually stands up, rather warily, but he still clowns around as usual.*

TABARY. Me? Why me? I'm a servant of the Crown!

RÉGNIER (*harshly*). Get that skin off you! Come on, make it snappy!

RÉGNIER *himself grabs him by the shoulder and shoves him out, tearing off the gown in the process.* TABARY *is dressed as in the scene at* MARGOT's. *He looks around uneasily at the other assessors but* RÉGNIER *pushes him into the witness box and he mumbles something with his hand on the Bible.*

VILLON. R-r-règne! Do you know who it was put the noose round your neck? R-r-règne?

RÉGNIER (*silencing him with a gesture; to* TABARY). You witnessed the accident?

> TABARY's *gaze wanders shiftily. The* BISHOP *gives an almost imperceptible nod.* TABARY *cheers up somewhat and in the course of the subsequent questions and answers even starts to show off.*

TABARY. Affirmative.

RÉGNIER (*aggressively and at a quickfire pace à la Perry Mason*). Did you see the assailant?

TABARY. Of course.

RÉGNIER. Where from?

TABARY (*indicating*). From over there.

RÉGNIER. Then you couldn't have seen his face.

TABARY (*with a smile to say: you'll not catch me out!*). Oh, but I most certainly could. Quite distinctly! I was standing immediately opposite to him! It was that man there!

RÉGNIER. Did he have a dagger!

TABARY. Yes.

RÉGNIER. His own?

TABARY. How should I know?

RÉGNIER. What did Ferrebouc say just after the blow was struck?

TABARY (*playing to the gallery*). What would you say if you'd just been stabbed in the leg?

RÉGNIER. What did he say?

TABARY (*ridiculing the question*). Nothing! He just rolled his eyes!

RÉGNIER. A lot?

TABARY. What sort of question is that?

RÉGNIER. How? (*Rolling his eyes.*) Like this? Or more so?

TABARY (*with a gesture to say: What a loonie!*). That's a great imitation, Monsieur. Yes, if my memory serves me right, it was just like that!

RÉGNIER (*rolling his eyes more and more violently and staring threateningly as he comes closer and closer to* TABARY). Like this? Exactly like this? Are you certain?

TABARY (*edgily*). If you don't mind, Monsieur –

VILLON. Règne!

RÉGNIER (*suddenly leaping on* TABARY *and seizing him by the collar*). And where did you see this from? You were facing the assailant!

This is a sign for uproar to break out in the court. The two BAILIFFS *strike the floor with their staves while shouting and artificially creating confusion.*

PICHART and MOUSTIER. All witnesses to leave the court immediately!

RÉGNIER (*gripping* TABARY). Do you want blood on your conscience?

PICHART and MOUSTIER. All unauthorised persons to leave the court precincts immediately or the court will be cleared!

TABARY (*crushed*). I shall make a confession.

An immediate silence of suspense.

I, Roger Dogis, born and resident in Paris –

PHILIPPE. The court is not quorate. (*Pointing to* TABARY's *empty place.*) There is an assessor missing.

TABARY. This year, on the Feast of St Boniface, I –

PICHART (*taking him by the shoulder*). That goes for you too, Dogis!

RÉGNIER. Speak, Dogis! Place this on record!

TABARY. – was instructed by two officers of the Royal Gendarmerie –

MOUSTIER (*handing* TABARY *his gown and starting to put it on him*). Come on, baby. That's the way. We'll talk about it all somewhere else. But now it's time you went!

RÉGNIER. Dogis!

TABARY (*while the two* BAILIFFS *are thrusting him into his gown and 'jamming' his confession with their shouts*). I stabbed Ferrebouc!

RÉGNIER. Did everyone hear that? Did you hear it?

TABARY (*a shriek of despair*). Villon!

The BAILIFFS *finish buttoning him in. Once in his gown,* TÀBARY *changes immediately: he assumes a tightlipped, impassive expression, pushes the* BAILIFFS *aside and puts the cowl on himself.*

RÉGNIER (*shouting*). Speak, Dogis!

MOUSTIER (*smugly*). Witness Dogis has left Paris, Monsieur. (*Slapping* TABARY *affectionately on the back.*) That's fine.

THE FATHER (*ringing the bell*). To your places, gentlemen!

Full lights. The ASSESSORS *apart from* RÉGNIER *stand up.*

BISHOP. Paris, Advent 1462 – According to law and in the name of God, François Montcorbier, known as Villon, is sentenced to death by hanging. The sentence to be carried out after the Christmas festival. I hereby declare the trial over. – Take Villon away.

VILLON (*more in surprise than horror*). What . . . Règne?

The BAILIFFS *push him out. The* ASSESSORS *disperse. The* BAILIFFS *try to hurry things along.* VILLON *looks back in bewilderment.*

Règne? . . . Règne?

RÉGNIER *remains alone on stage. He sits for a while motionless. Then he stands up, grabs the bundle of papers and hurls it at the wall. The papers fly everywhere.* RÉGNIER *sits down hunched on the ground. The* BISHOP *enters and gazes at him pensively. After a moment he says calmly.*

BISHOP. Counsellor.

RÉGNIER (*ignoring him defiantly and beating a rhythm on the floor with his fist while half-chanting, half-singing to himself*).

My – name – it – is – Fran – çois – a – las
born – in – Pa-ris – near – to – Pon-toise –

BISHOP. Calm yourself.

RÉGNIER. From a – length – of – rope – af-ter – Christ-mas.

BISHOP. Not so.

RÉGNIER. . . . my – neck – will – learn – the – weight – of – my – arse.

BISHOP. No. (*Picking up the bell and toying with it pensively.*) Your client will be reprieved, counsellor.

RÉGNIER (*looking up in disbelief; then, warily*). How come?

BISHOP (*smiling slightly*). I'd rather not go into detail.

RÉGNIER. So what was the point of those shenanigans in court?

The BISHOP *hands* RÉGNIER *the bell and sits down in the judge's place. Now he is neither malicious nor stupid. He is convincing in his way. The two of them converse with rare calm, reasonably, without superfluous emotion.*

BISHOP. My dear sir, there is no point in your getting so upset. Villon is not going to die.

RÉGNIER. So what was the point of all that tomfoolery?

BISHOP. The court will reconvene shortly and hand down an amended judgement.

RÉGNIER. Villon will be reprieved?

BISHOP. Of course.

RÉGNIER. And released?

BISHOP. Of course.

RÉGNIER. He'll be freed from prison?

BISHOP. Of course.

RÉGNIER. Fine. (*He turns as if to leave.*) Convene the court!

BISHOP. Of course. – The sentence will be: Banishment from Paris.

> RÉGNIER *instantly turns back. He stares at the* BISHOP *like one bewitched.*

> *Then he slowly removes his cap and tosses it on the floor, followed by his gown. He is revealed in modern dress.*

RÉGNIER (*astounded*). No.

BISHOP. I'm afraid so.

RÉGNIER. He is thirty-three years old. You can't bury him alive.

BISHOP. We shan't bury him.

RÉGNIER. If he's deprived of Paris, he'll never write another word as long as he lives. His fire will go out.

BISHOP. We are here and now. A Friday in Advent 1462. I am, by the Grace of God, the Lord Chief Justice of Paris.

RÉGNIER (*in a first show of emotion*). Here? Now? Shame on you, Chief Justice of Paris! (*Obstreperously.*) I am, by God's grace, the eye of time. I am, by God's grace, the ear of the future! – You know that if you banish that man you will destroy one of the greatest poets of all time.

BISHOP (*politely, emphatically, perceptively*). I do not know that. I cannot know that. I am not the eye of the future, I am the hand of the present, my dear sir.

RÉGNIER (*calm once more*). Then I shall tell you, my dear sir. – Do you know what a skid is? No, I see you don't: you are not the eye of the future. – On 9th January 1463, Villon is just leaving Paris when, just outside the city limits, he skids. (*Tapping himself on the temple.*) He skids up here. His words fly out of his hands and his talent slides away from beneath his feet with a clatter. He will never write another strophe. He will go on living for decades and won't write a single line. I call that capital punishment!

BISHOP. Here and now. – And I'm not allowed to accept that as an argument.

RÉGNIER *throws up his arms in frustration. He paces up and down. He stops.*

RÉGNIER. Imagine you are a crow, my Lord Chief Justice by the Grace of God. A crow here and now. Flying over France. In the evening. The deathly silence of the forests. Emptiness, snowdrifts. – And then you're over Paris. All of a sudden: Woosh! A fiery vortex of sound. Hubbub. A smoke of voices rises to the sky. Bells. Someone whistles. The sound of chairs scraping on the floor. Thoughts: Vroom! Vroom! – Paris is alive with sound!

BISHOP. So what?

RÉGNIER. Villon imbibes that sound! It is his life's blood! And only within that sound is that mish mash of voices turned into song!

BISHOP. My job is not to defend song, my job is to defend order.

RÉGNIER. Order? Order! (*He shakes his head.*) No, all there is the incandescent filament of time connecting everything, past and future. It passes through one in a million. Through him, but not us.

BISHOP (*calmly, reflectively*). You speak about time as if you had eaten it all up. Maybe you have for all I know. But for me time is not a filament. Time is a valley before the last judgement and it is my task to protect order in this valley.

RÉGNIER (*categorically*). I demand complete freedom for Villon!

BISHOP (*smiling slightly; good humouredly*). Freedom? There is no such thing as freedom. I thought you knew that. Freedom is only necessity in disguise and our task is to serve that necessity.

RÉGNIER (*gazing at him a moment more before giving a faint smile himself*). I beg to differ. Necessity takes care of itself. If there is something that needs our help, then it is freedom.

BISHOP (*smiling more openly, almost amiably*). Monsieur de Montigny. Had you not been hanged, thank goodness, a long time ago near Blois, I would banish you from Paris also. (*In a loud voice.*) The court is in sitting!

The ASSESSORS *enter.* THE FATHER *leads in* VILLON. *All take their places. The* BISHOP *rises.*

(*The* BISHOP). Hear the sentence of the court!

The bells of Paris ring out mightily, drowning his words. While they go on ringing, the ASSESSORS *disperse rapidly, leaving on stage* RÉGNIER, *who sits down wearily on the floor,* VILLON, *and the* FATHER *who starts to tidy up. He shuffles about absent-mindedly collecting files and straightening chairs. The bells finish ringing.*

VILLON. Did we lose, Règne?

RÉGNIER. Yes.

VILLON. Am I to live?

RÉGNIER. Yes.

VILLON. Am I to return?

RÉGNIER. No.

THE FATHER (*to* VILLON). The trial's over. We have to leave here now, my boy!

VILLON. The trial's over?

RÉGNIER. No.

VILLON. No?

RÉGNIER. We shall appeal!

Suddenly he stands up, takes his cap and gown and goes to his place. With emotion.

I appeal!

THE FATHER (*starting to extinguish the lights; to* VILLON). Run along, my boy, run along . . .

RÉGNIER. I demand that the case of François Villon be reopened!

THE FATHER (*pushing* VILLON *out*). It's time you were gone, lad!

VILLON. I have to go now, Règne!

VILLON *starts to leave. Just before he steps out of the light he turns and raises his arm in the same old salute.*

R-r-règne!

RÉGNIER (*ignoring him*). I wish to call witnesses! Is the court ready to hear their testimony?

On the traverse, the CHORUS *starts to perform. Shortly they are joined by the* TAPE-RECORDER. *The live singing and the recording mingle; it does not form a single musical item but is instead a deafening, disunited current, growing in volume all the time. Excerpts from* VILLON's *ballads, snatches from his texts merge into each other, and the wave of sound starts to drown* RÉGNIER*'s words, the last of which we manage to hear are:*

(RÉGNIER *yelling to make himself heard above the singing*). Here and now. Prague, March 23, 1979. I summon the jury!*

The singing now drowns his words while at the same time it becomes more organised until it unites in a single, mighty torrent of voices filling every corner of the theatre. THE FATHER *goes on putting out the lights one after another, oblivious now to what is going on. The stage is gradually plunged into darkness. The last lamp to be extinguished is the one above* RÉGNIER. *Singing continues to be heard from the darkness for a few moments.*

The End

NB. The author leaves it up to the producer the extent to which Villon's original texts are used in the play.

* The date and place given in the final line of the play are those of the particular production.

Appendix

Translator's note

Unfortunately I have not been able to locate in English as attractive a verse translation of Villon's poetry as that of Otakar Fischer or Jarmila Loukotková which the author uses in the Czech original. After lengthy and strenuous research – quite entertaining sometimes – I have decided to use verse translations from two sources: the celebrated translation of 'Les Neiges d'Antan' by Dante Gabriel Rossetti and others by Peter Dale, which I have taken the liberty of adapting slightly for the purposes of singability. In a couple of cases we have used my own translation from the original French, most importantly in the case of the Ballad written for the Contest at Blois. It is to be hoped that producers of the play will have access to songwriters capable of adapting the words for the musical numbers. The full text of Rossetti's translation of the Snows of Yester-year is appended.

A.G. Brain

List of Villon texts used and translations used, plus first occurrence in play:

*Ballade des dames du temps jadis
(Dites moi ou, n'en quel pays)
Where are the snows of yester-year
(Trans. D.G.Rossetti)
Page 144

Ballade des femmes de Paris (Il n'est bon bec que Parisienne)
Peter Dale (Selected Poems of F.V., Penguin Books, London)
(slightly adapted)
Page 154

*Ballade des menus propos
(Je connois bien mouches en lait)
Adaptation of Galway Kinnell's prose translation
Page 158

*Le Testament:
stanza CL (Item à Grosse Margot)
+
*Ballade de la grosse Margot
(Se j'aime et sers la belle de bon hait)
Peter Dale ibid
(slightly adapted)
Page 162

*Le Testament:
stanza CXIX (L'homme bien fol est d'en médire) .
Translation Gerald Turner
Page 168

*Le Testament:
stanza XXII (Je plains le temps de ma jeunesse)
stanza XXIII (Allé s'en est et je demeure)
Peter Dale ibid
Page 184

*Ballade du Concours de Blois
(Je meurs de seuf auprès de la fontaine)
Translation Gerald Turner
Page 189

*Le débat du coeur et du corps de Villon
(Qu'est-ce que j'oi – Ce suis je! – Qui? – Ton coeur)
Peter Dale ibid
Page 203

*Ballade de merci
(À Chartreux et à Célestins)
Peter Dale ibid
Page 210

*Quatrain (Je suis François dont il me poise)
Translation Gerald Turner
Page 217

The Ballad of Dead Ladies
(Where are the snows of yester-year)
Translated by Dante Gabriel Rossetti (1828-82)

Tell me now in what hidden way is
Lady Flora the lovely Roman?
Where's Hipparchia, and where is Thais,
Neither of them the fairer woman?
Where is Echo, beheld of no man,
Only heard on river and mere, –
She whose beauty was more than human
But where are the snows of yester-year?

Where's Héloise, the learned nun,
For whose sake Abeillard, I ween,
Lost manhood and put priesthood on?
(From love he won such dule and teen!)

And where, I pray you, is the Queen
Who willed that Buridan should steer
Sewed in a sack's mouth down the Seine? . . .
But where are the snows of yester-year?

White Queen Blanche, like a queen of lilies
With a voice like any mermaiden, –
Bertha Broadfoot, Beatrice, Alice,
And Ermengarde the lady of Maine, –
And that good Joan whom Englishmen
At Rouen doomed and burned her there, –
Mother of God, where are they then? . . .
But where are the snows of yester-year?

Nay, never ask this week, fair lord,
Where they are gone, nor yet this year,
Except with this for an overword, –
But where are the snows of yester-year?